BAD SPORTS

Billy Martin, who took one drink too many until the ones he took on his last tragic day ... Jim Brown, who liked more than one bedmate at a time ... Wilt Chamberlain, who kissed and told—about his 20,000 conquests ... Wade Boggs, and the woman he took with him on the road to feed his hungers and fatten his batting average ... Pete Rose, who had it all and threw it away as he made the hall of fame of losers ... Jose Canseco, who set some kind of wrong-way record with a combination of weapons possession, steroids, traffic tickets, D.W.I.'s and divorce from ex-Miss Miami ... "Big Daddy" Lipscomb and the shocking death that not even his closest friends could believe. . . .

Now a book of totally candid revelations and intimately truthful exclusive personal interviews gives you the real score about the stars who shine in public and sin in private.

SPORTS BABYLON

SPORTS
BABYLON

Jeff Rovin
with Steve Burkow

A SIGNET BOOK

SIGNET
Published by the Penguin Group
Penguin Books USA Inc., 375 Hudson Street,
New York, New York 10014, U.S.A.
Penguin Books Ltd, 27 Wrights Lane,
London W8 5TZ, England
Penguin Books Australia Ltd, Ringwood,
Victoria, Australia
Penguin Books Canada Ltd, 10 Alcorn Avenue,
Toronto, Ontario, Canada M4V 3B2
Penguin Books (N.Z.) Ltd, 182–190 Wairau Road,
Auckland 10, New Zealand

Penguin Books Ltd, Registered Offices:
Harmondsworth, Middlesex, England

First published by Signet,
an imprint of New American Library,
a division of Penguin Books USA Inc.

First Printing, April, 1993
10 9 8 7 6 5 4 3 2 1

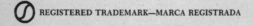 REGISTERED TRADEMARK—MARCA REGISTRADA

Printed in the United States of America

Contents

Acknowledgments

For their help in researching text and photos for this book, the authors would like to
thank Linda Kidd, Ann Meceda, Lynne Os-
borne, Kathryn Nist, and Paula Vogel.

Thanks, also, to editor Ed Stackler, for his
enthusiasm, interest, and wise suggestions.

Introduction

When football great Gale Sayers injured his knee for the last time, his wife, Linda, made a wonderful and very telling statement: "I suddenly realized that one of the reasons I was enjoying it (football) so much was that, through Gale, I was considered somebody."

In a way, Linda was speaking for all fans of sport. Through athletes, the rest of us armchair quarterbacks enjoy the vicarious thrills of competition, the satisfaction of winning, the emptiness of losing.

One thing we don't have, however, is the pressure: the fans adoring or booing us, the wealth and privilege, the media attention, or the humiliation of a quick, public trip to the showers or the doghouse. Or a whorehouse. Or a rehab center.

For many athletes, enormous fame and attention comes to them at an age when most of us are just out of school and figuring out which low-person-on-the-totem-pole job we were going to take—not which team we were going to sign with for what perks and how many millions of dollars, and what endorsements are best for us and our future.

A lot of athletes handle this pressure with grace. Did anyone carry himself with more dignity than Roger Maris the year he broke Babe Ruth's home-run record—or, more important, the year after, when some of the same fans who were cheering him turned on him for having dared to top the

Babe? He just went out there and did the best job he knew how. That's a hero.

Joe Louis and Fran Tarkenton and Jerry West and Elston Howard and Tom Seaver and hundreds of others not only went out and did their jobs like heroes, many of them lived exemplary lives as well. They are the people who define not just their sports, but the concept of what a sports hero should be: not *necessarily* perfect, but not flagrantly destructive or arrogant or scornful or hedonistic.

Unfortunately, many athletes who are heroes on the field are disappointments (or worse) off. Others were cut down before we got to know them—like Lyman Bostock—or after we'd gotten used to them—like Billy Martin—or even while we were busy criticizing them—like Roberto Clemente.

The self-destructiveness, misfortunes, and reversals are all a part of *Sports Babylon,* and you'll get a closer look at these men and others like them. In this book, we dwell exclusively on the pros; college and Olympic athletes require books of their own. We've also stayed away from athletes who fell victim to tragic diseases; not only were Lou Gehrig and Brian Piccolo as heroic in death as they were in life, but these acts of "fate" are random, uninfluenced by the human activities that create drug addiction or plane crashes, spur murders or suicides, cause players to be hit by a baseball or a linebacker. We have concentrated on those activities that run dramatically counter to the mental and physical perfection that sports demand.

Because of the controversial nature of some of the stories, many of the athletes who agreed to be interviewed did so with the provision that they remain anonymous. However, a number of athletes quoted herein made no such stipulation. Some of these men may have had problems at different times in their lives, but they've always said what was on their minds and have never hesitated to sign their names to it. Among these, the authors would especially like to thank Jim Brown and Floyd Patterson for taking the time to talk on occasions when a number of people were vying for their time and attention.

Sobering and sad as many of these stories are, we hope you'll come away from this book with a fresh respect for the pressures and dangers faced by people in the public eye, and for the athletes who have triumphed over adversity or managed to sidestep it altogether.

As for those who didn't, perhaps former Dallas Cowboys quarterback Don Meredith put it best. Several years ago, one of the authors spoke with him when he was *Monday Night Football*ing with Howard Cosell. Asked about the milieu of *Sports Babylon,* he came to the defense of his fellow athletes—even the fallen ones.

I don't know of any other business where you have to endure the kind of pressure you get in sports. I'm not even *talking* about the physical injuries, though there's that. I'm talking about the people. Athletes by nature have a tendency to be too hard on themselves. Fans can be truly wicked with them. Sportswriters and coaches are rough on them. And it's not only you who suffers, but your family. I'm not complaining—it comes with the turf. But people forget that a guy who stands six-four is still human, still breakable. What's amazing is not that guys *do* break, but that not more of them do.

If you're not crazy when you get into this game, it can surely make you so. There are easier and more secure ways of making a lot of money, and I have nothing but admiration for anyone who goes into a huddle or dugout or ring.

When all is said and done, we'll add a heartfelt "ditto" and the hope that even those whose stories are still unfolding—most notably Steve Howe, Pascual Perez, and Mike Tyson—will be able to muster the kind of stamina that made them winners in the first place.

Denny McLain:
"Mounds of Trouble"

It's like the old joke, "Those who can't do, teach."
In sports, the variation is, "Those who don't do
drugs, sell." And, strangely, the athletes and ex-
athletes who *do* sell them tend to end up in water
much hotter than the athletes who do them. The
users run afoul of the commissioners of their sport,
maybe get benched for a month and sent to rehab.
The sellers run afoul of the law—for example, one-
time baseball superstar Denny McLain.

Unlike the old Chicago White Sox pitcher Eddie
Cicotte, who was benched after 29 victories so his
boss wouldn't have to pay him a 30-win bonus, Denny
McLain was encouraged to win. As if anyone could
stop him!

For four glorious years late in the 1960s, Detroit
Tigers pitcher Dennis Dale McLain owned baseball. In 1966, the remarkable pitcher was 20-14;
in 1969, he was 24-9. But his miracle year was
1968, when he went 31-6—surpassing Dizzy
Dean's thirty-four-year-old record of 30-7. The Tigers won 103 games and took the World Series that
year, and sportswriters were pegging McLain as a
certain 300-game winner.

By 1969, after his seventh year in the sport, the
twenty-five-year-old had already earned an aston-
ishing 115 of those victories.

McLain wasn't just earning his living from base-

Denny McLain in his pitching prime. (*Author's collection.*)

ball, he was even married to it: his wife, Sharyn, was the daughter of shortstop Lou Boudreau, a Hall of Famer. McLain was headed for a big, fat entry in the history books, and he got it—though not just for playing baseball.

At the height of his fame and success, McLain

was an arrogant cuss with a smug smile and a short fuse. At the time, he said, "I want to be a billion-aire. When you can do it between the white lines, then you can live any way you want. Me? I like to travel fast and in first class. There's no other way to go, is there?"

McLain got his answer in 1970 when his entire professional output consisted of a 3-5 season. It wasn't entirely his fault: he only took the mound in 14 games. Seems that in his effort to become a big shot off the field, the kid had been involved with bookmakers in 1967. Baseball commissioner Bowie Kuhn suspended him for 132 days—then tacked on a month for packing a firearm and another week for drenching a pair of reporters with a pail of ice water.

Nor was that the end of the reckoning. Though McLain was earning $200,000 a year, he was shocked to find out that he was seriously in debt. Mr. High Liver had no choice but to declare bankruptcy that year.

McLain had been chronically insubordinate to the Tigers staff (he admits he had a "confrontational attitude about authority," the result, he says, of the untimely death of his father, who suffered a heart attack while driving to see him pitch in a high school game in Chicago). When McLain finally came back after his suspension, general manager Jim Campbell was waiting for him with his walking papers. McLain was traded to the lowly Washington Senators, where he had a miserable 10-22 season in 1971. It wasn't just that he was psyched out: he'd hurt his shoulder in 1965, and now his arm was on the way out. He was traded to the Oakland Athletics and then the Atlanta Braves, got nowhere, then went to play in the minors. Even there, without the pressure of the national press watching his every move, he couldn't perform like he used to. McLain's baseball career was over; he was twenty-eight.

Still yearning for the spotlight, he came up with a nightclub act, playing the organ, and it flopped. He tried to get back into baseball in 1975 by working as general manager for the Memphis Blues, a minor league team; the franchise went belly up before the end of the season, and in 1977, with $1 million in debts and $900 in assets, a dour McLain filed for bankruptcy a second time.

Hoping to start a small airline shuttle service, the McLains moved from Memphis to Florida, where a fire destroyed their Lakeland home in 1978. They lost everything; because McLain hadn't paid the premium, there was no insurance. Needing quick money, he turned to his hobby, golf, playing suckers—guys who were willing to lose some money for the honor of playing a two-time Cy Young winner.

"I enjoyed playing," he says, but also admits, "I enjoyed giving a guy three or four shots a side and beating his brains out."

In 1981, after a few years of playing the courses throughout Florida, McLain looked for something steady and went to work for First Fidelity Financial Services, which he describes as the "biggest mistake I ever made." Lured by the chance to make some really big bucks, he participated in loan-sharking, kickbacks, and bookmaking; the company used reputed mobsters to threaten borrowers into repaying loans, which included 130 percent interest.

Nerves and guilt drove McLain to drink and overeat and, despite Sharyn's pleas for him to watch himself, the once powerful athlete pushed himself over 300 pounds. Even after he had a heart attack, he refused to take care of himself: it was as though he wanted to die.

A year after McLain joined First Fidelity, the

state of Florida got wind of what was going on there and shut the place down. Having gotten used to making decent money again, McLain made an even bigger mistake: he became involved in drug smuggling. The Feds were watching him, though, and in March 1984 he was indicted for his activities at First Fidelity *and* for allegedly using his small plane, a Piper Cheyenne, to fly his golf bags, stuffed with cocaine, from Florida to New Jersey. By itself, intent to sell drugs carried a maximum sentence of fifteen years.

The trial in U.S. District Court in Tampa was a rout. McLain was found guilty of racketeering, possession of cocaine with intent to distribute it, and other charges. He was sentenced to twenty-three years in prison and exactly one year after he was indicted, the former Tigers superstar was sent to the Seminole County Correctional Facility in Sanford, Florida.

During his years in prison, McLain suffered from severe depression and even entertained thoughts of suicide. But he was a scrapper and, sparked by visits from his wife and their four children, and by long periods spent in the prison library reading up on the law and planning his appeal (phoning his lawyer, collect, whenever he found something), he kept himself from being beaten down. Ironically, while McLain was incarcerated, he couldn't resist temptation and pitched for the prison team: in his only game, he gave up three runs in six innings, his arm was in agony for two days after, and he retired from the game—permanently.

Fortunately for McLain, his hardworking attorney convinced an appeals court to overturn his conviction, proving that the trial had been rushed ahead with inadequate time to prepare a defense, and that Judge Elizabeth A. Kovachevich had allowed questionable behavior in court—such as allowing jurors to nosh during the trial and telling them it was okay to stand up and stretch when McLain's lawyer was cross-examining a witness. McLain was released after twenty-nine-and-a-half months, and he and Sharyn started a new life in Fort Wayne, Indiana, where Denny went to work for the International Hockey League's Fort Wayne Komets. The team had originally hired him just to play the organ at games, but when he met with the owner, McLain had such great ideas for filling the stadium that he was named their sales and promotion director.

McLain was happy and excited to be working in a legitimate enterprise, happy to have a stable home life once again and, most of all, happy to be free. For a while, it looked as though his joy was short-lived: though his conviction had been overturned, in October 1988 he was back before Judge Kovachevich to answer the charges anew. (A retrial is permitted when the conviction is overturned, but not the evidence.) Rather than go through a trial and risk another twenty-three-year sentence, he pleaded guilty. Judge Kovachevich gave him the maximum twelve-year sentence—though the chastened legal ump took into account the time he'd already spent in jail and let him out on five years' probation.

Today, McLain is happy with his life. He says, "I like getting up in the morning. It's a joy." Most important, and most satisfying, is that despite the lows he suffered and the mistakes he made, no one will ever be able to take from him those years of glory when he *was* baseball—a crown he may not always have worn with dignity, but which he earned with something that will always make him special: pure, beautiful talent.

Joe Pepitone:
"Pariah of the Yankees"

Expectations were high when another "Joe" joined the Yankee lineup in 1962, after four years in the minors. The team had won the World Series in 1961, Roger Maris had hit his 61 homers that year, Mickey Mantle and Yogi Berra were going great guns. The addition of Joe Pepitone—a powerful slugger and first baseman *and* a fine outfielder when you needed him there (he filled in for Mantle at center field when the Mick had knee problems)—should, theoretically, have made the team as unstoppable as they were in the glory days of 1927.

But Joe Pepitone was also one of the new breed of glamour boys who came to the sport in the 1950s, players like famed Yankees pitcher Don Larsen, who liked to work hard on the field and party seriously off the field (after Larsen plowed into a telephone pole following some late-night festivities, manager Casey Stengel brushed off the incident, stating Larsen "was probably mailing a letter.")

In contrast to the throwbacks like young Yankee second baseman Bobby Richardson, who didn't drink, smoke, or swear, Pepitone, like Larsen and others, liked to look great on and off the field, party into the wee hours with the likes of Frank Sinatra, and as Joe puts it today, have "a different girl every night, one after another, after another, after another." He blew his $20,000 signing bonus on a car

Joe Pepitone, as a Yankee at the top of his form.
(*Author's collection.*)

and a boat—which he used for entertaining—and
reportedly, some of his more disreputable party
pals offered to break the legs of Moose Skowron,
the first baseman behind whom Pepitone played in
his first season. Though Pepitone would have none

of that, the Yankees eliminated the problem by trading Skowron to the Dodgers before the next season.

Joe's first wife, Barbara, divorced him in 1964 after he went to Miami for a month for women and wine. His second wife, Diane, dumped him after she found a list of his sexual conquests in his pocket. Wrong kind of scorecard, Joe.

Obviously, you can't live like that and play your best. And because Joe did . . . he didn't.

In eight years with the Bronx Bombers, Pepitone was a disappointment. He started out fine enough: 27 home runs slammed in his first year. But then Mantle began to have problems, and Pepitone failed to deliver as well. The Yankees lost the Series in 1963 and 1964, then didn't even get into the competition for the next ten years. Though Pepitone guarded first base with the tenacity of Cerberus, his batting average hovered around the .270 mark; the Yankees finally traded him to the Houston Astros, who sent him to the Chicago Cubs (where, with a belated I'll-show-them-all attitude, he hit a career record of .307 in 1971), who sent him to the Atlanta Braves—all during the course of four years.

In 1973, lured by cold cash, Pepitone went to play in Japan, for the Tokyo Yakult Atoms, but he didn't lead the kind of lifestyle that pleased the Japanese, and he returned to become a professional softball manager. A stint as the Yankees' batting coach followed. Business ventures—such as restaurants and hair-styling parlors—all flopped.

Disheartened, the forty-five-year-old Pepitone made the mistake of getting involved with other party animals: drug peddlers. He had always enjoyed hanging out with gangsters, whom he admired for "doing their own thing and risking a lot of years in jail." Why not join their ranks? he decided.

Pepitone, as a con-to-be, as he's brought to a Brooklyn police station in 1985. (*AP/Wide World*.)

In March 1985, while Joe was driving through the Brownsville section of Brooklyn with two of his new pals, the car ran a red light and was stopped by the police.

"I'm Joe Pepitone of the Yankees," Joe told them, as though that would put up a red light where they were concerned. It didn't. The officers searched the car and found more than a kilo of cocaine, heroin, Quaaludes, a loaded gun, documents detailing drug deals, and various drug paraphernalia. Joe and his companions were arrested, and although Joe was acquitted on several of the heavier charges because he was only a passenger in the car, he was found guilty on a pair of misdemeanor drug charges and was sentenced to six months in jail. The judge got in some pointed digs during sentencing, chiding the ballplayer about trading in his Yankee pin-stripes for prison stripes, and having gone from a star first baseman to a second-rate drug operator.

When Joe was released after two months, he swore he was a new man: he settled down to a quiet life with his third wife and son, and went to work once more for the Yankees, doing various promotional and scouting chores. It was on one such assignment, on January 9, 1992, that he got in trouble with the law a second time—only this time, it wasn't his fault.

Staying at the Concord Hotel in the Catskills, where he was signing autographs to promote the Yankees, he went to the bar with comedian Sal Richards. There, shortly after 2 A.M., a twenty-one-year-old guest, John Capurso—who may have been drunk—began taunting Pepitone.

"You're washed up," he's reported to have said, "a nobody."

Pepitone ignored him.

The kid allegedly repeated the insults, then talked about the ballplayer with his two brothers, Ralph and Frank.

Pepitone continued to drink quietly with Richards.

"You're a real loser," one of the men is reported to have said loudly over his shoulder at Pepitone, apparently offering a last word on the matter. "Only a loser'd come to a hotel like this to have to earn a buck."

Now the ex-Yankee had had enough, and quietly told him to bug off—at which point someone in the Capurso party (it hasn't been determined who) jumped over and grabbed Richards, who looks like Pepitone and was mistaken for him in the dark bar. Pepitone immediately leaped to Richards's aid; the comedian backed off, two friends of the Capursos got into the fray, and suddenly there were six men brawling at the bar.

The state police were called, and it took four of them to break up the fight. All six participants were arrested and charged with assault and disorderly conduct; Pepitone pleaded not guilty, and no one served any jail time.

Ironically, the fight proved to be something of a vindication for the fifty-one-year-old Pepitone. As one of the officers said with open admiration after it was over, "Maybe he *is* washed up, but he took on five guys half his age and came out standing."

Though nothing will ever change the perception that Pepitone was a letdown for the Yankees, he takes a different view of things. Without denying that he might have played better ball if he'd kept more sensible hours, he says today, "I was young and I made mistakes; who hasn't? The difference is, mine were magnified because I made them in front of millions of people—fans and sportswriters, day in and day out. Living with that kind of scrutiny, with people who hate you and love you and don't even know you, can make anyone a little edgy." He laughs. "The partying wears thin after awhile, but the criticism never stops. Anyone who thinks that athletes don't earn their pay should try the lifestyle for a while!"

Today, if you spend any amount of time with Pepitone, you'll still see flashes of the streetwise kid with the hair-trigger temper who was often his own worst enemy. But you'll also see a wise, reflective man who, according to Howard Cosell, once explained the difference between being a star athlete and an athlete who's a star: "The star athlete gets ten years or so *more* on the playing field. When you look back," Pepitone said a bit wistfully, "it's surprising how much that matters."

Sam McDowell:
"I Was a Teenage Alcoholic"

Denny McLain and Joe Pepitone were undone by high living. In their wake, however, were many other athletes who were undone by living high.

In the eighties and nineties, pitchers like Dwight Gooden, Steve Howe, and Pascual Perez would make cocaine the substance of "choice" among baseball stars. Before them, however, one of the most promising major league careers of them all was ruined by something else.

Born in 1942, the six-foot five-inch southpaw joined the Cleveland Indians in 1961, but didn't really blossom until 1965 when he started retiring batters like they weren't even there: it was just McDowell, his blistering fastball, and the strike zone. He won five strikeout titles in five years, and only four other pitchers—Sandy Koufax, Nolan Ryan, Walter Johnson, and J. R. Richard—have twice sent home 300 batters.

Unfortunately, as much as he had always wanted the spotlight, he couldn't handle the pressure—first of trying to become the best, then of working to stay on top once he got there.

McDowell turned to drink to calm himself, and says, "I was the biggest, most hopeless, and most violent drunk in baseball." For years, he was able to control his drinking so that it wouldn't affect his on-field performance. That changed in 1971, when he went out and not only won a relatively piddling 13 games, but walked a whopping 153 batters.

Though the Indians were aware of his problem, McDowell wasn't interested in getting the kind of serious help he needed; he was traded to the San Francisco Giants in 1972, where he won only 10 games. He went to the New York Yankees and the Pittsburgh Pirates in quick succession, ending his career in 1975. By then, he'd struck out 2,453 batters; imagine what he could have done if he'd been sober.

McDowell obviously imagined it and, joining the better-late-than-never school, went for help. He cleaned himself up and went to work for the Texas Rangers organization, serving as an alcohol and drug counselor.

McDowell destroyed his career and ended up as a baseball footnote rather than as a superstar—but at least he didn't destroy his life in the process. The same can't be said for other athletes who felt that they needed more than reality and stardom to be fulfilled.

Eugene "Big Daddy" Lipscomb: "High Living"

In sports—indeed, in life—drug users fall into three categories: the people who get caught and get sobered; the athletes who get caught, get sobered, and go right back onto drugs; and the athletes who don't get caught and drop dead. What's most amazing about the last of these groups is that their teammates often don't realize anything is wrong until they read the bad news in the morning paper.

Like the teammates of Eugene Lipscomb.

One of the more familiar clichés uttered by announcers in every sport—especially in reference to larger-than-life physical specimens—is, "He was *born* to play this game!" Since sportscasters are given to hyperbole to keep an audience's attention, rarely is that statement applicable—or for that matter, true.

But with regard to Eugene Alan "Big Daddy" Lipscomb, the declaration actually borders on understatement. "Big Daddy" stood six feet six and weighed 288 pounds and, like Paul Bunyan, almost no one remembered a time when he was shorter or weighed less.

Life had demanded Lipscomb become a man at an early age. When he was eleven, his mother was stabbed to death while waiting for a bus; he never knew his father. Eugene went to live with his grandfather, who couldn't afford to feed or clothe

Eugene "Big Daddy" Lipscomb in July 1959—one of the most formidable figures ever to hunt a ball carrier. (*AP/Wide World.*)

him, so Big Daddy was forced to go to work on the graveyard shift at a local steel mill, after which, he once said, he headed home, "changed clothes and went to school."

In high school, besides playing football, he earned pocket money playing semipro baseball and basketball. As a result of his semipro activities, he forfeited any chance at college eligibility and, with no other options, he enlisted in the Marines, where he earned a formidable reputation as a lineman while playing at Camp Pendleton near San Diego. That was also where he earned his nickname. Since he had zero ability to remember names, he addressed all of his (usually smaller) teammates as "Little Daddy"; they took to calling him "Big Daddy," and it stuck.

The Los Angeles Rams heard about him, and in 1953 signed him to a $4,800 contract. But Big Daddy got to play very little, was waived, and signed on with the Baltimore Colts—fortuitously, at the same time as a young quarterback named Johnny Unitas. Fame and glory followed, along with back-to-back NFL titles, and Big Daddy proved to be an extroverted and funny member of the team: asked to describe his football talents, he said, "I just grab me an armful of men, pick them over until I find the one with the ball, then I throw him down." Even the opponents whom he ravaged noted a certain gentleness in the man; without fail, he would always help those he'd tackled back to their feet. "I don't want people or kids thinking Big Daddy is a cruel man," he once said. He believed very strongly in being the kind of role model he never had.

Even though Big Daddy was soon recognized by his peers as the preeminent defensive lineman in the game, and was regularly named "All Pro," he supplemented his income as a pro wrestler in the off-season—which paid him $40,000, twice what football paid. At the time, he said he was doing it because the memories of growing up poor continued to haunt him.

Maybe. But Big Daddy's lifestyle also apparently had something to do with his desire to make a few extra bucks. He loved fast cars (he owned five Cadillacs at the height of his career) and he loved women (he was married three times), though not quite as much as the cars. He once told a reporter, "I didn't mind losing the second wife as much as losing the 1956 Mercury to her."

All in all, Big Daddy's easygoing nature and his love of life made his death from a heroin overdose, abetted by a nonintoxicating amount of alcohol, on May 10, 1963, all the more shocking and mystifying.

According to a young acquaintance of Big Daddy's, Timothy Black, the football player first asked him to supply him with heroin at the end of the football season. Thereafter, says Black, he shot up three times a week.

Shortly after 3 A.M. on the 10th, he went to Black's apartment at 434 North Brice Street in Baltimore, drank for a while, entered the kitchen, cooked up heroin in a wine cap, and shot up. Shortly after Black did likewise, Lipscomb's lips began to tremble. A friend of Black's, Robert Waters, arrived then—just as Big Daddy slipped into unconsciousness. Waters tried to revive him with an injection of salt water, and when that failed Waters called an ambulance.

Waters left, and Black tried once again to bring Big Daddy around by slapping him; the big man fell to the floor, which is where the ambulance crew found him. He was pronounced DOA at Lutheran Hospital. Police went to the site of the crime, where they discovered a homemade syringe and other drug paraphernalia. Black later admitted to police: "I purchased a $12 bag of heroin around 4:00 P.M. in the afternoon. Big Daddy and I shared all of it." Black's charge of involuntary homicide was later reduced to possession of narcotics paraphernalia.

Like the sudden death of college basketball star and Boston Celtics number-one draft choice Len Bias nearly a quarter of a century later, Big Daddy's death caught everyone who knew him off guard.

Of course, there were some people who never believed Black's story; third wife Cecilia, for example. "He could never have put a needle in himself," she says. "He got a splinter in the bottom of his foot one time, and the way he carried on you'd have thought he'd lost his leg." She also points out that Big Daddy was *so* concerned about his image, about being a strong role model for kids, that he gave up wrestling when the promoters asked him to become a "villain" in the ring.

The others who never bought the story were just about every player who knew Lipscomb. Jim Brown says, "There wasn't one of us who believed he was on drugs. The reports of his death were so mysterious, we suspected wrongdoing." He says that several players got together and checked around, asked questions, but "they could never prove anything."

Unfortunately, the autopsy didn't lie. Dr. Rudiger Breitnecker found four needle marks and, when he looked for signs of previous injections, discovered a small strand of fiber in a healed needle mark inside the elbow. The fiber appeared to be cotton, which is often used to filter the heroin mix into the syringe.

His friends still didn't buy it. Close pal Buddy Young, an Illinois All-American, says, "If somebody told me Lipscomb died in an automobile accident or in a fight over a woman, I'd believe it." Echoing Cecilia's sentiments, Young says that Big Daddy "knew what his image was, because he had made it himself. He wouldn't destroy that with drugs."

The funeral of Big Daddy Lipscomb. With his head slightly bowed on the left is Baltimore Colts star Jim Parker; New York Giant Eric Barnes is to his left. Luke Owens of the St. Louis Cardinals is on the right, with Lenny Moore of the Colts and John Henry Johnson of the Pittsburgh Steelers behind him. (*AP/Wide World.*)

It isn't a cliché to say that Big Daddy was born to play football, but what did he die for? The sad conclusion has to be that his behavior that night in Baltimore was a deadly aberration, an experiment, something the high-living thirty-one-year-old wanted to try at least once in his life.

And so he did.

Thomas Henderson:
"High 56"

After the death of Big Daddy, the NFL started to take a closer (but not close *enough*) look at drug use. The league even came up with a euphemism for substance abuse: an NFI, a nonfootball illness. For far too long, the NFL didn't treat it with a suspension and forced rehab, but with counseling. Or a scolding. Or just plain looking the other way.

Unfortunately, some players have their own way of dealing with an NFI. In the case of star linebacker Thomas Henderson, it was to use more and more of the stuff that had screwed him up in the first place. What's particularly tragic about Henderson was that he had pulled himself up out of poverty, out of a shaky start with the pros, to become a star—and blew it all away.

Henderson was born in Austin, Texas, in 1953 to an unmarried teenager—a woman who had tried, unsuccessfully, to abort him with a coat hanger. Thomas lived by his wits as a child, working hard at odd jobs to earn money, hustling at pool, and even stealing when it became necessary. He gave that up only after the occupants of one house he tried to rob opened fire on him.

As a young teen, Henderson found himself drawn to drugs in order to escape, briefly, from his surroundings. He had his first experience with drugs when he did heroin and then "puked for two hours straight." He never shot up again, but started smoking pot every day when he was in high school—selling the stuff on the side so he could afford to buy more.

When he got older, he found another form of escape: football. He started playing in his senior year of high school, and knew if he did that well enough he stood a chance of getting a college scholarship. Henderson played defensive end, and proved himself to be a master of destruction. He won All-State honorable mention, and after reading how Wichita State University had lost its football team in a plane crash, applied to the school—and was turned down. He was understandably dejected ("I couldn't make a team that had no players on it," he lamented), but managed to get into Langston University, a small black college with a football team. There, his fellow students were into drinking, but Henderson stuck with pot.

A first-round draft pick of the Dallas Cowboys for the 1975 season, Henderson received a salary that was far less than that of white rookies—but more than he'd ever earned in his life, roughly a quarter-million dollars . . . for five years. He accepted that, glad to be playing in the pros, and also accepted a rough Tom Landry training camp that left him sore every place he had a muscle.

He accepted it all because he was able to relax whenever he could grab a moment's privacy behind a building or in his apartment: pot was his out. And after he was injured in his second game—a Cardinals helmet planted hard in his ribs—he also used pot as a painkiller. A lot. He took to wearing sunglasses inside and outside, he says, "basically to hide the fact that I was stoned."

The Cowboys went to Super Bowl X and, while they were down in Miami, the rookie met a famous young lady, a singer, at Joe Namath's new incarnation of his Bachelor's III pub. Curfew be damned, he went back to her hotel with her and, there, he was introduced to cocaine by a friend of hers. Even though he'd never tried it before, Henderson told his date that he didn't "turn down nothing but my collar," and sucked some up a gold straw.

Henderson recalls that there was no rush of ecstasy, "nothing tremendous"—just a sense of contentment he'd never known before.

Though Henderson played well and hard, the Pittsburgh Steelers won 21-17. Except for a lesser share of the money, Henderson had no regrets.

The next season was a time of rebuilding, and Henderson did well enough. Certainly he was having fun off the field. He met and partied with celebrities like Richard Pryor, in whose home cocaine was served by household help, brought around like hors d'ouevres. There were orgies at his own home, with sex and cocaine in ample supply. Henderson estimates that in his five years with Dallas, he slept with 1,000 different women. And when Henderson read that cocaine was dangerous, he says he did the only thing he could: he stopped reading.

All the while, Henderson was determined to keep improving as a player. During the next season, whatever his other faults, he gave his all on the field and studied the playbook off the field. The Cowboys won Super Bowl XII and renegotiated his contract—a five-year deal that earned Henderson $120,000 a season.

Feeling he had earned a larger share of the good life, he started hiring limousines to take him everywhere, an extravagance that earned him the nickname "Hollywood."

He improved his performance even more by taking speed and uppers before games. If he was short on cocaine, he had it sent by overnight mail. He began taking cocaine in tandem with crank—a speed and formaldehyde mixture. He was so screwed up that if he sneezed, he'd examine what came out: if the ratio of cocaine to mucus favored the former, he says, "I would eat the sucker."

Unfortunately, shortly before the 1978 season got underway, Henderson's nose started to go on him. He suffered a deviated septum and drank moonshine to ease the pain; yet, uncomfortable as he was, he wasn't happy *without* the drug. Henderson was often so impatient for a high that he wouldn't bother to chop up the cocaine, but would shove whole chunks of the stuff up his nose, which only exacerbated the problem by causing painful sores.

He was on an emotional seesaw as well, prone to extreme rages whenever he was ticked off—he would hit his girlfriend, threaten his trainers, and one time even vowed to jump off a taxiing jet when he found out he was on the wrong aircraft. Afraid of what the enraged player might do, the captain returned to the gate and let him off.

Henderson contracted hepatitis before the 1978 season—ironically, not from drugs or women but from bad fish—and ended up in the hospital, where he had cocaine smuggled in to him. When he got out, he was weak but determined to play. And as he'd demonstrated just getting to where he was, with Henderson, determination can make up for a multitude of failings.

Dallas had a terrific season, and Henderson positively glowed in a key game against the Los Angeles Rams, a performance capped by a 68-yard touchdown run following an interception. That one run practically killed him, though: he was so exhausted ("aged" by cocaine use, he says) that he couldn't even do his customary slam-dunk of the ball over the goalpost when he reached the end zone.

Nonetheless, the twenty-five-year-old's efforts and his big mouth (he'd predicted L.A. would choke) got him onto the cover of *Newsweek,* along with Terry Bradshaw—quarterback of the powerhouse Pittsburgh Steelers, whom Dallas would be facing in the Super Bowl.

Unfortunately, not only did the Cowboys lose (to a few bad breaks and some *really* bad calls) but by that time the poor little kid from Austin was so far gone on cocaine that he actually snorted on the sidelines *during* the game.

The following season, Henderson was getting into fights with just about everyone who looked his way, including coach Tom Landry—a guy with whom players just *didn't* mess. Landry put him on waivers. Henderson's only satisfaction came when the Rams creamed the Cowboys in the playoffs that year; he watched the game on TV, tears of joy in his eyes and a Baggie of cocaine in his hand.

Henderson went to play for the San Francisco 49ers, but suffered a mild concussion and back injury during the exhibition season, and was sidelined. He took to freebasing like "an animal" and, when he was all healed up, he went to play for the Houston Oilers. He was a key player in their making the playoffs, but he was totally screwed up otherwise. His new wife took their young daughter and left him. Paranoid that fellow player Mike Stensrud was out to get him—Henderson had decked him after some name-calling—he nearly put a knife into the man's throat as Stensrud approached him later . . . to apologize, as it turns out.

"Cocaine had almost made me a murderer," he said later.

By January of 1981, he says, "My body was going, my money was going faster than my body," and he knew he had to do something. He called Charlie Jackson, who was the head of NFL security, and spilled his guts. Jackson hooked him up with a psychiatrist and a drug treatment facility, but he found the experience frustrating: no one there seemed to understand the pressures that drove him to use cocaine, or the satisfaction it brought him.

He smoked pot to relax, and when he got out he had his nose fixed surgically . . . and went back to freebasing. When he ran out of money, he gave a dealer his beaver coat for a quarter-ounce of cocaine.

Because he'd gone public with his problem, he was now a player without a team. What's more, no one seemed to want him—though he convinced coach Don Shula of the Miami Dolphins to *please* give him a shot. Shula obliged, put him through the paces in May 1981, and Henderson made the team. That was the good news. The bad news was, he cracked several vertebrae during an exhibition season and ended up in the hospital—where, once again, he had cocaine smuggled in. When he got out, the Dolphins continued to pay him his $125,000 salary for that season, but his football career was over.

All his money, "every red cent," went to drugs. He sold his house. His Super Bowl rings. His Mercedes. He got a job as an executive headhunter and started drinking heavily at business lunches. Then, one day, he partied and freebased with some underage girls—and that, oddly enough, proved to be his salvation. He was arrested and put back into drug rehab, this time working with people who understood him, in particular a therapist who had himself been an addict.

Henderson got clean, was set to be tried on the sexual battery charge, innocently tried to pay the girls just to go away, and got hit with a charge of attempted bribery. His sentence: four years, eight months in prison.

He began serving his sentence in July 1984, and was released in October 1986. In between, he'd gotten married to a young woman, Diane, whom he'd met before going in. Her letters, her love, he says, "Helped me function as a person and not as a convict."

These days, Henderson travels around the country talking to groups about what happened to him—what he lost due to his addiction, and what he's gained since he's been clean. He still regrets how brief his career was, but takes comfort in how many other careers he might be able to save.

Incredible as it is to believe, though, in spite of his highly publicized fall and his many lectures to sports groups, there are still many athletes who haven't learned lesson number one about the dangers of drugs.

Eugene "Mercury" Morris: "Miami Vice"

Like so many athletes, Eugene "Mercury" Morris seemed to have the world by the tail. A powerful, fleet-footed All Pro running back out of West Texas State College, Morris was a key member of the Miami Dolphins teams of the early 1970s that appeared in three consecutive Super Bowls, winning two and completing an entire season of play undefeated and untied, something no other NFL team has done before or since. In 1972, he had made pro football history with teammate Larry Csonka when each gained 1,000 yards rushing. Accolades, a lucrative long-term contract, and a life filled with good times and beautiful people were his.

But like so many other football players, Morris found the gravy train derailed by injuries. Suddenly stripped of the abilities that defined his self-worth, he began a downward spiral that nearly ended in disaster on August 19, 1982, when, ratted-on by a gardener to whom he owed $400, and smoked out by a pair of undercover agents who came to buy drugs, he was arrested by Miami police who stormed into his home, seized cocaine, marijuana plants, more than $124,000 in cash, and assorted firearms in the course of the raid. (Morris had tried, unsuccessfully, to heave the cocaine into a canal outside the house, but the bag failed to go under.)

Initially, Morris denied the charges that had been brought against him. His mind clouded by extensive freebasing, he said that his cocaine use was personal and "medicinal." He claimed he'd turned to coke to alleviate excruciating pain he endured following a neck fracture administered by hard-hitting Pittsburgh Steelers cornerback Mel Blount in 1973. The bones had been surgically fused in 1980, three years after the injury forced him to retire from pro football. To bolster this contention, Morris pointed out that he'd brought an action against the Dolphins, charging that they'd concealed the serious nature of the injury and permitted him to continue playing. Morris added that the condition was aggravated when his car collided with a garbage truck before the 1976 season.

The truth was, ill-prepared for a life after pro football, his financial condition deteriorated by the fact that his half-million-dollar judgment against the refuse company was overturned on appeal, Morris found himself in a vicious circle. Whatever money he had went to drugs, and because he was unable to function in that state, he couldn't supervise his investments in real estate and other financial ventures. Things got so bad that one night, near a busy Miami intersection, Morris found himself listening intently to the voice of a demon that had materialized on his left shoulder. As cars crossed in front of him on a busy South Miami thoroughfare, Morris blinked repeatedly as sweat dribbled from his forehead into his eyes. He gripped the steering wheel tightly as the demon urged him to end his problems by speeding forward into traffic.

Why not? Morris thought, and lifted one of the feet that had blazed to glory in the Orange Bowl. He was about to slam down on the accelerator when, miraculously, something inside of him resisted. Today, he believes it was the hand of God staying him, saving him for a reason.

Despite gaining the upper hand on the road that evening, Morris was unable to do the same with his life. His drug use increased and financial problems mounted. His T-shirt and art print business floundered. Soon he was in default on his mortgage and his phone was on the verge of being disconnected. Things got so bad he couldn't even afford to buy formula for his five-month-old baby.

Ironically, just a month before the bust, Morris had turned in desperation to the 700 Club, a fundamentalist Christian organization that sent a local minister to Morris's home to have a chat with him. Morris recalls, "When I wasn't home the day my baby was born because I was out trying to hide (from creditors), I knew something was wrong so I called their 800 number. I didn't announce I was Mercury Morris; I said I was Gene Morris, a resident of Miami, and I had a problem with drugs and needed help."

Reverend Nick Schubert of the nearby Sunset Chapel went to talk to Morris. The visit didn't turn Morris's life around, but it pointed him in a direction; they met several times before the "sting." Indeed, when Morris was arrested, there was a well-worn Bible clutched in his hand.

Morris's worries were lessened somewhat by the fact that, a few days after his arrest, the state opted not to charge his wife, Bobbi—even though Chief Assistant State Attorney George Yoss maintained that there was probable cause to do so. He was free to concentrate entirely on his own defense. He was also free, literally, thanks to a $150,000 surety bond posted by an anonymous man whom Reverend Schubert had contacted. While he was free, Morris was arrested for having written a bad check for $498 to buy a gun. He was freed after another $1,000 bond was posted.

Mercury Morris listens as circuit judge Ellen Morphonios Gable sentences him to twenty years in prison, a minimum of fifteen without parole. (*AP/Wide World.*)

At his trial, which began November 1 and ended five days later, Morris and his defense lawyer vigorously contested the case against him, claiming that evidence had been illegally obtained. The jury returned in less than three hours with a resounding *not,* finding Morris guilty on four of six counts—one count of trafficking in cocaine, one count of conspiracy to traffic in cocaine, and two counts of possession.

In a scene that was to be mirrored ten years later during the sentencing of Mike Tyson, Dade Circuit Judge Ellen Morphonios Gable said, "I feel bad for you, Merc, I'm sorry," but pointed out that the law was clear on what had to be done, regardless of anyone's feelings or regard for Mercury Morris, football player. Morris was handed a staggering prison sentence of twenty years without parole.

Yoss later agreed that the outcome was harsh and "a tragedy. Nevertheless, he has to pay the price. The statute is tough. It says, if you do this, you're going to go to jail for a long time, even if you're Mercury Morris.

"We cheered when he caught the football," Yoss had said during the trial. "We booed when he fumbled. But he fumbled a lot more than a football game. He fumbled his life away."

Morris continued to protest that he'd been railroaded, though he later admitted, "I wasn't dealing. But I was freebasing. Freebasing so much that I was in danger of losing my wife and (three) kids." And in time, he would actually thank the judge who sentenced him for having given him a "determinative experience ... an event so monumental in its impact that it changes you forever."

The impact wasn't immediate. In fact, initially, the thirty-five-year-old had blamed others for his problems, claiming that while he would not disclose names, he was only doing what many other players had done. Even in jail, even as he read his Bible, he refused to accept the blame for what he'd done. He also felt sick for his family: Bobbi had to go back to work, as she put it, "to support my children and keep my household going." She said that in addition to being five months late on the mortgage, their car had been repossessed and all the utility bills were due. Fortunately, relatives and friends loaned her money, as did Morris's former teammates. For her part, Judge Gable generously told the state to pay for Morris's appeal, which he could repay when and if he were able.

Then, on November 7, 1982, Morris reached a moment of revelation. He was wearing his prison blues, sitting in a cold cement cell less than 3,000 yards from the Orange Bowl, where his teammates had gathered to celebrate the tenth anniversary of their first Super Bowl triumph. And it really hit him, then, that he couldn't do that for which he'd been so richly compensated just a few years before: run to freedom.

Slowly, rising to his feet and placing a hand on the bars, he listened as the stadium loudspeaker boomed introductions of all the team's players—all except one, Eugene "Mercury" Morris.

With tears in his eyes, he realized who his enemy was and what he had to do to defeat him. He said later, "Mercury Morris didn't have a cocaine problem; he had a Mercury Morris problem. I don't give the pigskin the credit for my success or the cocaine the blame for my fall." He said that throughout his career, he had always thought of life only in terms of growing older, never realizing that it was also "about growing up."

With inner peace gleaned from his Bible reading, and a keen reminder of human mortality after his mother died of cancer at the age of fifty-two while he was in prison (he was allowed out for one last visit), Morris not only survived but he began to thrive. He found self-esteem in his mind and heart, not in yards gained. In prison, through interviews, he spoke out against drug abuse.

In 1986, his lawyers were successful in their efforts to obtain a new trial (they hadn't been allowed to admit evidence of entrapment); instead of going through it all over again, prosecutors agreed that in exchange for a no-contest plea to one count of cocaine conspiracy, they'd drop the other three charges. The sentence was four and a half years in jail. However, impressed with Morris's changed attitude and antidrug messages, Judge Gable gave him a half-year off for good behavior; with the time he'd already served, that left Morris a free man.

Smiling broadly, he told reporters, "You're not going to see the end of this problem in drugs until you stop idolizing drugs," and said that after reacquainting himself with his family, he intended to do what he could to put an end to substance abuse. "Miami is a tough town," he said, "and drugs are the rule rather than the exception."

But rule or not, Morris took it upon himself to work with children and to speak out whenever a sports star found himself embroiled in controversy. His advice to other football players was to "attack the enemy, staring him in the mirror with the same ferocity he has attacked the enemy staring across the line at him."

The message is a good one but, more important than that, Mercury Morris has succeeded in living it himself.

Dwight Gooden:
"What's Up (Your Nose), Doc?"

Some athletes are lucky: they don't end up on a slab, like Big Daddy Lipscomb. Or ruined, like Henderson. Of course, *luck* is a relative term and they still flirt with disaster by using drugs. Some of them pull out of the tailspin; some of them don't. Here's one of the stories with a happy ending—so far.

At twenty-two, Dwight Gooden was the youngest pitcher ever to be honored with the Cy Young Award: he had finished the 1985 season, his second, with a record of 24-4, with 268 strikeouts and an ERA of 1.53, and the fastball ace from Tampa became the number-one hero of the resurgent New York Mets. (In 1988, the much-heralded Orel Hershiser won the Cy Young Award with a 23-8 record and a 2.26 ERA.)

Dwight Gooden was a hero, all right, but he wasn't quite the goody-two-shoes fans and sportswriters desperately wanted him to be.

Gooden was spotted hanging out at the Manila Bar and Restaurant in Ybor City, Florida—a known source for cocaine and other drugs. In December 1985, someone anonymously tipped off the Tampa police that Gooden had a great deal of cocaine in his possession. They put him under surveillance and, after six hours, stopped his car: they found $4,000 in cash, a gun, and a bag of what looked like

Even when he's clean, Gooden seems to attract trouble. One of the great bench-clearers occurs on August 9, 1990, when Gooden was hit by a ball thrown by Philadelphia Phillies pitcher Pat Combs. Seven players were ejected. (*AP/Wide World*.)

cocaine but turned out to be baking soda. They let Gooden go.

That didn't mean "Doc" wasn't using drugs, and he was way off his form the following year. The season started inauspiciously when Gooden got into an argument with a Hertz clerk at LaGuardia Airport in New York and Gooden threw soda in his face. He went on to tally a record of 17-6, with 200 strikeouts and a 2.84 ERA—not a disaster, but not what was expected. His playoff performance was even worse, losing his two World Series games . . . in spite of which the Mets took the fall classic from the Boston Red Sox. Gooden failed to show up for the ticker-tape parade the city threw to honor the team; they said he overslept, he said he had a stomach ache. Truth was, he'd had a major fight with his fiancée Carlene Pearson and was in no mood to be feted.

The off-season went from bad to worse. In November, his engagement to Pearson became a thing of the past. Not coincidentally, he acknowledged that he was the father of eight-month-old Dwight Jr., born to his old friend Debra Hamilton. Then there was strike three: on December 13, at ten minutes to eleven in the evening, Gooden's Mercedes was pulled over by Tampa police, who saw him weaving through traffic and screaming at other drivers. When Gooden was asked for his license, he started yelling and threw a punch; before long, the other passengers in the car—his nephew Gary Sheffield of the Milwaukee Brewers, his cousin Dick Pedro, and two friends—got into the fray. Fists and feet flew, ending when (inadvertently?) Gooden found his hand on an officer's holster and another policeman pulled his gun and pointed it at Gooden's head. End of fight.

Because the police were white and the Gooden party was black, there were charges of racism. But the bottom line was that Gooden pleaded no contest and was sentenced to three years probation.

What puzzled his teammates was that Gooden wasn't a violent guy. Quite the contrary. He was quiet. Thoughtful. Generous. He even taped a "Just Say No" antidrug commercial. So what was the problem?

The problem was that, since high school, Gooden had used cocaine on and off. He wasn't an addict, just an occasional user—rarely taking it during the season, and no more than once a week off-season—but it still affected his personality and judgment. For example, he used it shortly before the preseason drug testing he had to undergo and—surprise!—it showed up. Commissioner Peter Ueberroth gave him a choice: get help or leave the game. Gooden chose to get help, entering the Smithers Alcoholism and Treatment Center in Manhattan.

Gooden remained in the center for a month, his act apparently having been cleaned up. He married another old friend, Monica Colleen Harris, in November, and came back to the Mets ready to play. He went 15-7 that year, and 18-9 the following season. Except for a shoulder problem, Doc was back, and in 1991 he signed a hefty three-year contract that pays him more than $5 million a year. Unfortunately, that may not have been *all* that happened in 1991.

In March 1992, a thirty-one-year-old woman came forth and said that exactly one year before she was raped by Gooden and his teammates Daryl Boston and Vince Coleman. According to the petite, 100-pound architect, it was the "courage" of Mike Tyson's rape victim Desiree Washington during the previous two months that inspired her to come forward.

The alleged victim says that she was dating Mets pitcher David Cone at the time, and attended a party at Banana Max's (now Joxs) where the other men were present. She reports that Gooden asked her for a ride home—having previously told Boston and Coleman to go to his rented Port St. Lucie home and wait for them (she assumed). When they reached the house, Gooden reportedly invited her to use the bathroom before she headed back, and she accepted. The woman says that when she came from the bathroom, she was seized from behind and forced to the floor, where she was raped and sodomized. She took herself to a hospital, where doctors treated her—finding the kinds of cuts and stains (including semen on her clothing) indicative of rape.

The woman maintains that one reason she didn't come forward earlier was that friend Cone had talked her out of it, saying that she would never win against the famous players—especially Gooden, who now had the reputation of being a straight-arrow family man.

Gooden has said nothing, but his agent, Jim Neader, maintains that "no such incident took place." His attorney, Joseph H. Ficarrotta, was more insistent, declaring that "Dwight Gooden is a truly good person, and we would completely deny the serious criminal allegations." Which is what you'd expect him to say.

Unable to pursue her profession, the still-shaken woman has been seeing a therapist and working as a waitress and bartender. As of this writing, the men have not been indicted. Authorities seem to feel that the passage of time will make it difficult to make a case, and that even the semen samples (she saved the dress) will be inconclusive: The word around the clubhouse is that if there *was* sex with one or more of the three men, it was because the woman had consented.

On April 9, Florida State Attorney Bruce Colton decided that there wasn't enough evidence to prosecute the Mets. He cited that the lie-detector test taken by the Mets supported their claim "that some sex act took place but that the sex acts were consensual"; that the alleged victim failed a voice-stress test and was "deceptive" in some of her comments; and that, most problematic of all, there was no way around "the lack of corroboration available as to the issue of consent and the fact that the case boils down to the word of three individuals against the word of one individual."

After the matter was over, a friend of the accuser came forward and said that the "victim" had been "perfectly game" to leave New York and go down to Port St. Lucie and got turned off only *after* the encounter proved to be of the slam-bam variety. "Obviously, later on, she felt used and coerced. In her mind, she does believe she was raped."*

For his part, all that the obviously relieved Gooden had to say was, "I'd just like to get back to playing baseball."

Regardless of whether there's truth in the charges, one hopes that the tribulations of Dwight Gooden, of baseball genius compromised by high or reckless living, will help future players avoid his mistakes. Hopefully, Doc will help by using the media he's too often shunned to pitch some wisdom at fans and up-and-coming players.

---

*The offended party's efforts to resurrect an old wound had a domino effect, however: on April 11, a Spokane, Washington, woman, Victoria C, sued the Cincinnati Bengals—the organization *and* fifteen players—claiming that she was gang-raped for two hours in a Seattle hotel room on October 3, 1990, two days after a game against the Seattle Seahawks at the Kingdome. She said she waited a year and a half to press charges because the players had asked her several times after that not to say anything. The Bengals called the claim "groundless." In September, 1992 formal criminal charges were brought against nearly twenty former and current Bengal players.

Steve Howe:
"High and Outside"

In 1982, stating what every fan and sportswriter already knew, Montreal Expos president John McHale admitted that there were players on his team who were heavy cocaine users. One of the players, Tim Raines, actually kept the stuff in his pocket and took hits between innings.

A year later, four of the Kansas City Royals ended up in the clink for using the drug.

A great deal more about cocaine use came out in 1985, however, when seven Philadelphia men were indicted by a grand jury for dealing drugs to players. Baseball stars were granted immunity to testify against them—men like Keith Hernandez, who admitted he'd been using the drug for a while.

The seven "caterers" went to jail, and the trial revealed the heartbreaking fact that roughly 40 percent of the players in the major leagues snorted cocaine on a regular basis; several players even acknowledged that they'd bought drugs during exhibition games abroad and smuggled it home inside their gloves.

Of course, the revelations didn't stop cocaine use in baseball and a drug-testing clause was added to most major league contracts. Players who fought the clause were offered less money—on the average, 15 percent less. The owners were serious about cleaning up the sport *and* protecting their multimillion dollar investments in the players.

But there are ways of testing clean (such as not using the drug for a period before testing or substituting a non-user's specimen for your own), and a frightening number of players continued to snort. (Baseball instituted random testing for proven offenders, though that still hasn't rooted out everyone. Not by a longshot.)

One of the most relentless users of cocaine was L.A. Dodgers star Steve Howe. As a teenager growing up in Detroit, Howe wasn't happy at home, with his four siblings and autoworker parents, and he wasn't happy with himself. He just doesn't know *why;* even when he broke into the major leagues, and "The whole world was telling me, 'You're great,' I'd say to myself, 'What the hell's so great about me? I don't even like me.' " As a teenager, he expressed his self-loathing by getting drunk and picking fights. All it took was for someone to introduce him to cocaine.

In 1980, fresh from the University of Michigan, Howe won Rookie of the Year honors. At the presentation in Little Joe's restaurant in Los Angeles, he got nervous and headed into the bathroom to throw up. "I could pitch in front of fifty thousand fans," he says, but the press made him nervous. He *hid* behind his throwing, in which he had full confidence. But naked, with just himself—he couldn't handle that.

In the restroom, another player offered him some cocaine, told him it would calm him. Howe knew the guy was right: he'd tried the drug in college. He says he "took a big hit" and went out happy as could be. "The next day the newspapers said they loved me. And I don't even know what I said."

For a decade, Howe often didn't know what he said. Or where he went, often leaving for days at a stretch without telling his wife, Cindy, he was going anywhere. His fireball arm wasn't affected, he says, and he seems to have been right: in 1981, when he was doing up to 3 grams a week, he still helped the Dodgers get into and win the World Series. He was in top form in 1982 as well—though by this time, thanks to a private investigator, Cindy knew what was going on, and so did his teammates. So did one of the authors, who encountered him at an apartment tower in Marina del Rey, California, after a Dodgers game: Howe had made it to the building before the occupant did! Having parked in the garage, he was frantically trying to get inside, but didn't have the key.

"How do you get into this fucking place?" he snapped, without so much as a how-do-you-do. He was high-strung and clearly desperate.

He was told he'd have to go through the lobby, since the author didn't have a key to that particular door.

"Shit," he growled, pounding the glass door. "Where's the lobby?"

He was told, but seemed confused. He followed the author.

"You're Steve Howe, aren't you?" the rattled man was asked.

"Yeah—so? So the fuck *what*?"

"Are you okay?"

"I'm fine," he mumbled, then entered the elevator. He got off on a floor where a coke connection was suspected to live.

Shortly after the encounter, Howe was put into an Arizona rehab clinic, the Meadows; the day he got out, he went right back onto cocaine.

He continued to pitch like a demon. Unfortunately, despite his hefty $325,000-a-year salary, he spent all his money on drugs and ended up filing for bankruptcy. He became paranoid and even shorter-tempered. He missed games. Finally, he and manager Tommy Lasorda had a heart-to-heart

In June 1983, flanked by Dr. Joseph Pursch (left) and agent Tony Attanasio, Steve Howe explains how he's going to stay drug-free forever. Right. (*AP/Wide World.*)

in Lasorda's office, and Howe went back into rehab in May 1983.

Commissioner Bowie Kuhn had always been disinclined to view drug addiction as an illness, and made an example of Howe: when he went to the Care Unit Hospital in Orange, California, for thirty days, Kuhn fined him his salary for that period—$53,867—and put him on probation for three years. Kuhn often made some wacky calls during his tenure, but this one was entirely justified. Howe had let his teammates down. He'd let the owners down. Why the hell *should* he be paid?

Howe got out, continued snorting, and went back to Care Unit in the fall. Whether he got clean or not, Kuhn suspended him for the rest of the season. Howe didn't play baseball at all in 1984, and the following year he was traded to the Minnesota Twins. He was snorting anew, stunk on the mound, and the Twins let him go in September. He went back into rehab, but by the time he came out he found himself unofficially blacklisted and suspected that the new commissioner, Peter Uebberoth—who was the Eliot Ness of drugs—was behind it.

"Uebberoth couldn't fine me," Howe says. "But it was easy for him to secretly hit me with the ultimate penalty: banishment."

Since baseball was the only self-respect Howe had going, he went to pitch for the San Jose Bees, a semiprofessional team, in 1986. He was dismissed when he flunked a drug test. He was offered a chance to play in Japan, but went instead to Mexico, where he played with the Tabasco Gonaderos.

In 1987, the Texas Rangers offered him another chance to play in the majors. He jumped at the chance, did fine on the mound, then failed the drug test. He was booted off the team in January 1988. If ever a baseball player seemed washed up, it was Howe—and how. He was still doing cocaine, wasn't earning money, and had a wife and two children to support.

A year later, with the help of his wife and a local clergyman, Howe finally took charge of his life— for good, it seemed, of his own volition, he went to see the Yankees in spring training in Florida and asked for a chance to play with the team. General manager Gene Michael gave it to him. At thirty-three, Howe became an overnight success story— again. As former teammate, second baseman Steve Sax put it, "He's better now than he was during his rookie year because he's got a change to go with that ninety mph fastball."

Howe says, "I had to bottom out, get as low as you can. The old self had to die."

Maybe. That December he was arrested for allegedly paying $100 to a DEA informant in Montana, where the Howes have an off-season home, in exchange for a gram of cocaine. Howe had none of the drug on him when he was arrested; his home was searched and none was found there. Through his lawyer, Pat Sherlock, Howe said the federal agents had threatened "to take his pickup, take his home . . . and 'hang' him" if he didn't confess to having tried to buy cocaine.

In June, 1992 Howe decided to plead guilty to a misdemeanor charge of attempting to possess one gram of cocaine. However, U.S. Magistrate Judge Bart Erickson refused to accept the plea and set sentencing for August, when he ultimately placed Howe on probation. In the meantime, the proposed plea managed to put Howe's career on ice: declaring that "Steve Howe has finally extinguished his opportunity to play," Commissioner Fay Vincent suspended him for life.

Howe was surprised by Vincent's timing, since there had not been a legal outcome in court, and he wasted no time filing a grievance with the Players Association to overturn suspension. Howe maintained, in part, that "the suspension is without just cause within the meaning of the Basic Agreement and arbitration panels' decisions in areas of disciplinary suspensions." There were also allegations that Vincent tried to intimidate Yankee executives who wanted to testify on Howe's behalf at the grievance hearing, reportedly summoning them to his office for intensive questioning.

Don Mattingly was speaking for many of his teammates when he said, "I wouldn't be afraid to hold Steve Howe up as an example to kids of someone fighting an addiction. Steve's a good guy who works hard and has an addiction. I don't think what's going on is right. I know it's black and white (in court), but I know so much about the person." He added, "What happened to Steve ... is not something he should be banned from baseball for."

Apparently, Baseball arbitrator George Nicolau agreed. Because in early November, 1992, he reversed Vincent's edict and reinstated the often troubled, but ever talented reliever's Major League eligibility. Many baseball purists were appalled that in a game where batters only get three strikes, a known substance abuser, who brought misfortune on himself, would get another shot. Still others felt the decision meant that Pete Rose's lifetime ban should be reviewed, since if, as many medical experts contend, both drug abuse and gambling are merely forms of addictive behavior, why should a sport which lives and dies by having rules that apply to all, have two sets of standards governing conduct potentially extreme enough to affect the integrity of the game.

Emboldened by his new lease on life, Howe eagerly looked foward to fielding offers as a free agent. And few doubted, with the paucity of pitching and two new expansion teams, that he would have any difficulty hooking on somewhere.

While no one has ever questioned Howe's staying power on the mound, it remains to be seen whether ultimately he has the strength it will take to be victorious in the game that really counts—the one off the field.

Pascual Perez:
"A Fall in the Spring"

Meanwhile, sadly, one of Howe's Yankee teammates hadn't learned a thing from his fellow pitcher's experience, and continued down his own slippery slope to ruin. (He also showed a remarkable disdain for his teammates: with Howe temporarily on ice, the Yankees *needed* Pascual Perez. Instead, he risked banishment from the game to continue his habit.)

Perez, the lanky Dominican pitcher known for his windmilling style, came from a family of nine children and poverty to a life of plenty with the Atlanta Braves in 1983 and made quite a name for himself. But less than a year after his major league debut, the world found out just why Perez was so skinny: on January 9, 1984, he was arrested in Santo Domingo for possession of a half-gram of cocaine. He was sent to prison for three months, and hardnosed Commissioner Bowie Kuhn suspended him until May 16—though an arbitrator butted in and allowed Perez to return on April 28. Wrong message to send to this guy (and others like him), even though at first that didn't appear to be the case.

Things seemed to be going all right for Perez, and what problems he had apparently weren't drug related. On August 14, he started a brawl by slugging Alan Wiggins of the San Diego Padres; the fight ended up with thirteen people being ejected, and five fans arrested. He stayed calm for the rest of the season, and things started out promisingly the next—until he vanished from the Braves for three days, reportedly holed up with a psychic who was exorcising his demons.

Though Perez remained out of the headlines for everything but baseball over the next four years, things were not going well. He was still doing cocaine, and in 1989 ended up missing all of spring training with his new team, the Montreal Expos, so he could clean up in drug rehab once and for all. Seems he didn't try hard enough, however, and the Expos grew tired of watching him. Two months after the season ended he signed with the Yankees, a $5.7 million, three-year deal. However, he showed up late for spring training, claiming he had trouble getting a visa. After playing three games of the season, he's sidelined due to surgery on his shoulder. Comes back in 1991, rotator cuff nice and healed, though he's ten days late to spring training; again, he blames his tardiness on his visa. No partying was going on—he swears it.

Except for being told to get a haircut, nothing much happens this season. Comes 1992 spring training: this time he shows up five days late. Visa troubles? Nope, he says. This is when he was told to show up. He hadn't touched a baseball all winter, hadn't returned any of manager Buck Showalter's calls, but said he felt good and was ready to pitch. Nice of him, considering he'd started just seventeen times for the Yankees in the past two seasons. A few days later, he showed up an hour late for the team photo. No excuses, this time, he said; he just screwed up. He didn't even bother to show up at all the next day. No excuses again, but by then everyone knew what was wrong with the pitcher.

In 1990, Buck Rodgers, who had managed Perez

Pascual Perez in magnificent form after returning to action in May 1991. His return was to prove short-lived. (*AP/Wide World*.)

during the player's stint on the Montreal Expos, said that the pitcher was "a sick man . . . a time bomb that the Yankees will have to monitor closely." He said he never let Perez go anywhere alone, "even to the dentist," or he simply wouldn't show. The reason, he implied, was that Perez was still doing drugs and had to be checked "twice a week."

In March 1992, he tested and retested positive for drugs. Baseball has no fixed penalty for a repeat offense, so Commissioner Fay Vincent made up a proper one: Perez was suspended for a year, without pay. That boiled down to a loss of $1.9 million—and, most likely, his career with the Yankees. At thirty-four, that probably puts an end to his pitching career overall, but with expansion having come to Florida in 1993 and the desire of Latino fans to root for one of their own, who knows what team management might do to draw at the gate?

Perez's teammates were generally saddened and compassionate; only outfielder Mel Hall seemed to have his eye on the ball, though, when he said, "I think you have to be smarter than (Perez)." If you've got a problem . . . you have to get the problem solved." However, he also admitted, "I'm not a big drug-guy fan."

It's too bad there aren't more players like Hall. Maybe then, "hits" would mean what they used to in the sport.

Lyle Alzado:
"Helps Build Strong Bodies
Twelve Different Ways"

Not all drug use is intended to get into the system, provide a momentary high, and then—theoretically—leave the athlete unscathed. Some of it is intended to get in there and stay in the form of muscle.

While it can be argued that psychological problems lead to the use of cocaine and heroin, otherwise sane people have done the potentially more destructive steroids for one reason and one reason only: the pro lifestyle is intoxicating.

At some point, almost every young boy who has played sports has fantasized about growing up to be big enough, strong enough, and fast enough to be a professional athlete. Whether it's Little League baseball, Pop Warner football, or just friends at play in a school yard, something bigger is happening in each youngster's head: it's not his friend Johnny pitching, it's Red Sox flame-thrower Roger Clemens. The count's three balls and two strikes and it's the bottom of the ninth of the seventh and deciding game of the World Series. Bases are loaded and your team is trailing by one run—

Obviously, even very few athletes who are qualified make it to the pros. In fact, the statistics are so overwhelming against it that many prominent blacks have criticized black athletes for not encouraging more young people with athletic ability in high school and college to concentrate on their studies as much as on their athletic skills, so at least they'll have something to fall back on.

But the pro lifestyle is *so* intoxicating—and, more than ever, the purse is so rich—that some aspiring athletes are willing to become a part of it by artificial and life-endangering means—specifically, by taking "performance-enhancing" drugs. The lifestyle is so intoxicating, in fact, that even though Lyle Alzado has paid the ultimate price for having used steroids, you've got to wonder if young people *still* won't think twice about doing what he did. *Lyle was unlucky and got tagged. That won't happen to me . . .*

Alzado grew up on the streets of Brooklyn. As a standout six-foot three-inch, 190-pound teenager, he hadn't heard about steroids. But he *had* heard about the NFL, and he knew that his chances of a pro career were virtually nil because he lacked the size and speed to attract a scholarship offer from a top NCAA school. So he enrolled in a small Texas junior college, Kilgore, then transferred to Yankton College in South Dakota where his chances of being scouted were better. Still, he knew he had to bulk himself up. Eating six and seven meals a day and working out constantly with weights, Alzado was able to pack on 30 pounds of muscle. But even though his on-field play was excellent, Alzado knew that most offensive and defensive NFL linemen weighed a minimum of 250 pounds. Unless something dramatic happened, his best chance of reaching an NFL quarterback was to become a reporter and set up an interview. Then Alzado discovered Dianabol.

Almost overnight, his body was transformed into a 300-pound wall of solid muscle. He grew moody and was prone to explosive outbursts, but although these hurt and concerned his close friends, they proved to be an asset on the football field. Alzado was a bulldozer who suddenly had a legitimate shot at making the NFL. He was so strong, in fact, that he became a Golden Gloves star who years later would last eight rounds in an exhibition fight with Muhammad Ali.

Bingo. Alzado was drafted by the Denver Broncos in 1971. After developing a tolerance for Dianabol, he continued to build up his body with new and different steroids, orally and through injections. "It's hard to remember all the names now," he says bitterly. "I mixed combinations like a chemist." It never occurred to him to stop because he was a success: "I outran, outhit, out anythinged everybody," and the steroids "made me play better and better."

Alzado earned AFC Defensive Player of the Year honors in 1977 while helping the Broncos reach the Super Bowl. Indeed, Alzado's ferocious style of play so endeared him to fans that there was nearly a revolt when the Broncos traded him to the Cleveland Browns in 1979. Alzado's aggressive play helped the Browns get within one game of the Super Bowl in 1981 and made him a favorite in that town too . . . though he was also big among the players who used steroids because he had "ins" to get the goods.

Despite having established himself in the pros, Alzado did not curtail his steroid use. Indeed, he increased it. By the time he joined the Los Angeles Raiders in 1982, he was mixing potent pharmaceutical cocktails that made his metabolism run so fast that he could sleep only three or four hours a night. Tumors grew under the skin where he'd injected himself and had to be surgically removed; his cholesterol level reached 400-plus; and *still* he didn't get the message. "I was warned by doctors, but I didn't listen," he says today. He took the powerful

Bolasterone and Quinolone, some of the strongest steroids one can buy.

Keith Lee, a defensive back, says, "We all knew Lyle was a 'roid monster, but . . . the league was in love with size-plus-speed, and there was a lot of pressure on linemen. I thought of steroids as vitamins for big guys."

In addition, Alzado's personal life suffered. He went through two marriages faster than a bottle of pills. In public, he had a growing paranoia that people wanted to take him on. He couldn't relax. Ever. (His second wife, Cindy—the mother of Alzado's son Justin—says that her ex-husband beat her, but isn't able to blame it all on steroid use. "He was violent because he was mean," she says, "and he didn't want to change." In 1985, when she told him to leave, she says he broke her ribs and left her with a punctured lung.)

In 1986, after fifteen years in pro ball—including being named All Pro twice and playing on a Super Bowl winner in 1984—Alzado was forced to retire due to injuries, ironically, convinced his torn muscles and tendons were "a result of all the steroid use."

With his outgoing personality and rugged good looks, Alzado seemed destined to make the crossover from pro football to TV and movies, just like other defensive standouts such as Fred Dryer and Alex Karras before him. He landed roles in several films, guested on TV series, and opened a popular L.A. night spot and restaurant bearing his name. He made plans to franchise the place and open at least ten more immediately. However, it was clear to those around him that Alzado missed the NFL. He continued to work out almost every day, and continued taking steroids—a habit that cost him $30,000 a year.

In 1990, Alzado's off-field ventures stalled. That, coupled with the dismal play of the Raiders the

year before—particularly on defense—prompted
the forty-one-year-old to try and make a comeback.
Believing that steroids alone were not enough, Alzado decided to take human growth hormone, to
build up his muscle mass, along with the anabolic
steroid testosterone cypionate to increase his size.
Alzado felt that the ultimate reward—the prospect
of a $1 million contract with the Raiders—was well
worth the risk.

Fellow players were astonished at Alzado's physical appearance when he reported for preseason
practice at the Raiders' training facility in El Se-
gundo, California, in July 1990. His leg and arm
muscles were bigger than ever, veritable tree
stumps, with veins rippling just beneath the surface. Many of the guys knew what he'd been up to.

Though he was old enough to be the father of
some of them, Alzado could hardly have been described as paternal, showing the same on-field fero-
ciousness that had once led him to yank off New
York Jets tackle Chris Ward's helmet in the heat
of a playoff game and fling it at him. Alzado was
there to make the team, to become the oldest man
in pro football, and then to help the team win.

He might have succeeded, too, had he not torn a
calf muscle and missed two weeks of camp, and
then ripped cartilage in one of his knees almost
immediately upon returning to practice. The Raiders cut him. Alzado was forlorn and angry, and
made owner Al Davis promise to give him a call
if some of the younger players didn't live up to
expectations. Sure, Davis told him. He'd call.

Like many athletes who had been unable to accept the fact that his time had come and gone,
Alzado was adrift both professionally and personally. Worse, he was continuing to inject human
growth hormone and steroids practically every
day—not just to be ready when the Raiders called,
as he hoped they would, but because, "I liked the

Lyle Alzado (left) as fans want to remember him, zero-ing in on players—like the Philadelphia Eagles Harold Carmichael in November 1979. (Carmichael's catch broke an NFL record for passes caught in consecutive games—106.) (*AP/Wide World.*)

idea of looking the way I looked. I didn't even think about being sick." A few months later, while in a yogurt shop on Melrose Avenue in L.A. with Justin, Alzado felt a tickle in his throat. He went outside and started to cough, then fainted, falling on the sidewalk and breaking his nose. The incident marked the beginning of Alzado's rapid physical disintegration.

By February 1991 he was suffering regular dizzy

spells, and doctors told him he had an inner ear infection. In March, he married his longtime girlfriend, Kathy, and the dizziness continued; Kathy begged him to give up on the steroids. He refused.

On April 16, Alzado became embroiled in a bizarre altercation that eventually forced him to go public with his problem. When five-foot, five-inch, 110-pound L.A. County Deputy Marshall Linda Armstrong went to his tenth-floor Marina Del Rey apartment (ironically, the same building Steve Howe once tried to get into) to serve him with papers in a legal proceeding regarding one of his business ventures, Alzado took exception to being disturbed. It was 7A.M., and he reportedly pushed her toward the edge of a balcony 100 feet above the ground. She sprayed him with mace and called the Sheriff's Department for backup; Alzado was arrested and given a date to appear in the Culver City Municipal Court.

The incident caused both his doctor, Robert Huizenga, and his lawyer, Stephen Michael Lopez, to issue a statement: they said that Alzado was being given oral cortisone and daily chemotherapy treatments for brain cancer, which had been diagnosed on April 5, and he could not have done what he was accused of doing.

"Mr. Alzado had progressive dizziness over several weeks," they said, "culminating in a loss of right arm, right hand, and right leg coordination, slurred speech, and double vision." They said he's "quite unsteady when he walks (and) was incapable of committing any of the alleged acts purported to have occurred."

That was on Friday, April 16. The next day, he suffered a brain seizure and had to be hospitalized. None of it was for show. The man was in worse shape than any quarterback he had blindsided, sacked and nearly decapitated in the heat of gridiron competition.

Fans and sportswriters felt sorry for the athlete, and there was an outpouring of support—until he dropped the real bombshell in June when, in a nationally televised NBC interview with Maria Shriver, he said that not only had he used steroids and human growth hormone, but he and Dr. Huizenga firmly believed the drugs had caused his life-threatening lymphoma by destroying his immune system.

The public relations conscious NFL—knee-jerking as a legacy of former P.R. man Pete Rozelle's thirty-year tenure as commissioner—quickly categorized Alzado's case as the aberration, one individual paying the price for playing doctor without a license. Right.

"Ninety percent of the athletes I know are on the stuff," Alzado said in response. "We're not born to be 280 or 300 pounds or jump thirty feet. Some people are born that way, but not many, and there are some 1,400 guys in the NFL." Alzado added that he feared the fallout of his disclosure would *not* be a cutting back of steroid use: all it takes is to stop using steroids for a few days before a test. "If you cycle it the right way, you will test clean," he says. "The testing is a joke. I can beat the system any day and tell anyone else how to do it."

To his credit, Alzado did not ask for sympathy—only help. He wanted players using steroids and/or human growth hormone to stop, and those who hadn't started not to.

Weakened by a staggering weight loss, bald from chemotherapy, his speech slurred, and financially strapped from mounting hospital and medical bills, Alzado kept up a brave public face. Which made what happened in January 1992 even more pathetic. A dinner had been planned to honor Alzado and to help him financially in his battle. An event committee was formed, a hotel room was reserved, and dignitaries and entertainers were lined up.

Alzado in July 1991, with sports artist Joni Carter.
(*AP/Wide World.*)

The event was to cost nearly $200,000, but because
it was scheduled immediately after the holidays
and in the midst of an economic downturn, bene-
factors proved hard to come by.

To complicate things further, one of the men in
charge of coordinating the event suffered a heart
attack barely a month before the gala. The event
had to be canceled, but the news was never con-
veyed to Alzado. On the day of the event, Alzado
sat in his West Los Angeles home dressed in a tux-

edo, a happy man. A limousine was on the way to pick him and Kathy up and take them to the hotel. Then the phone rang and Alzado learned the heart-breaking news.

Trying hard to mask his disappointment, Alzado, ever the battler, refused to blame anyone for the fiasco. In fact, his illness helped him to put things in perspective: "I'm half the man I was, and not everything works," he said. What the *hell* else could he possibly get depressed about? As he put it, "My strength isn't my strength anymore. My strength is my heart."

In March 1992, Alzado opted to go to Oregon Health Sciences University in Portland to try their new, but still highly experimental "blood brain barrier" chemotherapy treatment. Though he fully intended to beat the disease, he died on the morning of May 14, 1992, after coming down with pneumonia, a common side effect of brain cancer and AIDS which many tabloids had speculated Alzado had..

Alzado went down fighting and damning the drugs that had brought him to this point. It's unfortunate, but at long last he became the hero he always wanted to be.

Earvin Johnson:
"This Magic Moment"

Just *how* intoxicating is the pro lifestyle? The money itself is alluring enough, but consider the other "reward": the women. For most athletes, getting a woman is as easy as walking into a hotel lobby or announcing a party at their home. Trouble is, sometimes sex is as dangerous and/or deadly as drugs. Take, for example, the sad saga of Earvin "Magic" Johnson—the "hero" who may have infected scads of women with the same disease that one of them gave to him.

Despite that, there's no taking from Johnson the wonders he worked on the court—the abilities that got him the fame and women and time bomb in his bloodstream.

Sports fans wouldn't be surprised if the Merriam-Webster people added a new reference in their dictionary: "To do the impossible on a basketball court, but make it look easy for twelve years, in eleven All Star Games and nine NBA Championship Finals." When Magic Johnson left Michigan State after his sophomore year to join the NBA, he accomplished two things. One was to work wonders in repopularizing the sport. In 1979, the NBA was at its low ebb. Television ratings were down, and even the league championship games were shown on a tape-delayed basis. There was even talk that CBS would not bid for rights when its contract lapsed, nor would the other two major networks.

The biggest problem was the NBA's players. Many were known to have used drugs. More significantly, although it was something the League disputed, was the fact that unlike football and baseball, the sport had few "white" stars. The demographics were "wrong" for advertisers.

Magic Johnson changed everything. His infectious smile so completely disarmed fans—black, white, and otherwise—that it was impossible for anyone not to love him, or to resent the $25 million lifetime agreement he ultimately signed with the Los Angeles Lakers. Whenever Magic played, whether his Lakers were ahead or losing, it was apparent that he was playing the game not because it paid him well, or opened other doors for his post-basketball career, but because he loved it. Fans knew that of all the professional players in the sport, Magic would play the game for nothing, anywhere, anytime. Such was the scope of his attachment to and affection for the game that when he built his dream house high in the hills of Bel Air overlooking Los Angeles, he had a basketball hoop built into the wall of his living room.

By the end of the 1980s, League attendance was at an all-time high. NBA teams had played games in Europe and Japan, and owners and players had agreed to do business with each other under the terms of a ground-breaking collective bargaining agreement that mandated players were to receive 53 percent of League revenues. All because Magic, and to a lesser extent Michael Jordan, Larry Bird, and others, brought excitement and wholesomeness back to the game.

Of course, if you had told any of this to Magic when he was growing up in Lansing, Michigan, one of nine children, he'd have thought you were crazy. Because if circumstances had been a little different, he might have ended up working alongside his father, Earvin Sr., who worked at GM during the day and hauled trash in the evening. But Earvin was *very* lucky. He was blessed with the body of a power forward and the quickness of a point guard. He was blessed with a father who made time to introduce him to basketball when Earvin Jr. was in elementary school, and taught him the fundamentals of the game. And he was lucky to receive the public support and encouragement of *Lansing State Journal* sportswriter Fred Stabley, Jr., who also gave the player his nickname.

Perhaps appreciating the opportunity that he had been given is what drove Magic to work so hard to hone his game. And perhaps the care and concern his parents showed him *and* his siblings—refusing to treat Magic differently despite his immense athletic talent and accomplishments—is what also made him the consummate team player. For all of his individual greatness and ability to score points, Magic never hesitated to do the "dirty" work, too—getting rebounds, setting picks, dishing off assists. Even though he individually outscored Larry Bird 24-19 when Michigan State defeated Indiana State for the 1979 NCAA Championship, Magic has said he'd have been just as happy not scoring at all, so long as his team won. And you had to believe him.

His enthusiasm carried over to the pros the following year: even teammate Kareem Abdul-Jabbar, the NBA's all-time leading scorer, was taken aback when Magic ran cross court to embrace him after Jabbar hit a game-winning last-second sky hook in Magic's very first pro game. Afterward, Kareem tried to remind the effervescent rookie that the game represented just one of 82 regular season contests and that if Magic tried to play each one with the same level of intensity, he would quickly burn out.

Little did Kareem know that Magic could play basketball no other way. And though not considered serious contenders for the NBA title that year, the Lakers surprised the experts first by finishing first in the Pacific Division, then beating the favored Philadelphia 76ers in six hard-fought games to win the title. Magic's performance in game six was one of the all-time great individual efforts in NBA history.

One of the more remarkable things about Magic is that despite the Lakers' constant contention for the NBA title, he worked virtually nonstop on improving his game. Between the Lakers first title in 1980 and their second in 1982, when they again defeated the 76ers, Magic worked on developing an outside shot, something that was to be a key to the Lakers beating their longtime rivals, the Boston Celtics, in 1985. When the Lakers again beat the Celtics for the NBA title two years later, it was due largely to Magic having developed a "junior sky hook," his variation on Jabbar's patented "sky hook."

After Laker coach Pat Riley retired in 1990, Magic and new coach Mike Dunleavy converted the Laker fast-break "Showtime" offense into a more deliberate, "Slowtime" half-court game. Despite a poor start, Magic made the new offense work and helped the Lakers upset heavily favored Portland to win the Western Conference title and reach the NBA Championship against Michael Jordan and the Chicago Bulls. In the aftermath of the Lakers' loss, Magic spoke of his determination to add new elements to his game so that the Lakers would be able to make a run at the Bulls' title in 1992. And no one doubted the venerable All-Pro's word.

At the same time, and somewhat ironically, during the 1991 NBA finals, Magic spoke for the first time publicly about retiring. While many were aware that for years Magic had been focusing on his life after basketball, the fact that he chose to speak openly about it caught many off guard. Fans and fellow players had understood and even envied Magic's foresight in signing with a top Hollywood talent agent as well as becoming a spokesperson for products ranging from Kentucky Fried Chicken to Pepsi to Converse basketball shoes to Nestlé chocolate and Nintendo games.

The maturing of Magic took another turn in September 1991, when he married his college sweetheart, Erleatha "Cookie" Kelly.

As the 1991–1992 NBA season loomed, the world literally seemed to belong to Magic. He learned that his wife was pregnant with their first child. He was one of ten NBA players selected to participate in the 1992 Summer Olympics in Barcelona. And because he had run three to four miles daily on a treadmill and lifted weights at the posh sports Club L.A. gym, all summer long, he reported to the Laker training facility in Palm Springs, California, in September in mid-season shape.

As part of their exhibition schedule, the Lakers went to Europe to play a series of games against top European teams, many of whose players Magic expected to meet in the 1992 Olympics. The Lakers returned from the tour victorious, but the trip seemed to have taken a toll on Magic. He was reported to be "jet-lagged" and suffering from the flu, forcing him to miss the last preseason game against the Utah Jazz in Salt Lake City. Then he missed the first three games of the regular season, and members of the press were both surprised and concerned. Nothing short of a severe injury had ever kept Magic out of the Laker lineup before. There were rumors of a heart condition.

In truth, what had happened was that on October 25, just before he was to leave with the Lakers to go to the Salt Palace, Magic received a call in his Salt Lake City hotel room from Laker team physician, Dr. Michael Mellman. From his office in Los Angeles, Mellman told him, "I need to see you in my office. Today."

He didn't tell Magic why, and the athlete assumed that an insurance physical he'd taken had turned up high blood pressure, from which his father also suffered.

When Magic reached the doctor's office, the physician dropped a bombshell: the routine blood test indicated that Magic was infected with the AIDS-causing HIV virus.

Magic lost his breath; he just sat there for a long moment, leaning forward in his seat, stunned. Dr. Mellman offered a glimmer of hope: he wanted to retest Magic immediately. However, he said that until his condition could be diagnosed for certain, it would be better for his own health as well as for the good of his fellow players that he not play with the team.

Magic nodded silently. Worse than the fears for his own health, though, were concerns for his wife, who was seven weeks pregnant. He went home, and when he told her the news he said he'd understand if she wanted a divorce. Her response? "She slapped me upside the head," Magic reports, "and said I was crazy." She, too, went in to be tested.

Nearly two weeks later, on November 6, 1991, after exhaustive tests, there were no more doubts, there had been no error: Magic was HIV positive. Fortunately, his wife and baby were not.

Johnson called his closest friends and told them: talk-show host Arsenio Hall and Larry Bird both wept openly; Pat Riley, Michael Jordan, and player Isiah Thomas were in shock.

The next day, like an earthquake, unconfirmed reports of Magic's condition began to be reported on radio stations across the country. Shortly thereafter, the Lakers announced that a press conference had been scheduled at the Forum in Inglewood, California, at 3 P.M.

No one wanted to believe it. Somehow, they hoped that the unconfirmed reports had been wrong, someone's idea of a cruel joke. And when Magic Johnson entered the Forum press club shortly after 3 P.M. and flashed his trademark smile as he walked to the podium, there was one last, brief flicker of hope. But then Magic calmly announced what sports fans worldwide hoped they wouldn't hear: "Because of the HIV virus that I have obtained, I am retiring from the Lakers today."

In an instant, a disease that had been identified essentially with gay men and intravenous drug users could no longer be pigeonholed: at six-foot-nine, 220 pounds, Magic Johnson didn't fit anyone's profile of a potential AIDS victim. He had been everyone's All-American, the red-blooded boy whose life had been—well, Magic.

Magic announced that he was dedicating himself to the fight against AIDS and, more specifically, to educating the black community about safe sex. He did not speculate how or from whom he might have contracted the virus, stating only that he assumed full responsibility for what had happened. In short, whoever gave it to him was not to blame; his own behavior, having unprotected sex, was.

The question was, where *did* it come from? He said later, "After I arrived in Los Angeles in 1979, I did my best to accommodate as many women as I could, most through unprotected sex." No lie: just a few months before, there had been a rowdy party at his Bel Air mansion in which strippers and porn stars had partied with Magic and other athletes. Word of orgies like these diminished the star athlete in the eyes of many: Martina Navratilova spoke for many when she said, "Magic says he was trying to accommodate these women. That is just terrible. Just think about the word. He's saying it's okay to be promiscuous as long as you use a condom. That's not good." The outpouring of support also irked her: "If I had the AIDS virus," she said, would people be as understanding? "No, because they'd say I'm gay—I had it coming. That's why they're accepting it with him, because supposedly he got it through heterosexual contact. There have been other athletes who died from AIDS, and they were pushed aside because they either got it from drugs or they were gay."

She had a point, but hers was a voice in the wilderness. Most who heard the press conference compared it favorably to the terminally ill Lou Gehrig's legendary Yankee Stadium retirement speech in 1939. Of course, there was a big difference between Gehrig's malady and Magic being HIV-positive, and Martina's telling choice of words—"supposedly he got it through heterosexual contact"—were echoed by many.

Magic was quick to respond. "I'm sure most of America has heard rumors that I am gay. Well, you can forget that. Some people started the talk during the NBA finals in 1988 and 1989 when I kissed Isiah on the cheek as a pregame salute to our friendship. I have never had a homosexual encounter. Never. I know that won't satisfy some people but it really doesn't matter what they might say about me. My skin is real thick."

The revelation that Magic Johnson's sexual partners had numbered in the thousands did not quell the panic in the heterosexual community. Across the country, AIDS hot lines were deluged with calls. In some major cities, the wait for the HIV blood test was four weeks or longer. Labs worked double shifts. Despite the difference between the number of sexual partners the average American has had and Magic—and, more significantly, Magic's sexual contacts with sports "groupies" who, in

Magic Johnson bids farewell to basketball. With him, on the far right, are Kareem Abdul-Jabbar and, between them, NBA Commissioner David Stern. (*AP/ Wide World.*)

turn, had had sex partners in the hundreds themselves—AIDS specialists were quick to point out that it only took one wrong partner and one wrong sexual experience to contract the deadly disease.

But if the public was sobered, fellow NBA players were horrified—especially coming, as it did, on the heels of Wilt Chamberlain's disclosure in his autobiography *The View from Above* that he had slept with more than 20,000 women. Where sex is concerned, so many athletes were like kids in a candy store who thought that a different set of rules applied to their behavior. Even the fans accepted that, which is why hardly anyone faulted

Magic's married Laker teammate, James Worthy, who was arrested in his Houston hotel room in 1990 for soliciting sex from two women he had ordered from an escort service, but who, in fact, were police officers participating in an undercover sting operation. (Worthy pleaded no contest to the charge, and accepted a thousand dollar fine and agreed to perform 40 hours of community service.)

With Magic's revelation, athletes were finally forced to confront the dangers of their lifestyle. "This has to scare everybody," said Dominique Wilkins, superstar forward of the Atlanta Hawks and one of the NBA's more eligible bachelors. "The more I think about it, the more scared I am. In fact, I'm scared to death." (Wilkins should know: the target of several paternity suits, he said that many women *discourage* the use of condoms. "They don't want safe sex, because they think if they have your baby, they'll be set for life.")

In the first few months after his announcement, Magic Johnson maintained a very active public profile, and AIDS victims and activists were encouraged. Previously, the only athletes to have died of AIDS had been gay—like former Washington Redskin tight end Jerry Smith, or Olympic decathlon luminary Tom Waddell—or drug users like Baltimore Oriole second baseman Alan Wiggins, race car driver Tim Richmond, and boxer Esteban Dejesus. And when Magic accepted a position on President Bush's National Commission on AIDS, it was widely believed that he would use the role to press the conservative administration to do more for AIDS victims.

But then, Magic's priorities seemed to change. He appeared to miss basketball so much that he was willing to risk his life by announcing that he was considering a basketball comeback. (And not for the money: he's worth $100 million.) This was undoubtedly fueled when fans voted Magic to be a starter for the Western Conference in the 1992 All-Star Game, where there were strong opinions pro and con about whether he should play. Some felt that Magic should participate to show that people who had the HIV virus could still lead active, productive lives. Others felt that if Magic's performance were lackluster, it would do a great disservice to the cause.

Despite the controversy, Magic opted to play. And play he did, accumulating 25 points, five rebounds and nine assists, en route to leading the West to a 40 point victory over the East in a performance highlighted by three consecutive three-point shots in the game's closing minutes, the last two while being closely guarded by Isaiah Thomas and Michael Jordan. Magic was the overwhelming choice for MVP. A week later, in a tear-filled, heart-tugging ceremony during half-time of a Los Angeles Laker-Boston Celtic game at the Forum, Magic's number 32 was retired.

Then, suddenly, in late September, after leading the "Dream Team" to the gold medal in Barcelona, Magic announced he was unretiring. But just as suddenly, on the eve of the NBA season, several pros, most prominently Karl Malone, publicly expressed reservations about playing their bruising, often bloody sport against someone HIV positive. Coupled with speculation he wasn't telling the "full story" about how he had gotten the AIDS virus, i.e., he had had homosexual contacts despite his repeated denials, Magic felt he had no choice but to retire for good, stating: "The controversies surrounding my return are taking away from both basketball and the larger issue of living with HIV". Despite Magic's uncertain future, former Laker coach, Pat Riley for one, remained optimistic. "He has the heart of a great warrior. He will not be beaten."

Jerry Smith:
"A Star Player"

Though the media and average sports fans would be quick to laud Magic Johnson and Arthur Ashe for the dignity they displayed when announcing that they were HIV positive and had AIDS, respectively, both sports stars were quick to add—lest anyone get the "wrong idea" about them—that they contracted their illness due to some cruel twist of fate. Neither man was gay nor had been involved in intravenous drug use.

But before either man stepped forward, another athlete made a similarly tragic announcement. A man who, in his own right, was just as gifted at his sport as Magic and Arthur Ashe were at theirs. An athlete who was, perhaps, even more admired because he was the first to "go public." That he has rarely been mentioned in the AIDS-in-sports debate is an insult to his memory, and a tribute to the shortsightedness of many sportswriters.

But then, Jerry Smith was a man whose life was filled with irony. Despite grabbing 421 passes for 5,496 yards and 60 touchdowns in thirteen seasons as a tight end for the Washington Redskins, and finishing among the NFL's top ten pass receivers for four consecutive seasons (1966–1969), Smith was reluctant to bask in the sunlight of his achievements. He was a shy man, one whose inherent gentleness stood in stark contrast to the violent world in which he earned acclaim week after week. At six-feet three-inches and 210 pounds, with stylishly cut, moppish long blond hair and clear blue eyes, Smith looked more like a movie star than like someone who had the daunting task of protecting legendary NFL quarterbacks like Sonny Jurgenson and Billy Kilmer from the mayhem a 260 pound-plus defensive end could inflict.

Unlike many other players who seemed to be out just for themselves, Smith prided himself on contributing whatever he could to help his team. That was never more evident than in 1972, when the Redskins reached Super Bowl VII where they lost 14-7 to the only team ever to complete an NFL season undefeated, the Miami Dolphins. Despite catching only 21 passes that year, seven of Smith's receptions were for touchdowns.

Team play was Jerry Smith's way. Ted Marchibroda, then offensive coordinator for the Redskins under George Allen, and now head coach of the Indianapolis Colts, flatout calls Smith "the most unselfish player I've ever been around. Mostly players want to know how much they'll be featured in the game plan each week. That didn't matter with Jerry."

Center Len Hauss said, "He never let you down. When there was a big catch to make, he made it. When there was a key block to throw, he threw it."

Smith was popular with his teammates for other reasons as well. At a racially tense time, when it was uncommon in pro sports for black players to share rooms with white players on road trips, Smith chose to room with defensive back Brig Owens. Not to make a point, but because he saw people as people, period. In a sport where hazing new teammates and rookies is extremely popular, Smith made it a point to make newcomers feel wel-

Rugged Jerry Smith of the Washington Redskins. (*AP/Wide World.*)

come. Dave Butz—the six-foot seven-inch, 300-pound defensive tackle who became a Redskins star—free safety Mark Murphy and kick return specialist Ricky Harris, all say that one reason they were able to catch on and succeed with the team was that Smith went out of his way to welcome them and help them fit in.

Yet for all his generosity, Smith remained an intensely private man. Following his retirement from pro football in 1978, he operated a construction company, opened a restaurant in Texas, and worked in the mortgage business. He also tried to find time to enjoy life, traveling and playing golf. Women who met him, and the wives and girlfriends of former teammates, often wondered why an easygoing, down-to-earth guy like Smith never married; if teammates and friends knew, they never let on.

But friends who saw Smith in the summer of 1985 chucked the code of silence among each other, openly wondering if something were amiss. He still had his All-American good looks, but he'd begun to lose weight and tired easily during workouts or biking or going out on the links. He consulted a doctor in Florida and, during the course of his examination, was given an HIV test. The initial results were negative, and although he continued to lose weight he did not change his lifestyle, possibly infecting a number of sexual partners.

By December of 1985, as his weight loss and fatigue increased, he was also being plagued by night sweats and bouts of the flu and diarrhea. Entering Holy Cross Hospital, he was again tested for AIDS: this time, the test came back positive.

At first, Smith quietly sought treatment at Holy Cross and at George Washington University. But his condition worsened quickly, and by June of 1986 he was incapable of keeping even the smallest morsels of food down. Sustenance was administered intravenously and he was almost constantly on painkillers. His mother and other family members visited daily and watched as he dropped to a skeletal 140 pounds and would, without warning, drift asleep in the middle of a conversation. At his request, no one outside his family or closest circle of friends was told what was wrong.

Just before the end, however, Smith began to think differently. He began to feel as though some good could come of what was happening, and told his mother, Laverne, that he was thinking of going public. Fighting back tears, she asked if he was afraid that the Redskins might not induct him into the Washington Hall of Stars at RFK Stadium that fall, as they had promised, if they learned about his disease.

In a voice barely above a whisper, Smith assured his mother that the committee would not change its mind and that his former teammates, the management, and fans would understand. Then, in an act braver than catching any pass while surrounded by defenders, Jerry Smith gave a *Washington Post* reporter a deathbed interview and, though he wouldn't discuss his lifestyle, he identified the opponent he was facing in the only game that really mattered—the game of life.

"I want people to know what I've been through and how terrible this disease is," he said. "Maybe it will help people understand and maybe it will help research. Maybe something positive will come out of this."

Something did—though not all that Smith had hoped. Many people were forced to change their view of what they thought an AIDS sufferer (read: gay man) was. It's difficult to say whether these people became more tolerant, but certainly their eyes were opened a bit. Smith had taken a small, first step in smashing stereotypes.

Unfortunately, his admission didn't destigmatize the disease, stimulate AIDS research, or spur the kind of awareness and fund-raising that Magic Johnson or Arthur Ashe were able to do a half a decade later. However, if the public wasn't quite as moved as he'd hoped, none of his teammates feared guilt by association. When the end came for the forty-three-year-old on October 16, 1986, there were only tears and words of praise. Indeed, former teammates Rickie Harris, who had played against Smith in college when he attended Arizona and Smith played at Arizona State, left his own bed at Holy Cross Hospital, where he was scheduled to undergo knee surgery, to attend Smith's funeral. Hall of Famers Charley Taylor and Sonny Jurgenson were two of Smith's pallbearers, as was Brig Owens, and among the mourners was Dave Kopay, who played for the Redskins during the 1969–1970 seasons and who later disclosed that not only was he gay, but that many other (unnamed) NFL players were as well.

Although the disease that had vanquished Smith was never mentioned by name at the memorial service attended by 250 mourners, his sister, Bonnie Smith Gilchrist, had portions of a letter that Jerry wrote to her read by pro football great Joe Namath at an AIDS Project Los Angeles ceremony. In many ways, Smith's words were more poignant than any eulogy or tribute he received:

> "I'm trying hard to fight AIDS the best way I know how, by letting people know that the past days have been hard, difficult, bad, but there is never anything so bad that anything good doesn't come from it. I've learned just how supportive and caring people can be. Relatives, friends, former teammates and people I've never met. These people have shown me there is a reason to fight on."

On November 2, 1986, before the Redskins's home game against the Minnesota Vikings, Jerry Smith was inducted into the Washington Hall of Stars.

Tim Richmond:
"Life in the Fast Lane"

Smith took some licks from ignorant members of the sport, but it was nothing compared to the reception accorded another AIDS victim, one whose sport was even less tolerant of the activities that can cause AIDS.

It was June 7, 1987; Pocono, Pennsylvania. For race car driver Tim Richmond, it was the best of times and certainly the worst of times.

Nicknamed "Hollywood" by his peers of the National Association of Stock Car Auto Racing—because of his shoulder-length hair, thick mustache, and penchant for sunglasses and loud clothes—Richmond was headed for the checkered flag when his hands tightened on the steering wheel and tears began streaming down his ruggedly handsome face. As he said later, "I cried all through the final lap, the first time I ever did that. I couldn't believe I was back ... I guess I'd thought about winning a championship so much, and when I won Pocono I proved (I) could do it."

He'd won the important Heinz Southern 500 the year before, but this was special because he knew it would be his last victory—certainly one of his last races. He was taking heavy doses of AZT to combat AIDS, and realized that at any time he could suffer a relapse like the one that had left him

91

hospitalized with double pneumonia at the end of the 1986 racing season.

Even as he entered the victory lane, savoring his win, he couldn't suppress a welling of bitterness that this was a too-early conclusion to his long-held dream of making the NASCAR racing circuit part of mainstream American sport, with himself as the linchpin.

When he first came to the sport, Richmond was an even flashier breath of fresh air than "Broadway" Joe Namath had been to football or snazzy Walt "Clyde" Frazier to basketball in the 1960s. And that had been his intention.

Most of the NASCAR drivers were good old boys, conservative Southerners who chewed tobacco, drank beer by the six-pack, and favored cowboy boots and blue jeans with big-buckled belts. Nothing wrong with that, as long as the guys could race.

But Richmond had a vision, a plan. Though race car drivers like Richard Petty and A. J. Foyt earned substantial amounts of money endorsing automotive products, Richmond wanted to interest Madison Avenue in drivers who could do all kinds of commercials: for breakfast cereals, clothing, appliances, you-name-it.

Raised in Ashland, Ohio, and later in Miami, Florida, by upper-middle-class parents, Richmond was always a young man in a hurry, determined to push himself and life to the limit. He learned to fly when he was just fourteen, and by the time he was seventeen he was licensed to fly multi-engine planes and helicopters. He dazzled some folks who knew him, and frustrated others; as his mother, Evelyn, puts it, "He wasn't the kind of young man who could sit still."

At the same time, he was a young man in search of an audience. At the Miami Military Academy, which he attended from 1969 to 1973, he found both satisfaction and attention as a football and

Racer Tim Richmond. (*Courtesy of Evelyn Richmond.*)

track star. But he decided that speed and cars was his thing, and he became interested in race car driving in 1976. The following year he drove in his first race, and the year after that he won the U.S. Auto Club Sprint Car Rookie of the Year award.

Enrolling in Jim Russell's driving school at Willow Springs International Raceway, he earned the distinction of becoming the fastest student in school history.

Amazingly, in 1980, even though he'd only run in five Indianapolis-style races, Richmond earned a spot in the Indy 500 field. Not only did he post the fastest time during practice, he finished ninth in the race and was voted Indy Driver Rookie of the Year.

Surprisingly—given Richmond's penchant for snappy clothes—the sleek, aerodynamic Indy cars didn't capture his fancy. He preferred stock cars, cars that resemble ordinary Buicks, Chevrolets, and Oldsmobiles, except for the fact that their engines are souped-up and their tires are more durable. To some race buffs, Indy car racing is viewed as a driver more or less just steering, hoping that an expensive piece of machinery doesn't break down. Conversely, the NASCAR circuit is a truer test of a driver's skill, a contest of man against man in machines that haven't been tested in wind tunnels or designed by computer.

Although shunned by veterans on the circuit who resented his family's relative wealth and his own tendency to showboat, Richmond could sure as hell drive, and he grudgingly earned the respect of his peers. In 1986, he captured seven racing titles—two more than his chief rival, Dale Earnhardt, who would later become the sport's top driver (1990–1991). Barring disaster, he was well on his way to becoming one of the sport's greats.

Thought by many to have been the inspiration for the character played by Tom Cruise in the film *Days of Thunder,* the outgoing Richmond secured his claim on the "Hollywood" monicker when he became a racing stunt double for Burt Reynolds, and spent some time in Hollywood taking acting classes. He told reporters that he planned to be Paul Newman in reverse—go from being a champion race car driver to renowned actor.

Unfortunately, Richmond's outgoing nature and strongly held opinions ("He saw things as black and white," his mother says today), while appealing to many fans, won him few friends in the business. His first run-in with NASCAR occurred early in his racing career, when he blew a tire in a race and went to the hospital to get himself looked at—only to be refused admittance. He understandably threw a fit, of which NASCAR did not approve.

Things got worse when he began showing up late for prerace drivers' meetings, and even fell asleep during one—the result of his full schedule and outside interests. Fellow drivers not only questioned his dedication, they reportedly asked NASCAR officials to informally investigate Richmond's lifestyle. No doubt some of the good old boys thought that his "Hollywood" ways just *had* to involve drugs. The suspicions became especially strong after his seclusion at the end of the 1986 season because of the double pneumonia, and his sudden, surprising withdrawal from the Southern 500 in 1987, when he complained of a persistent cough that he was afraid would cause a relapse.

Enter the conspiracy to destroy Tim Richmond.

Richmond's explanations were perceived by many to be a smokescreen for drug problems. Tragically, because of these suspicions, and not hard facts, he would run his last race—the Champion Spark Plug 400 at Michigan International Raceway—in August of 1987.

Before NASCAR would clear Richmond to race in the Daytona 500, he was ordered to submit to drug testing. He was amenable, though he had to take precautions. While educated folks realize there are many ways to contract AIDS, Richmond knew that in the macho world of stock car racing, "the word" among racers would be that he was either a drug user or gay. Since Richmond didn't want to have to deal with those allegations, he stopped taking AZT six weeks before the race, to make sure the medication wouldn't show up in tests and his illness would remain a secret.

Unfortunately, Richmond's test returned positive for opiates; he was stunned, and attributed the results to his having taken the over-the-counter, nonprescription, perfectly legal drugs Sudafed and Advil, to combat a sinus problem.

NASCAR banned him from racing when the initial tests came back positive, then rescinded the ban when retesting revealed the "opiates" to have been painkillers—just like Richmond had said they were. But NASCAR wasn't finished with "Peck's Bad Boy." Although they couldn't ban Richmond, they asked to see his medical records—just to prove that he didn't have a drug problem . . . or a problem of any other kind.

He refused. They had no *right* to ask that.

NASCAR hero Richard Petty disagreed. He regarded the organization's efforts as a form of self-preservation, and said, "I'm not for anybody or anything who tries to destroy what most of us have spent thirty years trying to build up, and this seems to be what he's trying to do."

Evelyn Richmond was convinced that NASCAR was simply trying to make life rough for her son, however, and she said later, "Tim knew all along they would pull something like this. They were out to get him. He was not an easy person to get along with, but he was a good person who cared about the sport. He wanted to see it grow and evolve. NASCAR wanted to keep things the way they were."

Outraged by the request, Richmond not only refused, he responded with a $20 million lawsuit against NASCAR for defamation of character. Unfazed, NASCAR made good their threat and he wasn't allowed to race. Hurt, Richmond responded by Peck-ishly hiring a plane to fly overhead with a banner that read, "Fans, I miss you. Tim Richmond."

Unfortunately, even though Richmond felt he had a very strong case against NASCAR, the suit was settled without comment from either side in January of 1988. Richmond's mother later said that he really didn't have the energy or attention to deal with it because "he was so devastated by having the disease that I can't even find the words to explain how he felt. He was very, very angry. He was angry at God, he was angry at everything." And, of course, he was thoroughly disgusted with NASCAR.

In time, the disease that Richmond had fought so hard to conceal took an impossible-to-conceal physical toll. He lived on a small boat near Ft. Lauderdale, Florida, occasionally stopping for a meal or drinks at one of the many small bars and restaurants along the south Florida waterfront.

People tended to let him be, but those who knew him could sense the anger he felt at being abandoned by his fellow drivers, and also at the press for the way they were speculating about the nature of his illness. He couldn't understand why it mattered anymore.

But Richmond did nothing to dispel the rumors and innuendo. He didn't speak to the press (which had failed to rally around him), and his physical appearance, which had meant so much to him, mattered little now. More often than not, "Hollywood" walked around haggard and barefoot. He loved tooling around on his motorcycle, but stopped after an accident in February of 1989 landed him on the asphalt and in the hospital with head injuries.

On August 13, 1989, at the Good Samaritan Hospital, the thirty-four-year-old Richmond left the rat race for good. Those who admired his skills and courage found it difficult to believe he was gone.

Initially, the cause of death was not revealed. Ten days later, however, his parents decided to go public in an effort to warn other young people about the hazards of unsafe sex ... and also to quiet other rumors. Evelyn Richmond admitted that although her son had died of AIDS, she told reporters most emphatically that he "was not a homosexual and he never used a needle."

To substantiate the claim, Richmond's personal physician, David W. Dodson, called a news conference in West Palm Beach, Florida, to announce that the stock car racer had contracted AIDS from an unknown woman. "There's no way of knowing who that woman was. Tim was a celebrity with a lot of charisma, a handsome guy. He naturally attracted a lot of women." (Shortly before the book went to press, Evelyn reiterated, "Tim had no idea where he contracted the disease, but it was a woman. There were always women.")

Not that it mattered, really. Sadly, very few of his fellow racers or colleagues came forward to eulogize him. In the fore was the classy Rick Hendrick, who owned some of the cars Richmond drove in his triumphant years, and who said of him, "As a driver, Tim had the most talent I've ever seen. He had that spark and charisma that could inspire awe in his driving."

The sad thing was that for Richmond, the illness not only took him from the sport he loved, it sent him into hiding. If he'd come along two years later, when someone else got "caught" after enjoying the kinds of "opportunities" afforded to one who is a sports superstar, things might have been considerably different. . . .

Arthur Ashe:
"A New Kind of Open"

On April 8, 1992, forty-eight-year-old Arthur Ashe stood before the press at the New York headquarters of Home Box Office—for which he worked as a sports commentator—and addressed them with the same kind of grace and dignity that have characterized his thirty-two years in the public eye.

With his wife, Jeanne, on one side, and New York's peripatetic Mayor David Dinkins on the other, he said, "Some of you have heard that I've tested positive for HIV, the virus that causes AIDS. That is indeed the case."

With those words, the six-foot one-inch Richmond, Virginia, native became the second sports figure in less than a year to announce that he was fighting a life-and-death struggle with the dread disease. Unlike Magic Johnson, however, Ashe did not get AIDS from unsafe sex. He got it from a blood transfusion which, at the time, could not be screened for the virus.

During his historic career, which began when he won the National Junior Championship at the age of seventeen, UCLA graduate Ashe won an amazing 33 professional tennis singles titles, including a Grand Slam championship in 1970 and Wimbledon in 1975 (his only championship there), whipping Jimmy Connors for the title. He was the first Amer-

Arthur Ashe faces John Alexander in their World Cup Tennis Tournament match in 1979. Ashe won, but his luck was about to change. (*AP/Wide World.*)

ican player to earn over $100,000 in one year (1970).

However, what Ashe did off the field was often as impressive as what he did on. He came to prominence in a time of social unrest, and says, "In the sixties, being a black athlete in the middle of the black social revolution, you were obliged to get involved in that issue." He was being modest: though he adds that he had "a terrific willingness to do that," he fought hard and diligently for civil rights, doing so in a way that was both reasonable and effective. And he struggled for the rights of blacks not just in this country, but in South Africa as well, becoming an early and vigorous opponent of apartheid. He also spent a lot of time and money working on behalf of underprivileged children.

Despite his activism—which, however just, tends to scare off many sponsors—Ashe was so articulate, and was such a champion, that he had no trouble earning big money as a spokesperson for Coca-Cola, American Safety Razors, and other products. Unlike many athletes, he also had a remarkably stable home life, having married photographer Jeanne Moutoussamy when she came to shoot him at a sports function in 1977. Though he had plunged in the tennis rankings by the end of the decade, life was good for the superstar.

Then, in the summer of 1979, Ashe went to the hospital after experiencing chest pains. Doctors discovered that he had suffered a heart attack and, later that year, Ashe underwent quadruple bypass surgery. He recovered quickly, and not only resumed his civic duties and endorsement schedule, but spent two years as the National Campaign Chairman for the American Heart Association.

Unfortunately, the surgery wasn't entirely successful and in the spring of 1983 Ashe was back under the knife for a double bypass. It was during this operation that he was unwittingly given the HIV-infected blood. Screening of the blood supply wasn't instituted until two years later.

In September 1988, shortly after the publication of his black sports history book *Hard Road to Glory,* and the birth of his only child, daughter Camera, Ashe suffered a new setback as he lost all motor function in his right hand. In an effort to find out why, doctors did a biopsy of his brain tissue and found the cause to be toxoplasmosis. The parasitic infection is regarded as a "marker" for AIDS, and doctors discovered that he was indeed suffering from a fully established case of the disease (as opposed to being HIV positive).

Ashe's initial concerns were for the health of his wife and daughter, and his burden was eased considerably when tests revealed that they were HIV negative. He was placed on AZT four times a day, an antibiotic three times a day, an antifungus medicine, and a treatment—administered once a month—to prevent pneumonia. He says that since that time he responded exceedingly well to the medication and has "six good days for every one bad day. I can function very well." As a result of his illness, he began spending more time with his family and marginally less in the public eye.

Cut to March 1992. Only Ashe's close circle of friends knew he was sick, but—apparently—one of them leaked the story to a sports reporter at *USA Today.* The reporter phoned Ashe and confronted him with the information, saying he would publish the news only if Ashe confirmed it.

Ashe recalls, "It put me in the unenviable position of having to lie if I wanted to protect our privacy." He couldn't do that, and told the reporter it was true. Even though the paper didn't run the story, Ashe knew it was only a matter of time before some paper did—and, after thinking about it until three in the morning, decided to go public.

He reluctantly canceled a meeting with Washington, D.C., area kids he was to address and flew from his home in Virginia to New York.

Billie Jean King had known about his illness since 1988. When he called her—as he did thirty of his closest friends—she said, "I cried a lot because he really didn't want to talk about it."

Errol Campbell, the Davis Cup coach, also hurt for his friend, but said, "The more I think sports figures come forward, top stars, I think the government will put more money into it."

As for Ashe, though he knew he'd be in a position to do good, he resented being forced to reveal his secret.

"I am not running for some office of public trust," he said at the press conference, "nor do I have stockholders to account to. It is only that I fall under the dubious umbrella of 'public figure.' "

It wasn't just the invasion of privacy that bothered him, although that *was* an issue. The unspoken truth was that he knew he'd have to use some of the precious time he had left to become an AIDS spokesperson, à la Magic Johnson.

Again, Ashe has *never* been backward about trying to move causes forward. But he also wasn't naive. He says, "I assumed three-and-one-half years ago that I wouldn't be here now. But not only am I here now, I'm doing very well." He added, however, "Since the day I found out, what proscribes what I can do more than anything else is, *I don't have much time*. And I've got to try and squeeze whatever I want to do into a smaller period of time."

Suddenly, that time had been reduced considerably by what he knew he would be asked to do to encourage efforts to fight AIDS.

Then too, he said that there is, unfortunately, still a stigma attached to AIDS.

At the press conference, Jeanne—taking over when her husband was briefly overcome with emo-

Arthur Ashe is momentarily overcome during the new York press conference in which he announced that he had AIDS. (*AP/Wide World.*)

tion—read from a prepared statement, "Camera already knows that perfect strangers come up to Daddy on the street and say hi. Even though we've begun preparing Camera for this news, beginning tonight Arthur and I must teach her how to react to new, different, and sometimes cruel comments."

In an interview after the press conference, Ashe

elaborated. "The quality of one's life changes irrevocably when something like this becomes public. Reason and rational thought are too often waived out of fear, out of caution, or out of just plain ignorance."

He added that he expected to experience "a loss of control, the loss of some freedoms to pursue things that I had wanted to pursue. But," he said with his typical calm and intelligence, "I'll just learn how to adjust to that." And once again thinking of the public good, he said that although his own earning ability may be compromised, "With each revelation that comes out, each time the public is educated a bit more and I think there is a bit less hysteria and a bit more realism about what the true nature (of the disease) is."

Whether Ashe's words prove prophetic or merely wishful remains to be seen. But as he did when he broke down barriers in tennis, Ashe proved himself to be a man of poise, class, and determination.

Magic Johnson was quick to respond to Ashe's action: "It takes great courage and strength to make such an announcement," he said. "I applaud his decision to make his condition known and I'm eager to speak with him so that we may join forces in our efforts."

His manager, Ray Benton, spoke what was on the minds of many when he said, "It simply isn't fair that one of the truly good people in the world has had such a run of bad luck on the medical side." Then, he added, "The AIDS movement has really gained a great asset."

Since his press conference, Ashe has repeatedly shown that he would not let his condition inhibit his efforts to help others, even if his own health was put further at risk. In September, 1992, shortly after being arrested for participating in a demonstration protesting the Bush administration's policy of repatriating Haitian refugees, Ashe suffered a heart attack; fortunately, prompt medical attention was available to save his life.

Wilt Chamberlain:
"20,000 Babes Under the C"

Arthur Ashe was a faithful husband, and he got AIDS. He was unlucky. Wilt Chamberlain was a satyr, and he didn't. He was lucky. It's a strange world.

In any case, this matter of basketball legend Wilt Chamberlain (self)-reportedly having slept with 20,000 different women certainly deserves a place in *Sports Babylon*, if not in the *Guinness Book of World Records* and *Ripley's Believe It or Not*.

Twenty *thousand* women.

Assuming Wilt the Stilt started when he was fifteen (which is what he claims), that makes—by his calculation—1.2 women a day. *Different* women. And that doesn't include seconds or thirds with the same women.

Wilt Chamberlain is a big man, and a gracious one. At a book-signing shindig for his autobiography, he was asked about the claim, and said with a laugh, "My pro stats are pretty amazing too, but nobody questions those."

"True," he was told. "But we *saw* those."

He looked down with an expression like *Why are you bothering me, little weasel?* Instead, he simply asks, "So you think I'm lying?"

"No," he's told, quickly. "Exaggerating, maybe?"

He smiles and shakes his head. Signs a book. Says, "Why would I need to exaggerate? If the number were five thousand women, would anyone be less amazed? Do I gain something by inflating that?"

He's got a point. As he modestly explains his appeal in his book, "Many young ladies . . . want to try something different. *I* am the most different thing they can find." He also implies that the number would have been greater if he had dallied right before games, which he didn't (unlike fellow Laker James Worthy, who was arrested for reportedly trying to pick up a pair of undercover agent "hookers" a few hours before a game).

Actually, the total isn't as incredible as some of Wilt's individual stats—for example, his claim that he pleasured fourteen of those women in one night. But, again, we'll just have to take the former Los Angeles Laker's word for it.

Steve Garvey:
"Base Ball"

Obviously, not every athlete who has slept with a number of women has the HIV virus. Wilt is proof of that. But sex presents other kinds of dangers: the wrong kind can ruin careers. For instance—

The first baseman with movie-star good looks who did his best to be the kind of player everyone could look up to. When he was in his prime, just to shake his hand was a thrill for most of us. Whether he enjoyed being a hero to give kids a role model (as he's said) or for his own ego (as his ex-wife Cyndy has suggested) is moot: he was out there giving his all to the fans and to the game. If he had the flu, he was in the field, playing. Once, he had to take twenty-two stitches in his face . . . but he was at his post, ready to field and hit. He set a National League record by playing in 1,207 straight games. If there were a charitable cause, he was at this auditorium or that dinner or some other fund-raising function. If you wrote to him, he wrote back. If a hospital needed someone to cheer up kids in a ward, he went. Garvey didn't need a limo: he drove himself.

He refused to socialize with the other players, whom he felt were too loud, drank too much, or lasciviously ogled every skirt that passed their way. He was quiet, thoughtful, and preferred to hang out with older men, quieter folks like coach Tommy

Lasorda. He never swore; not once. Even when he was having trouble in his rookie season, and fans would confront him outside the stadium or even call him at home, he would hear them out—like a flagellant. He honestly felt that if he couldn't deliver the goods, he deserved the scourging.

Above all, this churchgoing straight arrow seemed devoted to his wife and family. In public, or in photographs, they were always holding hands, hugging, smiling. Steve Garvey and beautiful Cyndy Truhan had met when they were both students at Michigan State University. Her dream was to go on to medical school; his was to play baseball for the Los Angeles Dodgers, the team he'd revered since he was a child. They married in 1971, and Cyndy put her own ambitions aside so that he could pursue his career.

His rise to the top was quick, and when he got there he stayed. Not only did he make it onto the Dodgers, he was a ten-time All-Star. And when the Dodgers wanted younger blood, he helped the San Diego Padres win their first, and to date only, division title. To say that he gave his team 100 percent is an understatement.

Unfortunately, after ten years, Cyndy didn't feel there was much of a marriage anymore. Her husband was never around, and his daughters Whitney and Krisha rarely got to spend time with him. Home was just a pit stop as he played or spoke to groups or played golf or worked for his charitable Steve Garvey Foundation.

Other women? "I never suspected another person," says Cyndy, "because Steve's image was too important to him."

After painful deliberation, Cyndy decided to move out of the house with the girls. But the separation—for which the press gave *her* a lot of flak— seemed to work, and after a year they sold their home. (Even there, however, Cyndy ended up going it alone because Steve couldn't find the time to help out.)

While Cyndy was busy clearing out the belong-ings she'd left behind, she began to have second thoughts. She wanted to talk to Steve, to be abso-lutely sure, to see if the separation had made him see things differently. And to see if a bad, final year with Los Angeles had made him realize that there were things more important than baseball and fame.

Sobbing and confused, she went to his office at the Foundation, just a five-minute drive from the house: when she walked in the door, Steve's secre-tary literally ran from the office. Steve wasn't there and, curious, Cyndy looked around. There were photos of Steve and his secretary on the wall. She began going through his date book and saw ski trips, dinners, and other outings the two had taken.

There was a cot in the office.

Despite what she'd believed, her husband didn't limit his swinging to the baseball diamond.

Cyndy left the office, and when she confronted her husband later, he said that the relationship had come about *after* she said she was leaving him. And even then his secretary did nothing more at first than help him cope with the separation—just like a sister might do, he said. Cyndy didn't believe him, pointed out that one doesn't sleep with one's sister, and that was the end of that.

Cyndy went into therapy for more than seven months, but Steve's therapy was to keep playing—for the San Diego Padres, following his slump in L.A. in 1982—and also playing around.

The couple was divorced in 1983, and Steve im-mediately took up with businesswoman Judith Ross, whom he had known for two years. They moved in together and were happy until, in the summer of 1986, Steve was interviewed by CNN in Atlanta and met assignment editor Rebecka

A photo signed by Steve Garvey in happier days. (Author's collection.)

Mendenhall. The two fell in love and—without Judith knowing about Rebecka or vice versa—they carried on a long-distance relationship.

Meanwhile, Steve also had the energy to date a medical product saleswoman, Cheryl Ann Moulton, whom he met in San Diego, and he was so attracted to her he admits that there were "times we never left her apartment."

In July, six months after they met, Moulton became pregnant. When she told Steve, he was stunned: "I was led to believe she was taking responsibility for birth control." (Making the kid was easy; it took a court order in October of 1989 to make him come up with child support.)

Steve felt it was time to settle down and, because he didn't want to marry Moulton, in November 1988 he proposed to Rebecka and they made plans to marry in April. Then, in January, Judith says he told her, " 'You're the one I see myself married to.' "

Later that month, he learned the Rebecka was pregnant with his child . . . and, once again, he was shocked: he thought she was using birth control ("She walked into the bathroom beforehand," he says of their liaisons. "What am I going to do, follow her?").

Three women—bases loaded. And what was Steve's solution to all this personal chaos? On February 18, 1989, he married thirty-year-old interior decorator Candace Thomas, whom he met in January at his yearly Special Olympics ski classic in Deer Valley, Utah.

Judith and Rebecka were stunned—even more so when Judith happened to find photos of Rebecka and the two finally learned about one another.

Meanwhile, Cyndy was faring much better. She had a happy new relationship with composer Marvin Hamlisch and was hosting the cable TV show *Motherworks*. When Steve failed to pay her $25,000 in legal expenses, however, she made it difficult for him to see his daughters. (He claims it was the other way around.) They went to court, where Cyndy was declared in violation of the custody agreement that gave Steve visitation rights, and she was sentenced to 130 days in jail. She was handcuffed, escorted from the courtroom, and tossed in prison—she was only there a day, agreeing to go along with the original accord.

Meanwhile, Steve became a free agent in 1987 and retired in 1988 when he failed to get to first base with any of the clubs he talked to. And there was worse news for him. After seventeen years of professional play, during which he'd earned more than $9 million, Garvey was broke. His Garvey Marketing Group—a sports marketing enterprise, designed to counsel players how to save money they made during their careers and help them make the adjustment to post-athletic life—didn't work out as he'd hoped, and a pilot he'd taped with cohost Fawn Hall, *Tickets to a Dream,* about big-time lottery winners, failed to sell. His sexual escapades also cost him a kids cable TV show about baseball; Reggie Jackson did it instead. His financial woes were so severe that, at one point in 1989, he owed the government a half-million dollars in back taxes.

So where does all of this leave Steve?

Today, he earns some $110,000 annually from a radio show, roughly half of which goes to support his children and ex-wife. He had always hoped that when his baseball career ended, he'd be able to go into politics, make a run for the U.S. Senate—and he still hopes he can do that. The good news is, by the time he quit the sport, much of the dirty Steve Garvey laundry had already been aired. The bad news is, it's enough to keep him in private life for the foreseeable future.

Steve tries to remain pragmatic about it all as he puts his life back together. "When I signed with the Dodgers, I was sure that was the only team I'd ever play for. When I got married, I was sure it would be to one woman the rest of my life.

"Some people have a midlife crisis," says Garvey with a trace of bitterness. "I had a midlife disaster."

Wade Boggs:
"Swinger"

Samson had Delilah. The *Titanic* had its iceberg. Wade Boggs had Margo Adams.

On the surface, it would have seemed that the five-time American League batting champion and seven-time All-Star was an unlikely candidate for controversy of any sort.

Anyone familiar with Boggs's career and his style of play regarded him as a throwback to the players of yesteryear, the ones who always took extra batting and fielding practice and who weren't afraid to get their uniforms dirty diving for balls or sliding into bases. Furthermore, the fact that Boggs was not a graceful athlete, had worked hard to improve his skills, and had labored in the minors for many years, suggested that he would do nothing to risk a career that had not been easy for him to come by in the first place. Finally, the fact that Boggs's life had been twice touched by tragedy—immediate family members had been killed or badly injured in auto crashes—had given him the appearance of someone mature beyond his years, not only grateful for what he had but determined not to do anything to jeopardize it.

Baseball players are by nature a superstitious lot. If they pick up a teammate's bat and that day get three hits at the plate, it's likely the teammate will never see the borrowed stick again—that sort of thing.

Wade Boggs's superstition had to do with chicken. It was practically the only food he'd eat on game days. He had favorite dishes, but would even eat chicken cooked a new way before he'd sample the choicest New York steak or the freshest Pacific red snapper. Teammates teased him and the media wrote about it, but it worked for Boggs and he stuck to it.

By 1988, Boggs had a career batting average of .344, the fifth highest in the history of Major League Baseball, and a mark equaling the career average attained by the fabled "Splendid Splinter," Ted Williams. With his pronounced crouch, ability to go with the pitch and hit to all fields, as well as his impeccable sense of the strike zone, Boggs was often impossible for opponents to get out for long stretches of the season. During these hot spells, Boggs would follow the same daily routine, scared that any deviation would end his magic at the plate or, worse, send him into an irreversible tailspin.

Viewed in this light, it makes sense that after Boggs met sultry, curvaceous thirty-year-old red-head Margo Adams in the bar area of an Orange County restaurant, he would insist on seeing her again. He met her after a Red Sox road game against the California Angels in 1984, and soon embarked on an awe-inspiring hitting tear. It didn't take long for the "friendship" to blossom into something more.

Soon, Adams was accompanying Boggs on road trips. Her chief duties were to reserve rooms with certain numbers and wear specific outfits to the ballpark—such as no underwear after he went four for five on a day she didn't wear panties; *that's* how convinced Boggs was that these rituals paid off for him on the field. Because she made more than sixty trips with Boggs over the next two years, it meant

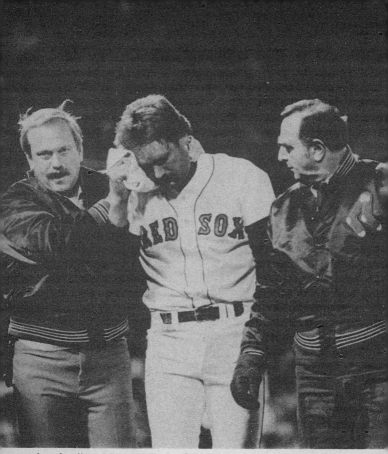

In April 1984, trainer Charlie Moss helped Wade Boggs off the field, after Boggs was bloodied trying to field a fly ball. The pain was mild compared to what was waiting around the corner. (*AP/Wide World*.)

that their relationship was hardly a secret among his teammates; indeed, Boggs allegedly boasted that in the same way he maintained there were hits in the chicken he ate every day, "There's hits in Margo, too."

Remarkably, Boggs's wife, Debbie, was clueless.

She was at home with their two children, Meagann and Brett.

By 1988, Boggs had tired of the relationship and tried to end it; obviously, the thing had taken on a life of its own, independent of his hitting prowess, and he just didn't want it anymore. Unfortunately for Wade, Margo wasn't merely a woman scorned, she was a woman unemployed. At least, that was the version of things she presented.

She claimed that she had given up a lucrative career as a mortgage broker at Boggs's request and in return for his promise not only to support her, but to compensate her for her time and efforts arranging his travel plans and working as his valet and secretary. She sought $12 million in damages.

Boggs vehemently denied even knowing Adams at first, then admitted that he *had* met her, but disputed that they'd been lovers. At the same time, Boggs attempted to intimidate Adams, arranging for friends to pose as FBI agents and appear, unannounced, at her doorstep one morning to suggest that she would find herself in a bad way unless she dropped her suit. Adams not only refused to relent, she played a trump card: seems she had intimate photos and other souvenirs of her years together with Boggs.

When Boggs found it a bit difficult to explain what he was doing with his arms wrapped around Adams's narrow waist, smiling like a couple on their honeymoon, his credibility was dealt a severe blow. He countered with a one-two punch of his own, however. His lawyer, Jennifer King, took the view that even if her client had slept with Adams, the relationship was purely sexual and the law expressly precludes compensating anyone involved in such a "meretricious" relationship.

That was the legal tack. As for saving face in public, Boggs did what public figures have done for years when caught with their pants down. He wrapped himself in home and hearth, portraying himself as a devoted husband and loving father. Debbie was willing to forgive his indiscretion, and he patiently posed for pictures at the ballpark with his family, confessing that while he may have erred, his ability to do right by his family now was being prevented by this madwoman.

But Margo knew how to use the media as well. Initially, she wasn't coming across as sympathetically as she wanted, and started throwing in things like Boggs was a racist (false). Or that she hadn't been out looking to tie up with a baseball player (dubious). And she certainly presented her case more spectacularly, by doing a nude layout for *Penthouse* as part of the two-part "tell-all" story she wrote for the magazine in February and March of 1989. In addition to the revealing photos, the article featured detailed accounts of the sexual acts he preferred (oral sex), his habit of shaving her privates, and—the final indignity!—his rating on Margo's lover scale: behind Steve Garvey.

The old saying, "When things go wrong, they really go wrong" was true in Boggs's case. Because his sex life was an open book, the Red Sox were desperate to trade him. And off the field, he narrowly escaped serious injury when he and a friend were attacked by a group of knife-wielding crazies outside a Florida bar one night. They felt that *he* was dragging the sport down. What they were doing was fine, though.

Fortunately for Boggs, the Red Sox could find no takers and Margo—apparently discouraged by court decisions whittling her potential recovery, and also facing mounting lawyers' fees—agreed to an out-of-court financial settlement, the terms of which were sealed by court order. (While her suit against Boggs was in progress, Margo was arrested for shoplifting, fueling suspicion by Boggs supporters

Margo and Wade in 1985. (*AP/Wide World.*)

that, while the affair did take place, Margo was an unbalanced individual strapped for cash.)

In view of the new wave of morality that seems to have swept baseball in the past few years—especially the ruling that Pete Rose is ineligible for the Hall of Fame because of his gambling, and Orlando Cepeda is ignored due to his conviction for cocaine possession—one must wonder whether Wade Boggs's torrid affair with Margo Adams will impact his Hall of Fame prospects. In a larger view, will it reach the point that players will feel the need to get out in front of problems in their personal lives to head off embarrassing disclosures? And if so, what type of behavior will be deemed tolerable or excusable, considering the growing number of impressionable youngsters who visit the Hall of Fame annually? Will Babe Ruth be ejected because he had countless affairs and umpteen paternity suits? Joe DiMaggio because he reportedly beat his wife Marilyn Monroe? If we judge Hall of Famers by anything other than how they played baseball, we're going to have some mighty bare walls over in Cooperstown. (Tangentially, no one asked Michael Jackson about his personal life when they gave him armload of Grammy Awards, or Kirstie Alley about her cocaine habit when she won her Emmy Award. Kids pay attention to what these people do; are *they* fitting role models?)

In an ideal world, baseball players would be perfect gentlemen and devoted husbands. We all would. But this is the real world, and in an era when the media is constantly looking for a scandal, and action off the field is often more interesting than the action on the field, baseball had better do some soul-searching before it destroys its bright—if randy—stars and, in so doing, destroys itself.

Jose Canseco:
"Miami Vice"

In troubled economic times, it's tough to feel sorry for a superstar athlete like Texas Rangers slugger Jose Canseco, who earns $5 million a year, drives expensive foreign automobiles, is married to a beautiful woman, and is also a "close" personal friend of Madonna's. Canseco may be right when he claims that fans don't appreciate the pressures he has to contend with—living in the spotlight twenty-four hours a day. But many people would probably make that deal with the devil and trade places with him; smarter people might even take some of the money Jose has paid over the years for bail bonds, lawyers, and court fines, and hire someone to protect them from themselves.

What may be most amazing to the average fan is not how someone with all that money can get into so much trouble, but how someone possessing all that talent can do so much to jeopardize his career. But Canseco has. In fact, few players in the history of baseball have become embroiled in controversy—and to this degree—so soon after establishing themselves as a superstar.

It's arguable who was the key player that enabled the Oakland Athletics to reach the World Series three straight years, starting in 1988. Certainly major contributions were made by star reliever Dennis Eckersley; leadoff hitter and all-time base stealer Rickey Henderson; and dependable pitcher Dave Stewart, who overcame the personal trauma of being arrested for soliciting sex from a transsexual and being discarded by both the Los Angeles Dodgers and Texas Rangers. However, no one can dispute that the six-foot four-inch, 215-pound Canseco played a crucial role.

Born in Cuba, Canseco came to Miami with his parents and identical twin brother, Ozzie, at the age five. He starred in a variety of sports in high school, before settling on baseball and signing with the A's.

Canseco literally powered his way through the minor leagues to the majors. While no one questioned the free-swinging youngster's ability to hit tape-measure home runs, some wondered whether he would be able to hit for average and play the outfield. Canseco was determined to prove he could to it all, and not only became a steady hitter but a first-rate defensive player as well.

Hitting 33 home runs during his first season helped make Canseco the overwhelming choice for the 1986 American League Rookie of the Year Award. Two years later, Canseco went on a home run tear which, were it not for a minor late-season injury, would surely have enabled him to become the first American League player to hit 50 home runs since Mickey Mantle and Roger Maris did for the 1961 Yankees. Still, Canseco's .304 average and 42 home runs earned him the American League's Most Valuable Player Award, and in his first World Series game Canseco hit a grand slam home run.

Unfortunately, that game also marked a turning point of sorts in the charmed life of a young man who, until then, was the very embodiment of the immigrant who had made good. For when L.A. Dodger Kirk Gibson came off the bench to pinch hit a dramatic two-out, ninth-inning home run, it not only propelled the underdog Dodgers to victory in that game, but gave them the momentum to pull off one of the biggest upsets in World Series history, stunning the heavily favored A's in five games. Ironically, the grand slam proved to be Canseco's only hit in the Series.

There were some who speculated that Canseco's subsequent performance in the Series might have been affected by news reports appearing at the time, suggesting that not all his gifts were God-given, but the by-product of steroid use. Although there had been "whispers" around baseball for some time to the same effect, the charges had never before been made public. He denied the reports and shrugged them off, although the attention had to have affected his play.

Still, in the aftermath of the Series disappointment, Canseco appeared to bounce back. He married former Miss Miami, Esther Haddad, on October 25, and after returning from their honeymoon, worked out regularly in preparation for the 1989 season.

But when 1989 arrived, so did trouble. In January, Canseco's personal secretary, David Valdes, was detained in a Detroit airport for carrying a concealed weapon. Also found in his possession were steroids. The media reopened its examination of Canseco's possible steroid use, openly wondering why Ozzie, also an outfielder in the Oakland A organization, was so much smaller than his brother. Once again, however, the charges were never substantiated. Just for the sheer spite of it, a lot of people wanted to see the new sports idol knocked off his pedestal—and, unfortunately, Canseco did nothing to establish himself as a man who deserved anything but.

In February 1989, he was arrested for driving 125 miles an hour in suburban Miami. Ten days later, without explanation, he failed to appear—as promised—at a baseball card show in Rochester,

New York, which would have paid him $20,000 for signing autographs for three hours. When he subsequently received three traffic citations during spring training in Phoenix, speculation mounted that "something" was affecting his behavior. The topper, however, occurred when the season was less than a month old and he was arrested near Oakland for carrying a loaded 9mm semiautomatic handgun in his 1989 Jaguar. Canseco's wife had to post $5,000 bail to get him out of jail. He later pleaded guilty and in lieu of serving six months in jail was placed on probation and ordered to perform 80 hours of community service.

Despite all the controversy and resulting bad press, Canseco played a significant role in helping the A's capture the American League Pennant once again, then sweep crosstown rival San Francisco Giants to win the earthquake-delayed World Series. Fans and the press both noted that he seemed more relaxed and at ease with the pressures of stardom, speculated that maybe he was settling down. But within a month he was in trouble again, detained at McCarren Airport in Las Vegas after causing a disturbance on a flight from Los Angeles for refusing to wear his seat belt. A few months later, after the Giants signed Will Clark and Kevin Mitchell to long-term, multimillion dollar contacts, Canseco complained publicly about the A's refusal to do the same for him.

What was the matter now? Why this sudden swing back to confrontation? Teammates privately speculated there might be trouble on the home front.

Throughout spring training, tensions ran high. Manager Tony LaRussa was put in the difficult position of not wanting to offend his star but, for the sake of team unity, not appearing to coddle him either. Canseco brooded and on April 21 told the media that "racism" was the reason the A's hadn't awarded him a long-term pact. Management denied that vigorously, but to no avail. The rift had been created.

A tempestuous season ensued, with charges and countercharges of bad faith and prejudice; eventually, the A's relented and signed Canseco to a landmark five-year, $23.5 million contract. The team once again won the American League pennant, only to be humiliated in the World Series, losing four straight to the Cincinnati Reds.

In many ways, defeat at the hands of the Reds was more shocking than the upset by the Dodgers two years before. Many had dismissed the earlier setback as a case of the immensely talented but very young A's team suffering a case of World Series jitters and running into the incredibly hot Dodgers pitcher Orel Hersheiser. No such excuses could be made this time. Their hearts weren't in it. They simply, flat-out stunk.

Grumbling and finger-pointing among the A's spilled from the privacy of the locker room and onto TV screens and sports pages across the country, particularly after Canseco's wife called A's manager LaRussa "a punk" for benching Jose in game four—overlooking that Canseco's misplay in the outfield in game two in Cincinnati had cost the A's that game and shifted the Series momentum irreversibly to the Reds. In Canseco's defense, he *had* suffered a late-season shoulder injury of which manager LaRussa was aware, so perhaps he shouldn't have been playing right field in the late stages of a close ball game in the first place.

Despite all of this, Canseco was hoping to put these controversies behind him and just lie low in the off-season. But he never got the chance. In December, foreclosure proceedings were instituted due to his failure to pay $4,264.44 in maintenance fees on two Florida estates worth more than $2.3 million. Barely a month later, Canseco stunned friends when he filed for divorce from Esther in Florida, a separate property state, claiming the marriage was "irretrievably broken." Esther promptly countersued for divorce in California, a community property state. Personal animus flew between the two like electricity during the winter months of 1991, but by spring training they had reconciled—some observers wondering if Jose were motivated by emotional or financial considerations.

But this seeming resolution to Canseco's marital problems proved to be just the lull before the storm, as 1991 proved to be not only a tumultuous year for the slugger personally, but a disastrous season for the A's. Rickey Henderson, the 1990 American League MVP, reported late to spring training, complaining—rather incredibly, if you stop and think about it—that the four-year, $12 million contract he had signed barely a year before, and which had been surpassed by a dozen deals other clubs had made with players since then, was tantamount to playing for slave wages.

But Henderson was only one problem. A's third baseman Carney Lansford was lost for most of the season because he tore knee ligaments while riding a snowmobile. Then, the usually reliable Dave Stewart and Dennis Eckersley pitched poorly once the season started, and first baseman Mark McGwire hit only .200, well below his weight. That meant opposing pitchers could concentrate on pitching around Canseco.

In spite of this, Canseco somehow made the best of things and went on a massive home run tear, pitting him in an exciting race with Detroit Tiger slugger, Cecil Fielder. Given that Canseco's efforts were the one bright spot in the A's otherwise dismal year, he expected members of the press and fans to offer encouragement. Instead, Canseco's rampage seemed only to inspire sarcastic asides. These became especially thick shortly after

Canseco was spotted leaving rock star Madonna's Manhattan residence early one May morning. The visit was downplayed by both Canseco and Madonna as nothing more than a chance for two superstars, who happened to be mutual fans, to commiserate about the pressures of fame. But neither Canseco nor Madonna would describe exactly what happened when they were alone, nor, for that matter, would Canseco categorically deny to reporters that he had ever been with another woman since he married Esther.

The tabloids and the weekly news magazines had a field day with the story and, lashing out like a spoiled brat, Canseco demanded to be traded. There was speculation that a trade which would send Canseco to one of the New York teams was in the works.

Canseco argued that whatever went on in Madonna's apartment was no business of anyone but the Material Girl and the Boy of Summer. However, that just isn't the way things work in the real world. You're living the good life, you're making the big bucks, you're a sports hero—people are going to be interested in you. Right or wrong, that's the trade-off. And it happens to be a good one: if it weren't for gossip-mongering public watchdogs keeping an eye on stars of sports, screen, or politics, there's no telling what they'd try and get away with. It's important to have checks and balances in any system.

Much later, Canseco cooled down enough to comment on what happened up there. He said when he was eighteen, he had first seen Madonna perform and had been taken with her *as a performer*. "You think I ever thought I would meet her?" he said. Well, when the opportunity presented itself, he jumped. However, he swears that "It was nothing but a business meeting. There may be some future stuff on movies." After they talked, he said,

Jose Canseco signs a Freudian autograph. (*Author's collection.*)

"She showed me around her apartment." No affair; no romance. Case closed, as far as he and the press were concerned.

Astonishingly, by season's end Canseco managed to tie Fielder for the American League home-run crown. But with the A's out of the World Series for the first time in three years, Canseco resolved—swore to himself and his friends—that the off-season would pass without incident. Perhaps, at twenty-seven, he had finally become aware of the new fiscal reality in baseball. Ball clubs were entering into fewer long-term contracts and, in any event, he wouldn't be able to play the game forever. Additionally, insofar as Canseco wanted to capitalize on his fame while he was still an active player, he realized he had to display a certain maturity to attract corporate sponsors. Finally, with an expansion team set to begin playing in his hometown of Miami in 1993, Canseco probably sensed that it would be easier for the team to bid for his services when his contract with the A's expired if he were less controversial.

Canseco held to the course for all of five months, until the early morning hours of February 13, 1992, when he was arrested and charged with aggravated battery for crashing his 1985 Porsche into his wife's 1991 BMW, causing more than $10,000 in damage. According to reports, the Cansecos had been quarreling at home. When Esther left in her car, Jose followed in his, and they continued heatedly at a 24-hour gas station around 4:30 A.M., apparently about his ongoing "friendship" with Madonna.

During the shouting match, Canseco suddenly grabbed Esther's purse so she couldn't go anywhere. When he finally returned it, Esther jumped into her car and sped away. Canseco followed, reportedly pulling alongside and spitting on the driver's side window (helluva range!), butting the car on the side and nearly running her off the road, then ramming the car twice in the rear. An onlooker called police, and when they arrived and started to arrest the enraged Canseco, Esther tried to intervene on her husband's behalf, claiming—incredibly, if not schizophrenically—that the police were taking Jose into custody not because of what he'd done but because they just didn't like him. Although Canseco was released on a $5,000 cash bond, he faced charges carrying a maximum fifteen-year prison term and $10,000 fine and quietly worked out a plea bargain with Dade County prosecutors.

Asked to comment on Canseco's latest off-field adventure, Sandy Alderson, the A's beleaguered vice-president, remarked wearily at the time, "I'm not a defense lawyer, a marriage counselor, or an auto mechanic, so I don't know what I can add."

Apparently, the incident took its toll on A's management. As successful as the club was with Canseco, it was decided the franchise would be better served in the long run without him. Thus, despite being embroiled in a pennant race, the A's traded the heavy-hitting outfielder to division rival Texas in late August, 1992. That about sums up the story to now, anyway, of Jose Canseco—another young player who went too far too fast and doesn't seem mature enough to deal with it all. But he's still got a lot of years ahead of him and, hopefully, Jose Canseco will end up in the Hall of Fame instead of Baseball's Hall of Shame.

Martina Navratilova:
"Mixed Doubles"

Among athletes, there isn't a more cooperative, outgoing, and personable superstar than Martina. If you've got a reason to be around her, she'll be a gracious host. If you've got to interview her, she'll be open and entertaining. But if you've got a double-standard—watch it. She expects the same kind of fairness and honesty from those around her that she displays for them.

Unfortunately, events in Martina's life have focused unwanted attention on her private affairs, and made her the victim of winks and sniggering from the male-dominated sports press.

Born in Prague, Czechoslovakia, in October of 1956, Martina played tennis at the small club where her parents enjoyed friendly games— a four-year-old batting balls against a wall with a warped wooden racket. She began playing on a court two years later, and throughout her school years could think of nothing but tennis. When she got to see powerful Australian superstar Rod Laver play in Prague, she knew that that was what she wanted to do with her life.

Martina's father and mother encouraged and practiced with her, and at the age of nine she began working with George Parma, a former tournament player. Martina came along quickly, began playing in tournaments around the world, and in 1975 embarked on a tour that brought her to the United States—for good. She asked for and was granted asylum, lived in Beverly Hills for a year, then bought a ranch in Dallas. She later applied for and was granted citizenship (despite her fears that having openly embraced a nonheterosexual lifestyle would work against her).

Martina had defected so she could enjoy the freedom of coming and going as she pleased, of playing tournaments when and where she wanted. She also had expected to enjoy greater freedom in her private life: certainly greater tolerance. But that proved not to be the case.

Martina had had her first sexual experience with a woman after she came to the United States. She says an earlier sexual relationship with a man "hadn't made me all that eager for a second one," and when the woman seduced her she said she "never panicked and thought, Oh I'm strange, I'm weird." Martina says she experienced "an outright, head-over-heels case of infatuation." She adds, rather naively, "I didn't imagine my sexuality would become a major issue to anybody. It seemed like *my* business somehow."

The press didn't make much of that relationship, which lasted six months, but when Martina took up with writer Rita Mae Brown in 1978, things were different. Martina describes their courtship as a wonderful time of "wine, suede and lace and silk instead of Gatorade and warm-up suits," but when they moved in together the supermarket tabloids and even the "legitimate" press jumped on them, often painting them as freaks. The relationship lasted three years, the author eventually becoming jealous of the time Martina spent on the road or working out.

When they separated, Martina took up with Women's Basketball League star Nancy Lieberman, who not only was thrilled with Martina's blossoming career, but helped her get into the best physical condition of her life.

Sadly, 1981 was the same year that Martina's close friend, tennis star Billie Jean King, was rocked with a mortifying palimony suit filed in May by Marilyn Barnett, a former hairstylist who had become King's secretary and her lover. Though Billie Jean had been married since 1965, she acknowledged the seven-year affair after initially denying it (she couldn't have ducked for long: Marilyn had letters, and threatened to make the intimate details public).

King triumphed in court after spending a quarter of a million dollars in legal fees and suffering what she said was irreparable "emotional damage to me and (husband) Larry, and my folks."

The publicity *was* damning and Martina was indignant, not just because of the suit but by the threat the coverage posed to women's tennis. Sponsors were uneasy about being tied to gay players, and Billie Jean lost a number of lucrative endorsements because of the suit.

Martina should only have known what lay ahead for herself.

The relationship with Nancy overlapped Martina's close friendship with Renee Richards—aka New York eye specialist Richard Raskind, who had undergone a sex-change operation (which included a near-suffocating attempt to reduce his Adam's apple by drilling through his throat). Raskind had been a highly ranked men's amateur and, in 1977, tried to qualify to play in the women's tour. That was when Martina first met Renee, although their friendship didn't blossom until they met again in 1981, and Renee helped Martina improve her game while Nancy worked on her strength and stamina. The press disparagingly dubbed the trio Team Navratilova—though the irony was that Renee and

Nancy spent a lot of time "studiously avoiding each other," according to Martina.

She broke with Richards in 1983, and Nancy followed in 1984. Martina says, "After the women's league went down, Nancy . . . tried to take full control of my business—and my life." For several years, she'd let her; now it was time to take it back. For her part, Nancy had become disgruntled being known (erroneously) as Martina's gofer/friend, and agreed to split—though there was some brief legal acrimony as Nancy sought to be compensated for business she'd handled (Martina had *thought* as a friend) during their years together.

Nancy—now Nancy Lieberman-Cline—says that while she will always resent the "nickel and diming" Martina subjected her to at the end, she's "not ashamed" about the time they spent together. Today, the two are sociable, if not chummy.

Rebounding from that relationship, Martina became close to nine-years-older Judy Nelson, a tennis fan she met at a tournament. The former beauty queen left her surgeon husband to move in with Martina, but after seven years of living and loving together, things turned sour.

In 1986, the two women "solemnized" their relationship by signing a "non-marital cohabitation" document. In essence, the partnership agreement gave the two an equal share of anything they (read: Martina) made from that point forward. Not only was the document signed in front of witnesses, the event was videotaped. Point, Judy.

The time the two spent together was among the most enjoyable for Martina. They bought a place in Aspen, Colorado, and skied; they rode horses on the Texas ranch; and Judy jet-setted the world with Martina to various tournaments. Martina earned $9 million during those years.

Cut to 1991. Martina becomes interested in a U.S. Olympic skier, Cindy Nelson (no relation), who is eight years younger than Judy. Martina breaks off with Judy in April, and her ex-companion is understandably upset: she says, "For seven years, I've supported and assisted Martina, sacrificing many of my own personal goals in the process." Now, Judy went on, "She's left me and pursued another relationship." The divorcée said she could live with that, but when she pressed for her share of Martina's income, the nine-time Wimbledon champ said no way. Martina claimed that, at most, all the agreement entitled her to was earnings from the *businesses* they had started together, not from Martina's career.

Martina said, "Judy and I had a very good relationship. I not only took care of Judy, but I looked after her family, provided help with her parents and kids, flew people all over the place to tournaments and on vacations. That wasn't enough, I guess."

Darn right, said Judy, who returned Martina's smash in June with a palimony suit, demanding what she felt was hers. In an additional move intended to put pressure on the star to settle, Judy also asked the court to restrict the amount of money Martina could spend on travel and luxury items, lest the athlete spend *her* money as well. Private photos of the two from Judy's "album" also appeared in *The National Enquirer,* suggesting that the spurned lover was willing to let the supermarket tabloids rake Martina over if the matter weren't settled quickly and fairly.

Martina was furious, declaring that she had "trusted Judy as I have never trusted anyone else" and felt "betrayed." The public humiliation notwithstanding, Martina was willing, if not happy, to let the matter go to court.

That it did in Fort Worth, Texas, in September, Judy stating simply, "I think that we would both

like to see the pain and the suffering stop so we
can get on with our lives."

Despite the stiffness of her backbone in June,
Martina had not counted on the emotional toll of
going to court and confronting Judy, of watching
the videotape of their signing. No sooner did she
take the stand than she broke down in tears, looking at Judy and her two grown sons and weeping,
"I feel sorry for me, for everybody involved."

As the second day of the hearing got underway,
Martina decided she didn't want to go through the
wringer and instructed her legal team to come to a
financial settlement with Judy. The terms of the
settlement were not revealed. (Martina's old friend
Rita Mae Brown had served as an intermediary between the athlete and Judy; ironically, during this
process, Judy and Rita Mae fell in love and moved
in together shortly after.)

As younger players begin to take the championships that Martina once won with ease, she is
thinking of slowing down her professional activities and devoting more time to charity, particularly
her Martina Youth Foundation, which helps the
underprivileged.

To say that she has recovered from the pain of
her legal bout with Judy or, for that matter, with
Nancy, would be inaccurate. But as with everything else in her life, Martina assimilates her expe-
riences and grows—which, after all, is the hallmark
of any champion.

Lance Rentzel:
"Double Exposure"

Athletes' sexual escapades with other women make headlines, but they're usually of the same sort: All-American hero falls for young model/cocktail waitress/choose-your-euphemism. Marriage is ruined. Career goes down the dumper. He writes a book and then drifts into some other business.

Martina obviously put some new twists on that, but none were as dramatic or shocking as those of Lance Rentzel, who followed the pattern except for the first part: he went for *very* young girls.

Rentzel's escapades with underage girls didn't exactly make him unique; he wasn't even a record-holder. Philadelphia Phillies first baseman Edward Bouchee was arrested for exposing himself to a six-year-old girl in 1958, underwent two months of psychiatric care (seems he'd done this four times previously) spent three years on probation, then returned to play on the first New York Mets team. Nor did Rentzel suffer the singular indignity of being arrested *during* a game, which is what happened in 1983 to twenty-six-year-old Boston Red Sox utility shortstop Julio Valdez. The married Valdez was accused of having had sex with a fourteen-year-old girl in a hotel near the stadium, and detectives came to get him during a home game with the Seattle Mariners. He was let go by the officials when the girl admitted she'd lied about her age, and was also let go by the team when his batting average dropped to .120.

In 1987, an entire *team,* the Oakland Athletics, was investigated for having consorted, the previous year, with underage hookers during a stop in Minneapolis, Minnesota, to play the Twins. The pimp was sent to jail but the players were let off, their names never made public.

But Rentzel did his twisted little deed in an era when the news media jumped on scandals like pit bulls at a barbecue: they were beginning to feel their oats after the fall of Camelot, and were ripe with righteous indignation. In Rentzel's case, they hit hard and didn't let go. Which isn't to say that the newspapers were to blame; Rentzel did a lot to bring himself down all by his lonesome.

When Lance Rentzel, football player, was "on," no one could stop him. You wouldn't wrest a ball from the guy if you hit him with a forklift. When his heart wasn't in a game, no one had to stop him: he stopped himself. Fumbled. Missed passes. Slipped.

But that was part of the fun of watching Rentzel: you never knew whether you'd be cheering a dashing hero or booing a butterfingers.

Off the field, however, there's no question about who did Rentzel in. *He* blamed the press. "A pro football player with a glamorous blonde for a wife," he snorts. "The media ate up guys like that." But the truth is, Lance Rentzel was done in by no one but Lance Rentzel.

Born in 1943 to a well-to-do family, Rentzel graduated from the University of Oklahoma in 1965 with a degree in computer sciences. He was a second-round draft choice of the Minnesota Vikings and, despite his rich-kid image and good looks, the six-foot two-inch halfback (later, wide receiver) was devoted to his sport. Unfortunately, he got off to a shaky start, and things got even worse with the breakup of his relationship with girlfriend

Marcia and suffering a sprained ankle, which kept him on the bench.

Climbing into his car after practice one afternoon in September 1966, he drove around St. Paul and finally stopped in the Highland Park area, where he saw two girls playing.

He watched them for a moment and, "feeling useless," he says he had a sudden urge to be a care-free child again . . . to impress someone, to play, "Look at me. Look at what I've got."

Without getting out of his car, he called the girls over. When they reached the vehicle, he exposed himself to them and drove off; the whole thing took "maybe ten seconds," he says.

Back at his apartment, Rentzel felt "strangely relieved," and over the next few days he thought about the incident less and less. But someone had seen what happened and, together with the girls' descriptions and a description of the car, police were able to trace the incident to Rentzel. Charges were pressed and, following his lawyer's advice, Lance went to see a psychiatrist. This was a pre-emptive strike to show that Rentzel wanted to find out what was wrong . . . and make sure he wouldn't do it again.

According to Rentzel, the doctor "did not feel that I had a serious emotional problem," and although the player was booked, the charge was reduced to disorderly conduct. He pleaded guilty and was ostracized by some teammates, warmly supported by others; when the season ended, he was traded to Dallas.

The Cowboys were an up-and-coming team at the time, and Rentzel enjoyed growing with them—even though their reputation for choking during the big games frustrated him and his teammates, especially quarterback Don Meredith. Still, Rentzel himself was doing fine, and in 1968 he was the third-ranked receiver in the NFL.

On a trip to Los Angeles in 1968, where he cut a record for Columbia, Rentzel met entertainer Joey Heatherton, and the two were wed in April of 1969. He bought a house in Los Angeles, though the couple lived in Dallas during the season.

Professionally, the year was a good one for Rentzel. (Football-wise, that is. The record was a stiff.) He led the league in average yards gained (22.3), and scored a league-high 12 touchdown catches. Married life was also good, initially: he and Joey were America's Sweethearts, and she enjoyed the attention and the novelty of the football crowds. Then, in 1970, things began to sour all around. There was no work for Joey in Dallas, so she prepared an act and took it to Caesar's Palace in Las Vegas, which kept them apart. Rentzel was co-owner of a Dallas nightclub, the Warehouse, which proved to be a financial sinkhole. And as a harbinger of things to come, Rentzel dropped the very first pass of the first exhibition game of the new season: that psyched him out completely, and he—as well as the team—got off to a lousy start.

Not surprisingly, the team meeting on November 17, 1970, was filled with rage and hostility. When it was over, Lance was unable to reach Joey at Caesar's Palace, so he went to the movies, then went home and took a sleeping pill—though he says he was tempted to take many more.

The next day, he was still filled "with a sense of vast futility, of emptiness, of desolation." After an unsuccessful practice, he got in the car and drove around aimlessly, and he felt familiar stirrings. He tried to suppress them but failed and, "drawn by the sight of a young girl playing in the front yard" of a big house in the Dallas suburb of University Park, he pulled up to the curb. Smiling, he called the ten-year-old over to ask directions, exposed himself, and drove away. Unknown to him, her father had witnessed the entire thing.

Lance and Joey, America's Sweethearts. (*AP/Wide World.*)

Rentzel slept well that night, and says that the next day, "I was a new man." The Cowboys won that Sunday. But the girl's father, prominent attorney Paul Adams, had filed a complaint and, on November 23, the police came for Rentzel. They were deferential, even apologetic as they brought Rentzel in, but he admits, "I guess I would be outraged if I had a daughter and a man exposed himself to her. I felt deeply ashamed of what I had done."

But that wasn't good enough. On December 14, the case went before a grand jury; Rentzel was indicted and the story became national news. He wept when he saw the first headlines, but facing his teammates was even tougher—as were the jokes on TV, on the radio, and in the press:

Rentzel was going to be traded to the Montreal Expos.

The charges were going to be dropped because it was no big thing.

The evidence wouldn't stand up in court.

He was propositioned by gay men, received vicious letters and phone calls, and once again was the object of either scorn or compassion from his teammates. There were rumors that he was a rapist, a child molester, and that the Dallas ownership had covered it up. He was now seeing a psychiatrist twice a week, and couldn't believe that someone who had a problem but was *doing* something about it should be the focus of such derision.

The worst punishment was still to come, however. As the Cowboys began to soar, he wasn't permitted to play. He had to sit out the Super Bowl when they played against Baltimore, and when they lost he blamed himself: he was convinced (with some justification) that things would have gone differently if he'd been in the lineup.

On top of everything else, Lance still had his legal problems. In Texas, exposing himself like that was not considered a sickness, but a crime, and Adams intended to see the case through. If Rentzel were found guilty, he could go to prison for two to fifteen years. On April 8, 1971, shortly before the trial was due to begin, there was a meeting in which the prosecutor, Adams, and Rentzel's attorneys came to an agreement: there wouldn't be a trial *if* Rentzel pleaded guilty in court, and if the court ordered a lengthy probation.

Rentzel's inclination was to fight, but his lawyers convinced him otherwise. After considering the matter, Judge John Mead set the athlete's punishment at five years probated sentence and continued psychiatric care. Not bad, although he wondered if anything he ever did would remove the stigma that he was a pervert. Joey was understanding, and stood by him—but what about everyone else?

The answer was as unpleasant as it was unexpected. Before the new season began, the Cowboys traded him to the Los Angeles Rams. Rentzel was "despondent" over the move, but coach Tom Landry defends his decision: "When he was upset, his playing efficiency dropped off drastically." Feeling that Rentzel would still be the object of unwanted attention, Landry says, "I was confident that this was best for Lance."

Landry wasn't wrong a lot, but this time he was. Whenever Rentzel took the field for the Rams, opposing players would taunt him mercilessly with, "Flasher," "Pervert," "Hollywood Fag," and the like. Rentzel was distracted, and he played lousy ball. But there was one game he wanted desperately to be up for: one year after his arrest, he was back in Dallas playing against the Cowboys. The Rams lost, and he was severely depressed. His mood soured and even his wife couldn't help him anymore: on September 17, to no one's surprise, Joey filed for divorce.

Rentzel's teammates believed he'd hit bottom,

and the betting was he'd pull himself out of his depression. They were wrong. In Los Angeles, Rentzel had fallen in with the "Hollywood crowd," and started behaving more carelessly off the field than he did on. In January of 1973, a telephone repairman working at the home of film producer William S. Bellasco saw Rentzel walk in with a shopping bag stuffed with marijuana: he told police, who searched the two men's homes. They found pot, cocaine, amphetamines, barbiturates, codeine, and other "paraphernalia"; Rentzel was arrested, a conviction for selling the substances carrying a two- to ten-year prison sentence.

Once again, Rentzel was able to do some broken field running: he pleaded guilty to possessing marijuana, and the charges of furnishing marijuana for sale and the possession of codeine without a prescription were dropped.

Judge William Caldecott fined Rentzel $2,000 and sentenced him to ninety days in jail, suspended, and in July, hard-nosed Commissioner Pete Rozelle issued a suspension of his own: for "conduct detrimental to pro football," Rentzel was benched for a year. In fairness to Rozelle, the last time Rentzel pleaded guilty in court, the commissioner had only put him on probation.

Though Rentzel was allowed to return to the game in May of 1974—not-so-coincidentally, the day after a *New York Times* article quoted him as considering "very good offers" from three World Football League teams—the State Court of Appeals upheld the lower court conviction and the sentence stood.

Lance returned to the Rams in 1975 for the exhibition season only to find—just a few months shy of age thirty-two—that they didn't want him anymore. He was placed on waivers, and said at the time he still wanted to play. "I would hate to end my career on a negative note. I want to show what

I am still capable of doing." No one snapped him up, however, and that was the end of the playing career of Lance Rentzel.

He tried to be pragmatic about it. "I've been in this game five years longer than the average player, and I have to accept I'm old and youth can replace the old. You can't play a game forever. You can't lose sight of the fact that one day it will end and you'll have to come back to earth. This is a rude awakening for most athletes."

Rentzel felt he was somewhat immune to that because he had something to do: he remained in Beverly Hills and, rather than "take a PR job somewhere or play golf and host," he turned to writing and perhaps emboldened by the success of former Dallas teammate, turned novelist, Pete Gent, tried to peddle various novels and movie ideas based on football themes. But there were no takers, and he drifted off into private business selling computer systems.

It can be argued that although the legal punishments against Rentzel were lenient, the judgments of fans, players, and sportswriters were unduly harsh. They didn't want to accept that this man who looked and moved like the Greek god Apollo was flawed. Gods can drink, gods can carouse, but gods can't do small, cheap things. As the New York Giants' Joe Morrison aptly put it at their training camp in Bridgeport at the height of Rentzel's troubles, "You open your mouth in this game, you're asking for trouble. You open your zipper, and you've got it."

Mike Kekich and Fritz Peterson: "The Ultimate Trade"

If Lance Rentzel represented a man undone by his own personal exhibition season, the quartet of Mike & Susanne & Fritz & Marilyn proved that even private *legitimate* sexual choices could become very public controversies. Mike Kekich and Fritz Peterson experienced this firsthand as, right before the start of the 1973 season, the two New York Yankee pitchers who decided to trade wives—not for a night, but permanently.

Marilyn and Fritz Peterson were married in 1964, Susanne and Mike Kekich a year later, and maybe what they did was a natural outgrowth of two couples who had settled into a traditional lifestyle at a time when other young people were participating in political rallies and enjoying the sexual revolution, or else searching for greater self-awareness through nontraditional arrangements like communal living. Or maybe—as the cynics said—it had to do with the fact that both were left-handed pitchers who, among baseball aficionados, always have been regarded as being a little "different."

Not only had Kekich and Peterson been teammates, they were roommates on the road and the closest of friends since April 1969, when Kekich joined the team. They lived just eight miles apart in New Jersey; their wives were also very friendly and the two Peterson sons and two Kekich daughters got along just fine.

But "closeness" took on a whole new meaning after the two couples went to the movies one night in July 1972. They had a few drinks and began discussing the possibility of exchanging families. Susanne recalls, "We laughed about it like a bunch of high-school kids and thought the whole thing was a big joke."

After a few weeks, however, they began talking about it in earnest. As Susanne puts it, "We were all attracted to each other and we fell in love." Okay—that's not unusual among close friends. Sometimes mates are even swapped under the circumstances—out of curiosity as much as attraction—and there the "swapping" ends.

Finally, though, late in the summer, they were all at a party and decided to give it a try. Marilyn and Mike went home together to her house, and Susanne and Fritz went to the Kekich house. The next day, they met at a restaurant to see how they had all liked it: very much, as it turned out. The men went home to stay with their new mates, Kekich describing his new life as "a fantastic, storybook relationship," said with all the heartfelt-at-the-time sincerity of any man scratching a seven-year itch. After Thanksgiving, just "to make sure," according to Kekich, the men returned to their respective homes for two weeks. They discovered that the swap had been much better for everyone, and made it official. All four sought no-fault divorces.

When they informed their teammates, the players and their wives were split on the controversial move. Manager Ralph Houk said pragmatically, "You've got to remember that you only go through life once," but Commissioner Bowie Kuhn took a harder view: "It's appalling, regrettable, and deplorable," he said, and openly bemoaned the fact that "the powers of the commissioner do not reach this particular situation." Nothing would have pleased him more than to see these two men out of baseball for the good of "the image of the game."

As it turns out, Kuhn didn't have long to wait. By March of 1973, Marilyn had gotten cold feet and, as Mike put it, the relationship "fell apart." Things worked out better for Fritz Peterson and Susan Kekich, who married. Unfortunately, in the process, the Peterson-Kekich friendship frayed ... though, as Kekich said, he had to stay sociable with his ex-pal because "Fritz is going to be the father of my kids."

In response to a reporter's question at the time, he said, "When was the last time I was happy?" but just shook his head and walked away.

The players continued to be teammates until the summer of 1973, when the Yankees traded Kekich to Cleveland. Despite denials from the Yankees, conjecture was ripe that clubhouse tension and the discomfort among other players' wives prompted the team to make the move. Protests from offended fans also had something to do with it.

Kekich's career went into the dumper after that: he played lousy ball, and the Indians released him at the end of the season. He went to the Texas Rangers, winding up in the team's Spokane farm club. Resentful and not earning what he needed to make ends meet, he jumped to Japan for big bucks—all in the space of a year. Unhappy in Japan, he returned to Texas in 1975, was let go the next year, then went to the Seattle Mariners for a short stay. He played in South America and in the Dominican Republic before giving up on the game. He married again in 1978 and opened a medical services firm in New Mexico.

As for Peterson, he went to the Indians after Kekich's departure and remained for two seasons. When the Rangers let Kekich go, Peterson went there, stayed less than a season, then retired from

From the left: Marilyn & Mike & Susanne & Fritz. The picture was taken in August 1972, right after they made their notorious family switch. (*AP/Wide World.*)

baseball. He and Susanne moved to Barrington, Illinois, where they became realtors and got themselves involved with "wonderful Christian people" and went to work spreading the word of Jesus.

Talk about "born again . . ."

Mike Tyson: "Heavyweight Chump"

There's nothing funny about what happened to the life-swapping Yankees or to Lance Rentzel, but as sexual escapades go, what those people did was comparatively victimless. The girls who witnessed Rentzel's display are fine today.

Obviously, reputed beatings and rape are a different matter. The question is, in our newly confused post-Anita Hill/Clarence Thomas episode, which has polarized supporters of women's and men's rights, can we always see past appearances and tell who the real victim is? For example, William Kennedy Smith got off for rape, yet a lot of people still think he's guilty. Mike Tyson didn't, and a great many people still think he's innocent.

Going into the trial, Tyson had two disadvantages. First: he was black. Like it or not, that still matters to jurors and law enforcement officials. Just ask Jim Brown.

Second, he's a fighter. He makes his living by breaking people. As a rule, these guys don't get off because, for the most part, they don't understand that you can't whip people outside the ring. For example, there's the case of Tyson's former opponent Trevor Berbick who, in October 1990, was found guilty of raping a woman who worked as the family baby-sitter. Not only was Berbick found guilty—after changing his story three times—but his behavior at his sentencing only underscored his irrational nature. The fighter gave a rambling, 45-minute speech in which he not only reiterated his innocence, but blamed "secret agents" for having framed him. Despite the urging of family members who implored him to sit down, Berbick became more and more agitated, waving his arms and alternately sobbing and screaming, and the judge finally ordered him to be taken away for a mental examination.

Or there was the case of former middleweight champ Carlos Monzon who was, in 1989, found guilty of having argued with his longtime lover Alicia Muniz and then choking her and throwing her from a second-floor balcony, killing her. Before that, there was young Tony Ayala, the junior middleweight—undefeated in 22 bouts—who, on January 1, 1983, wandered into the apartment of a young blonde, tied her up, and brutally raped her. Because this wasn't his first offense (he was accused of attempted rape six years before) he was sentenced to thirty years in prison.

Other well-known professional boxers have had serious encounters with the law over women, going all the way back to August 12, 1924, when middleweight champion Kid McCoy shot his girlfriend Teresa Mors in the head—an accident he said. The jury believed him, returning a verdict of manslaughter. (McCoy, however, was a hell of an actor, fond of feigning weakness in the ring to draw a foe in, then suddenly coming to life and destroying him—hence the origin of the expression, "Is this the real McCoy?" He was so despondent that his melodramatic performance in court didn't get him an acquittal that he later took his life.)

So—did Mike Tyson get a fair trial? Has Tyson been his own worst enemy? The answer to the first may never be known. As for the answer to the second, that's an unqualified *yes*.

Former world heavyweight champion Floyd Patterson once said, "I'll tell you what it is about Mike. He's got raw power but he doesn't just *unleash* it. He bottles it up then channels it out hard. Smart?" Patterson laughed. "I don't know. But he thinks when he fights, I'll tell you that."

Patterson was talking about the Tyson that matters to his fans and foes, the fighting machine who is beautiful to watch inside the ring. Outside the ring, though—that Tyson is a very different beast. Maybe his birthdate had something to do with it: June 1966—666. He was bound to have some of the devil in him. That was particularly true where women were concerned.

Mike Tyson was raised in Brooklyn by his mother, Lorna Smith Tyson; Mike's father, Jimmy Kirkpatrick, was Lorna's ex-boyfriend. Mike was close to his older sister Denise and older brother Rodney. As a child, Mike wore glasses, which were constantly being stolen by neighborhood bullies; Mike took the abuse—for a while, accustomed as he was to having his "butt kicked" by Rodney. One day, though, he had had enough and decided to fight back: he was in the second grade, his opponents were two years older, but he recalls, "I kicked the shit out of them." That became Mike's response to being tormented, and soon, he says "word spread throughout Brooklyn" that he was a tough little cookie.

For a thrill, Mike began stealing—candy, fruit, doughnuts, pigeons (which he raised)—anything he could put his hands on. He also drank and smoked, used girls to pick up guys so he could rob them, and became an expert pickpocket. He went to reform school, did time in prison, and in 1979, prison athletic coach Bobby Stewart introduced him to boxing manager Constantine "Cus" D'Amato, who lived in upstate New York with his friend Camille Ewald. Even though Tyson stood only five-foot-six,

Stewart felt that he had a future in boxing; for his part, Cus hadn't bred a champion in more than a decade. Cus agreed that Mike had potential, and the young man moved in with the couple. Both Cus and Camille made sure that Mike maintained his studies as well as his physical training.

In 1981, Tyson was a standout in the heavyweight division of the Junior Olympics, a competition for ten-to-sixteen-year-olds. He also began winning against adults in "unofficial" exhibition fights, though he failed to make the Olympics in 1984 because he battered opponents rather than finessed his way to victory, and the judges dumped on him. As Pat Nappi, the U.S. Olympic boxing coach explained it to Cus's friend, fighter Jose Torres, Mike's foe in the trials (Henry Tillman, who went on to win the gold medal) simply "understands the amateur rules and style better than Tyson." (In a nontitle fight in Las Vegas in 1990, Tyson knocked Tillman out in the first round. Revenge is sweet.)

Despite the depressing setback, Tyson remained a focused fighter who was well on his way to heavyweight competition. He also drank a fair amount and spent as much time with women as he could get away with. Cus didn't protest too much about the women; unlike most trainers, he felt that a bit of relaxation would enhance rather than distract his fighters. But Tyson came to regard women as his just reward and, according to Tyson's friends, the muscular fighter was not turned away by many of them.

Tyson became a pro in 1985, and slaughtered his adversaries one after another. After winning his first nationally televised fight, with Jesse Ferguson, Tyson was questioned by a reporter about whether he was trying to floor Ferguson with an early uppercut; Tyson replied that, actually, "I was trying

Mike Tyson, on top of the world. (*Author's collection.*)

to push his nose bone up to his brains." He may
have been jesting, but Tyson didn't smile.

Sadly, Cus didn't live to see his charge become
champion: he died on November 4, 1985, and
Tyson won the heavyweight crown on November
22, 1986, stopping Trevor Berbick by a TKO in 2

minutes and 35 seconds of the second round. He was just twenty years old. He kept on hammering all comers in the ring and proved that a kid who makes an estimated $100 million needs a stern but loving Cus D'Amato to look after him.

Just as when he was growing up in Brooklyn, Tyson did what he wanted—only now his crimes were not robbing fruit stands, and his audience was not a judge but the whole world. Unfortunately, there were hints of trouble even before he won the title, although none of his handlers was smart enough (or forceful enough) to rein him in.

On February 20, 1986, he was in a mall in Albany, New York, four days after the Ferguson bout, and he made sexual overtures to a sales clerk. When she spurned him, Tyson became both verbally and physically abusive and was ordered to leave. Later, he was thrown out of a movie theater when the same thing happened all over again with a candy clerk.

The following year, on June 21, after attending a rap concert at the Greek Theatre in Los Angeles, Tyson was smitten with a woman who worked at a parking lot and tried to kiss her. When a male co-worker attempted to stop him, Tyson slugged the guy and was charged with misdemeanor assault and battery. The fighter paid $105,000 to settle the matter out of court.

Tyson's handlers hoped that when he married actress Robin Givens on February 7, 1988, he'd settle down. But those close to Tyson began to worry when Robin and her mother, Ruth Roper, asked for access to Tyson's bank account so they could buy a $4.5 million mansion in Bernardsville, New Jersey. Mike obliged. Before long, however, he became frustrated with Robin and Ruth: people close to him whisper that the women are manipulating him, using him. He confronted Robin, and when she denied it he smacked her around. Often. She stayed with him because she wanted the marriage to work . . . not just because she was fond of Mike, but because she was already perceived as a golddigger. Leaving with a hefty financial settlement would only legitimize such talk. Still, she told the press about the beatings, just to go on record that she was putting up with physical abuse in order to stand by her man. Her sister, Stephanie, reported how Tyson had shown up drunk on the set of Robin's TV series *Head of the Class* one day and trashed the set. Stephanie confirmed that Mike beat Robin, saying, "He knows how to hit her and where to hit her without causing any real damage."

Mike didn't learn from the public humiliation. On May 8, 1988, he had a minor accident with his $183,000 Bentley in Manhattan. When police arrived, he waited for them to write up the accident, then gave the car to a pair of Port Authority officers; he couldn't be bothered having it repaired. Here was a man whose sense of values was seriously screwed up, and again no one close to him could tell him he was wrong. When his manager Bill Cayton tried, Tyson turned on him and took him to court to get rid of him. They ended up with a compromise that saw Cayton's cut reduced from 33 to 20 percent.

In the meantime, in July, businessman Donald Trump had become a part of the Tyson advisory team, and it was hoped that he could be a steadying influence on the fighter: money can reason with money, it was thought. But it was no-go. Just a month later, on August 23, Tyson got into trouble again, this time for fighting another boxer, Mitch "Blood" Green—at 4 A.M. on the streets of Harlem. (The "Blood" came from Green's tendency to give up blood, not draw it.) Tyson was picking up some clothes at the Dapper Club Boutique, which was open round-the-clock, when Green entered (possibly having been tipped off that Tyson was there).

Words were exchanged about money Green was allegedly owed from a 1986 fight, and Tyson threw a right at the boxer; the former suffered a fractured bone in his hand, the latter a badly swollen eye. Though Green wanted to take Tyson to court, he was persuaded to let the matter drop in exchange for a title shot. (Later, Green ended up in prison for a drunk driving conviction. When he got out, he filed a $25 million suit for Tyson having reneged on a rematch. Tyson, in the midst of his rape trial, didn't pay much attention.)

Unused to all the attention, and without anyone he could turn to, Tyson was emotionally unstable: he suggested publicly that he believed he was a manic-depressive. On September 3, he went to dinner with Camille, stayed at her home, then had a phone argument with Robin the next morning. Leaving the house in the rain, he crashed into a horse-chestnut tree on the property—"A tree that has been hit by a hundred cars," according to Camille.

He was knocked unconscious (or faking; he suffered no concussion), and was taken to the Columbia-Presbyterian Medical Center, a half-hour away in Manhattan. He was determined to be fine, physically—but speculation was rampant that he'd tried to commit suicide.

There were more fights in the home, and three days after Givens told Barbara Walters during a prime-time interview that life with Tyson was "pure hell," Mike made it even purer: he threw a fit at the house, tossing furniture out the window and forcing Robin and Ruth to flee. When police arrived, he tried to chase them off, calling them "scum" and suggesting that they "get off my property and fuck off." Robin didn't press charges, but five days later, on October 7, she filed for divorce. Just over a month later, Robin sued Mike for $125 million, claiming he'd libeled her and her mother by calling them "the slime of the slime." Robin withdrew the complaint in March of the following year; the divorce became final in June.

There were other brushes with the law. In April, he was accused of hitting a parking lot attendant for refusing to move his car. The charges were dropped. That month, he got a ticket for doing over 70 in a 30-mph zone. He got another speeding ticket the following month and was fined $300 and ordered to do community service. Professional troubles plagued Tyson as well. His relationship with Trump unraveled, and he signed with Don King. He lost the title to the surprising James "Buster" Douglas on February 19, 1990.

After Robin left, however, nothing plagued Tyson like his problems with women. In October 1989, he had an affair with New Yorker Kimberly Scarborough, who bore his child; he owned up to it in March 1991. Then he admitted having fathered a second love child, D'Amato (an honor or effort to tweak the boxer's heart?), this one with Natalie Frears. In December, he was charged with grabbing computer operator Sandra Miller's breasts and butt at Bentley's Disco Lounge in Manhattan; she sued for $4.5 million, but a jury awarded her only $100, taking into account that the location and circumstances might have been conducive to his behavior. A few days later, recreational therapist Lori Davis joined Sandra and charged him of grabbing her butt that same night. Her $7 million suit was settled out of court.

There were other complaints of a similar nature—from Robin's assistant Phyllis Polaner, hooker Candy Washington, actress Robin Young, and dancer Trena Archie, who also claims he fathered *her* child.

Ignoring the paternity suits, J. Morris Anderson, director of the Miss Black America pageant, called Tyson a "serial buttocks fondler," and Anderson knows whence he speaks: it was Tyson's behavior before the pageant in July 1991 that caused his world to cave in.

On July 18, Tyson showed up in the lobby of the Omni Hotel in Indianapolis, to attend the opening ceremonies of the week-long Indiana Black Expo, which includes the Miss Black America pageant. The pageant contestants were in the lobby as well, and Tyson flirted with them; they flirted back. Contestant Noemi McKenzie says, "We were all happy. We all said, 'Let's get pictures.' We crowded around him." (One person who was *not* happy was Rosie Jones, Miss Black America of 1990, who said that when they posed for pictures, Tyson "grabbed my rear end. And then I took his hand and knocked it off my behind and I said to him how I didn't appreciate that." She hit him with a $100 million civil suit a month later.)

That evening, Tyson met eighteen-year-old contestant Desiree Washington at a concert and, later, called her at her hotel room. He asked her if she wanted to go for a sightseeing ride in his limousine and she agreed—even though it was 1:30 A.M. As soon as she got into the car, she later said, "He grabbed me and tried to kiss me. I kind of jumped back, and he said, 'Oh, you're not like these city girls. You're a good Christian girl.'"

He reportedly did nothing else until he said he had to go to his room (666!) at the Canterbury Hotel to make a phone call (despite the fact that he had a phone in his limousine). Even after the assault in the car, Desiree went with him. There, she said, they sat on the bed and watched TV for a while and talked—and then Tyson asked her, "Do you like me?" She said, "I don't know you." Then she said he told her she was turning him on—and she became frightened. She says she got up, headed for the bathroom, and told him, "When I come out I want to see Indianapolis, like you said." Sure,

Tyson replied. But when she came out, all she saw was Iron Mike stripped to his underwear. He grabbed her arm and pulled her onto the bed, where he allegedly used his forearm to pin her down. Then he tore off her clothes, raped her ("It was excruciating," she said. "It just felt like something was ripping me apart."), and left her to make her way back to her hotel.

Initially, Washington wasn't going to report the incident, but then decided she wouldn't be able to live with herself if it happened to anyone else. She told the police and, after an investigation, Tyson was indicted for rape on September 9.

Tyson is a soft-spoken guy, but he vehemently disagreed with Washington's account: "She knows what happened in that room. I didn't hurt no one." He said they talked, his hand on her leg, and then they began kissing. After she came back from the bathroom, he said they had oral sex and then she asked him to make love to her. He admits that he didn't go back to her room with her because he was too tired to go downstairs, but he invited her to stay with him.

Not surprisingly, the devoted Camille, then eighty-six, also had something to say about the charges: "If a girl comes to a man's room at 1:30 A.M. she is only coming for one purpose—to sleep with him. What is she coming for? To hold hands? She came for it—she asked for it."

When the trial began on January 30, Tyson's lawyer, Vincent Fuller, attempted to portray Washington as someone who "found herself treated as a one-night stand" and didn't like it, and also "has a compelling desire for money." Contestant Madelyn Whittington concurred. She told the jury that when she bumped into Washington and asked where she was going, the woman replied that Tyson had asked her out. "He's got a lot of money," she reportedly said. "He's dumb. You see what

Tyson goes to court on January 30, Camille Ewald is on the right. (*AP/Wide World*.)

Robin Givens got out of him?" Contestant Cecillia Alexander corroborated Whittington's account.

But the jury didn't buy any of that. Washington's mother testified that her daughter was a changed woman since the attack—that she wanted her to be a happy, smiling girl again. She made one juror weep, and on February 10 they found Tyson guilty.

At his sentencing on March 26, Tyson said to Judge Patricia Gifford, "I'm not here to beg for mercy, ma'am. I don't see any good coming out of this. I've been crucified. I've been humiliated worldwide."

True, but Judge Gifford hadn't liked Tyson from the get-go. He was candid but crude on the stand,

and in sentencing him she said, "Something needs to be done about the attitude you displayed here." Tyson's punishment was ten years on each of three counts of rape, with four years suspended on each and the remaining six years to be served concurrently. Good behavior will get Tyson out in three years, but he'll also have to serve four years probation and get psychiatric help when he gets out.

A petition for bail during the appeal process was denied, and Tyson was hustled right off to prison. There, he immediately got into trouble with authorities for signing autographs for inmates *and* guards, and for refusing to take solid foods. (Who the hell can blame him for not having an appetite?) Defeated defense attorney Fuller said bitterly, and with some justification, "What I fear most is that years of incarceration would do nothing for Mr. Tyson but put him back where he came from and make him worse."

Tyson failed in his bid to get the Indiana Supreme Court to let him remain free on bail pending on appeal. When he learned of their decision he said, "Today, for the first time in my life, I was trying to cry. I couldn't. It's terrible not to be able to cry, especially when you know that you didn't do anything wrong."

Alan Dershowitz—the superlawyer who worked wonders for Claus von Bulow but couldn't keep Leona Helmsley or Mike Milken out of jail—is handling Mike's appeal, though he vigorously denied a published report that he plans to ask for a new trial since important evidence was never presented: that Tyson was out of control due to steroid use.

Unfortunately, the ham-fisted Donald Trump hurt Iron Mike's cause further when he offered to give $3 million to set up a rape crisis center in Indiana if the state let him walk (and earn money by fighting in one of Trump's facilities, naturally).

The public outcry was swift and quite properly negative, and Indiana prosecutors threatened to hit Trump with charges of obstructing justice if he dared to approach Washington with any kind of deal. It's amazing how Trump misunderstood the meaning of "paying for one's crimes."

Not that the nongold-digging Washington came out looking like an angel in the aftermath of the trial. She got herself on the cover of *People* magazine and went on TV's *20/20* with Barbara Walters, claiming that she wasn't in this for the fame or riches: she pointed out that if it were money she was after, she'd have taken the $1 million offered by an anonymous friend of Tyson's (one of the Dons?) to drop the charges. She said she was going public for one reason and one reason only: to encourage women to speak out if they've been raped.

The sentiment was both wise and generous. But the whole thing still seemed tainted. *People* and Walters had helped to contribute to the Tyson circus for years; it would have been better if Washington had gone through less show-bizzy media—*Ms.* magazine, perhaps, or even PBS; something with the trappings of substance and clarity of purpose. Worse, although the now-ponytailed Washington entered a small New England college and said she only wanted to get on with her life, "to learn to trust again, to smile the way I did, to find the Desiree Lynn Washington who was stolen from me and those who love me," as soon as the publicity started to die down she retained a top New England attorney to pursue a civil suit against Tyson, one that could net her millions in damages (i.e., she may never feel comfortable with a man or in a hotel room again). On June 22, deciding that "the feeling of remorse is obviously still not very high on his list," Desiree made the suit official, seeking an unspecified amount of money.

Legally, she may well be entitled to the money.

However, *appearances* give a boost to the gold-digger claim, and erode some of the important issues the case raised. Indeed, Desiree's actions have gone so far as to call her credibility into question. Days after she filed the civil suit, the Rhode Island Supreme Court revealed that it had information that "might well have an effect" on the verdict—namely, that during the trial Desiree had testified she had no contingency arrangement with a lawyer to seek civil damages against Tyson. Yet her attorney told the court that that was precisely the kind of arrangement he had with Ms. Washington. The court said, "It is not the function of this court to determine whether the victim in the rape trial testified falsely or whether defense counsel failed to fully explore the issue in examination of the victim." But if this information was "overlooked," isn't it possible that other details of the case were also overlooked or even misrepresented?

Then there's an aspect of the affair that never came out at trial and deserves comment. According to a source close to Tyson, the issue never was rape. Supposedly, the source says, what happened in the hotel was consensual sex followed by Tyson's alleged request for an uncommon act—one that caused Desiree to freak and charge rape when he tried to do *that*.

The reason Tyson's people never trotted out this fact is that when he gets out of prison, he could still have a career—but maybe not if this reported fascination were to become public knowledge. He'd be the unrelenting butt of jokes in every bar on earth. Better, says the source, to take the prison time and keep his secret.

There's no telling what's in store for Tyson. One month after going to jail, he wrote to Camille, "It saddens me deeply to be serving time. Right now it's not an easy thing to deal with but I'll be okay."

But will he? Suppose he doesn't get out of prison

while he's still young enough to fight: Fuller's words may prove prophetic. Tyson's fortune has dwindled to a few million dollars, and he has no other skills. Tested in prison, he was found to have the reading, writing, and math skills of an eleven-year-old. Nintendo has dropped him as a video-game hero, and he certainly won't be doing any endorsements when he gets out of prison. What will he do? Wrestle? Become a sideshow freak?

Justice may—*may*—have been served by his incarceration, but in burying Tyson society may have provided the stuff from which a future Frankenstein monster may be built. Though the fighter is no gentleman where women are concerned, the truth is he wasn't a *lot* of things. He wasn't a good husband. He wasn't articulate. While we're at it, he certainly wasn't a good driver either.

Still, he had it in his power to do worthwhile things with his position and wealth—perhaps to lift other kids from the ghetto, to save other teens from jail, to get young people committed to physical fitness. As he wrote to friend Rory Holloway from prison, "There are a couple of guys here who are doing life. They are sixteen years old. I feel sorry for them. I talk to them all the time because I'm in the next cell." He's got the sensitivity; it's in there, somewhere. Anyone who saw him interact with fans—male or female—knows that as messed up as he was in the bedroom, he's got a heart.

That the courts did not come up with a way to use that, to let him atone by doing good instead of time, may ultimately be the greatest tragedy of all.

David Cone:
"Negative Charges"

Whatever Desiree Washington may or may not be—
victim, opportunist, gold-digger, foolish young kid—
she showed courage on the stand. To come forward
and face an excruciating grilling, with all the details of her sexual life laid bare—few women can
muster the courage to do that just for publicity or
revenge or the hope of a hefty financial settlement.
But there *are* exceptions.

In 1952, Jim Rivera, a rookie outfielder for the
White Sox, was charged with raping a local woman.
A grand jury was convened and Rivera was found
innocent of any wrongdoing, but Commissioner
Ford Frick put him on one year's probation anyway. Frick said at the time that he was sending a
message to players that he would tolerate nothing
less than "the highest standards of morality among
all men who are connected with the game." This,
even though Rivera was innocent. Kenesaw Mountain Landis was alive and well.

With the passage of years, it was no longer necessary for the baseball commissioner to step in and
make an object lesson of any player. He had the
press to do that for him.

On July 29, 1991, twenty-three-year-old Sandra
Salarimatin went to a game between the New York
Yankees and the Oakland Athletics at Yankee Sta-
dium. Afterward, she went home to her apartment

on East 74th Street, got into an argument with her husband, Johannes, then headed downtown to the bar of the Grand Hyatt Hotel where the ballplayers were having a small party. There, she met married A's star and former Yankee Rickey Henderson— the all-time stolen base leader and the previous season's MVP.

According to Sandra, she and Henderson began chatting, and when the bar closed she went up to his room on the twenty-sixth floor. She said she *thought* a girlfriend she'd met at the bar was also coming up, and when she didn't show, Sandra tried to leave. At that point, she said the thirty-two-year-old Henderson began smacking her around. She managed to get away and complained to hotel security personnel, who contacted the police. When the police arrived at 4:37 A.M., they found Sandra "drunk and belligerent."

Sandra was taken home, and the next day— sober—she admitted that what had happened up in the room was that Henderson had received a phone call and, because she was giggling, he'd smacked her once to quiet her down. Smacked her? the investigators asked. Well, no—it was more like a tap, she admitted.

Henderson denied that even *that* much had occurred: he said, he talked with her at the bar, but that was it.

"I don't know why she got so mad and went running around making up this story," he said later. "Maybe she got home late and her husband was upset."

Whether or not Sandra went upstairs with Henderson (of *course* he had to say she didn't), and whether or not a girlfriend was supposed to meet them is beside the point. The moral of the story is that one drunk woman was able to cry wolf and get Henderson two days of brutal headlines.

A more outrageous event occurred in October

1991, when a twenty-three-year-old New Jersey woman said that on the Saturday night, October 5—the last weekend of regular season play—she had gone with her sometimes boyfriend, Mets pitcher David Cone, to his room at the Hilton Towers in Philadelphia. There, she says he stripped and she was giving him a massage—when suddenly, he demanded to have oral sex with her. When she refused, he proceeded to rape her.

Cone told the police that, yes, he was with the woman, but he vehemently denied the charges. "No way," was all he would say to the press.

Police investigated. They learned that Cone had been eyeing another woman earlier that day at the hotel, which made his companion jealous. They discovered that later in the evening, hours after the alleged rape, they were overheard arguing about a completely different subject. And finally, as Cone's lawyer Walter Phillips later said, "She reportedly admitted to at least one person that she fabricated the allegation to extract money from David."

The police investigation took less than three days to complete. No charges were pressed, yet Cone *was* damaged by the affair. When he returned to his Manhattan apartment from Philadelphia, he found the media waiting for him. Later, in an interview, he said, "Once the media got ahold of it, arguably the damage was irreparable. I had headlines that rivaled Clarence Thomas and William Kennedy Smith," alluding to two other men found innocent of wrongdoing, but crucified by the public. He received hate mail every day, and prank calls at all hours of the night.

He said, "From a baseball standpoint, it's not damaging. Any bitterness I had I channeled into a nineteen-strikeout performance. I wish I could bottle those emotions," he added with a laugh. Then he continued more seriously, "The feedback I've gotten has been pretty positive. I know most people realize I was the victim here. But from a marketing and endorsement standpoint, the damage may be irreparable."

True enough. But what does this clown do in the aftermath of the charges? Keep a low profile, as one would expect? Not at all.

Okay, he's a bachelor, entitled to do as he pleases. But on St. Patrick's Day, 1992, he was spotted in the parking lot of the Jensen Ale House with teammate Bret Saberhagen—who is married—hoisting a young pickup into the air ("Like you'd inspect a ripe tomato," said disgruntled eyewitness and reporter Andrea Peyser) and then driving off with her.

Of course, even if Cone had behaved himself, he still would have been in deep yogurt; maybe he felt he had nothing to lose. In September 1991, three women hit him with a lawsuit, claiming that during the summer he'd charged into the stands to lambaste them for allegedly having harassed the wife of teammate Sid Fernandez—whom one of the women, dental hygienist Debra Hittelman, had dated for three years. The relationship ended when Fernandez tied the knot with someone else.

The charge itself was relatively minor, but with no settlement in sight, it was amended in March 1992 to include two other rather explosive incidents.

The first reportedly occurred on May 7, 1989, when Hittelman was still dating Fernandez. Cone invited her and her two friends, Phyllis DeLucia and Joan Twohie, to the bullpen to collect an autographed baseball before a Houston Astros game. According to Hittelman, when they arrived, Cone "was sitting on a stool, his pants and underwear below his knees, and he was masturbating." She called him an animal and left.

A second additional charge claimed that later in the 1989 season, he'd gone to the hotel room of two of the women at 3 A.M., was admitted, stripped off his underwear, and hopped "uninvited" into bed with them.

As of this writing, the various suits are still pending.

Clearly, Cone is overexposed, and not *all* of the wrongdoing may be *his* doing. But one day maybe it'll dawn on him and his fellow baseball stars that they can't afford to live like the rest of us mortals. Not only are they too big and rich a target, but as much as they may resent this, they owe their young fans role models worth emulating.

Cone's problems aren't isolated incidents. On November 30, 1991, Kevin Mitchell, then a San Francisco Giant, was arrested and accused of forceable rape, rape with a foreign object, and false imprisonment and battery. The woman subsequently decided not to pursue the matter, but the Giants made a judgment of their own: less than a month later, they traded Mitchell, a former National League home-run king, to the Seattle Mariners for three unproven players.

Baseball players aren't the only perpetrators/victims. In 1990, David Wingate of the San Antonio Spurs was basketball's contributor to the sexual misconduct sweepstakes when a twenty-one-year-old woman claimed that he had sexually assaulted her after she had a drink with him at a local nightclub. This, just three days after Wingate had been charged in Maryland with the rape of a seventeen-year-old girl. Both charges were subsequently dropped, but to no one's surprise Wingate is no longer a member of the Spurs.

If there's a moral in all of this, it's the same one that many movie stars and politicians learn: fame may make you a big person, but it also makes you a big target. Athletes must learn to go out of their way to lead exemplary lives, not just for their image and viability in endorsements, but for the sake of their very liberty.

Rubin Carter:
"The Fight of His Life"

In all of sports history, there may not have been a bigger target than Rubin "Hurricane" Carter, and his story is one of the saddest in all of sports history.

In 1966, Carter was the number-one ranked middleweight fighter in the world. He had already fought once for the title, losing a controversial split decision to Joey Giardello in 1964, and was training for a bout against then-champion Dick Tiger. With his shaved head, scowling countenance, and tautly muscled body, the ferocious puncher—who had the ability to take out most opponents with one mighty left hook—at once epitomized the grace and power to which every professional boxer aspired.

He also personified a sense of black pride that was beginning to happen at the time. It's impossible to underestimate the impact that Carter and other athletes of the middle sixties had on young blacks: they proved that socioeconomic conditions in the ghetto did not condemn those born to poverty to a life of poverty. Carter had escaped his past as a teenaged gang leader in New Jersey— arrested at the age of twelve for attacking a man he'd accused of sexually assaulting him, then spending four years in Trenton State Prison for purse snatching.

Like Mike Tyson years later—in *many* ways, like

Tyson—Carter was able to channel and direct his anger. He learned that he didn't need to prey on society, discovered that all he really wanted was a fair fight, an equal chance. Boxing gave him that.

What he couldn't know, at the time, was that he would not face his fiercest opponent in the ring, but in a different arena.

In the dark morning hours of June 17, 1966, two black men walked into the LaFayette Bar in Paterson, New Jersey, fired a shotgun and pistol, and instantly killed the establishment's bartender, James Oliver, and a patron, Fred Nauyaks. Within a month, a second patron, Hazel Tanis, died of wounds suffered in the attack and another customer, William Marins, was left partially blinded.

Despite the fact that witnesses had described both killers as being light-skinned blacks about six feet tall, and that the man with the shotgun had a pencil-thin mustache, the police detained a car they spotted containing Carter and nineteen-year-old John Artis, who had no criminal record and was due to start college in the fall. The police took the men to the hospital, where Marins was being treated: he was unable to identify them. Subsequently, the two were given lie-detector tests and passed. And at a grand jury hearing that followed, the investigator in charge of the case pointed out that both killers had been described as having been wearing dark clothing, whereas on the night of the shooting, Carter was wearing a white jacket and Artis a light V-necked sweater.

Nonetheless, nearly four months later, on October 14, 1966, Carter and Artis were arrested and charged with murder. It seems that the state had found two eyewitnesses: Alfred Bello and Arthur Dexter Bradley, both of whom said at the ensuing trial that Carter had been one of the gunmen. Never mind that both witnesses were felons with multiple convictions. Never mind that the state couldn't suggest a motive for the crime. Carter had been in jail as a youth. He was in the vicinity. Most important, he was black. On June 29, 1967, he was sentenced to one concurrent and two consecutive life sentences.

An understandably defiant Carter protested his innocence and, when brought to Trenton State Prison, he refused to abide by the rules, such as surrendering his wristwatch and ring, or shaving his goatee. As a result, he spent his first three months in the "hole"—solitary confinement. When the warden finally let him join the prison community, he persisted in his stubborn ways by refusing to wear prison clothes (he held onto his identity by holding onto his tie-dyed jeans and sweaters) or undergo psychiatric evaluation. He wasn't a criminal and there was nothing to be gained by seeing a shrink.

All he needed was to get out. Then he'd be just fine.

In the meantime, Carter passed the time by spending countless hours in front of an old typewriter, slowly writing the story of how he'd been wronged.

Although many public figures had expressed outrage over Carter's conviction, nothing came of their dander and prisoner number 45472 faded from the public's mind and conscience. If possible, however, the original outrage was dwarfed by what was to follow.

In 1974, both Alfred Bello and Arthur Dexter Bradley told a public defender that Paterson police had been so eager to solve the shootings quickly that they pressured the pair into lying in exchange for reward money and lenient treatment for the crimes they'd committed. "I was twenty-three-years old and facing eight to ninety years in jail," said Bradley. "I lied to save myself."

Suddenly, Carter became the civil libertarians'

flavor of the month; Bob Dylan even wrote a song about the fiasco, "The Ballad of the Hurricane," which made the national top ten. Despite the enormous public pressure, however, New Jersey officials refused to act. Then, a tape recording surfaced of an interview that had been made with Bello in October 1966, one in which the prosecutor made it clear that Bello would receive favorable treatment if he managed to be *positive* that Carter and Artis were the perpetrators of the crime. That jarred Bello's memory. Yeah ... he was positive.

Armed with this new and very clear evidence that the prosecutor had violated the rights of the accused (specifically, the U.S. Supreme Court's "Brady Rule," which requires prosecutors to give exculpatory evidence to the accused in a criminal trial), Carter's lawyers were able to persuade the New Jersey Supreme Court to give the boxer a new trial.

Once again, however, Carter found himself sitting in a courtroom wondering if he was hearing the same testimony as the jury when, despite Bello's admitted perjury, he and Artis were once again convicted of murder and their previous sentences reinstated.

Returned to prison, Carter withdrew, refusing all visitors.

Growing more bitter every day, Carter began to rebel more aggressively than before. He refused to stand up during cell count, seeking a confrontation with prison guards. He knew that they'd overwhelm him by sheer numbers, but he also knew he'd be able to mete out some punishment as well. Carter got what he wanted, and prison officials finally had enough of him; they transferred him to Trenton State's Vroom Readjustment Unit.

Since Carter talked to no one during this period, it's difficult to say whether or not he ever gave up hope. However, even after the New Jersey Su-

preme Court upheld Carter's conviction with a
four to three decision in 1982, Lesra Martin refused to give up.

In 1980, Martin had become interested in the
case and began writing to the jailed fighter. Convinced of Carter's innocence, Martin worked with
Carter's lawyers Myron Belbock and Louis Steel,
and constitutional scholar Leon Friedman, to as-
semble a lengthy brief chronicling the numerous
contradictions in the testimony of the key prosecution witnesses. Late in 1985, Carter's lawyers
brought a writ of habeas corpus before U.S. District
Court Judge H. Lee Sarokin. That meant, in essence, that Carter was to be brought before the
court for an investigation as to whether he had been
imprisoned illegally, pilloried by a system fearful of
racial tension and urban unrest.

Sarokin's decision, delivered on November 7,
1985, read in part, "The extensive record clearly
demonstrates that (the) petitioners' convictions
were predicated upon an appeal to racism rather
than reason, and concealment rather than disclosure. (To) permit convictions to stand which have
as their foundation appeals to racial prejudice and
the withholding of evidence critical to the defense,
is to commit a violation of the Constitution as hei-
nous as the crimes for which these petitioners were
tried and convicted."

Sarokin ordered Carter to be released, but the
state of New Jersey wasn't finished. Judge Sarokin's decision was appealed all the way to the U.S.
Supreme Court, where his ruling was upheld. On
February 26, 1988, the indictments against Rubin
Carter and John Artis were finally, formally
dismissed.

On that day, his head covered with short, stylish
hair, and wearing a neatly trimmed mustache and
wire-rimmed glasses, Carter looked more like a
lawyer than a prize fighter. It was difficult to ascer-

tain whether time had changed him, or if the system had; maybe it doesn't matter. Carter decided to move to Canada, applying for immigrant status while retaining his U.S. citizenship.

Moving to a 10-acre farm just outside of Toronto, Carter now has plenty of time to reflect on his past and on his future. That future includes continuing his fight against injustice, which he does by regularly visiting college campuses, including Harvard Law School, and talking about what happened to him ... describing his ordeal with passion and intelligence.

"It is not finished," he tells listeners. "I still feel the loneliness. I still feel the pain. I feel *everything*."

And he always will. But the important thing is that Rubin Carter never went down during the longest and most important bout any boxer has ever fought. More than anyone else in his sport, he has defined the meaning of "world champion."

Lyman Bostock:
"Playing with the Angels"

Sometimes, athletes self-destruct. Sometimes, because of the amount of time they spend flying and traveling, the odds simply catch up with them and they get nailed.

And sometimes, they just happen to be in the wrong place at the wrong time. Like Lyman Bostock, the star outfielder of the California Angels, who died over a woman—literally.

In 1977, Bostock signed a five-year, $2.5 million deal with the California Angels that, at the time, made him one of the highest-paid players in baseball. For Bostock, who had toiled in relative anonymity for the Minnesota Twins, the Angels' contract was not only lucrative—to say the least—but it gave him the opportunity to return to Los Angeles. His wife was from there, and he'd played college baseball at California State University, Northridge. Most important, he'd always wanted to do something about the poverty that plagued sections of the city. Now, he'd be able to do that by helping to raise money for the needy by making personal appearances, organizing charity games, and letting poor kids come to the stadium to watch the Angels play.

Nor was Bostock's generosity "just for show." In order to play for the Angels, he turned down the opportunity to sign a far more generous contract offer from George Steinbrenner's New York Yankees—and when he started the 1978 season in a horrendous batting slump, he went to Angels owner Gene Autry and pleaded with him, "Take back my salary. I haven't earned it!" The kindhearted Autry refused, reassuring his shaken star that things would improve for him and the team. Instead, Bostock donated his salary for April to charity.

Gradually, things did begin to fall in place for Bostock and the Angels. His batting average started to approach .300 and the Angels closed the gap separating them from division-leading Kansas City.

Following a night game against the Chicago White Sox on September 23, 1978, Bostock decided to travel to Gary, Indiana, to visit his uncle, Thomas Turner, whom he loved very much and visited whenever they went to the Windy City on road trips.

Bostock went out one night with his uncle and his two godchildren, sisters, Barbara Smith and Joan Hawkins. Bostock was in the backseat with Barbara, enjoying the warm summer evening; less than a half-hour after they'd set out, Barbara spotted the car of her estranged husband, Leonard Smith, pulling up beside theirs. She told Thomas to get them away from there.

Thomas sped away, going through a pair of red lights before he was forced to stop at a busy intersection. When he did, Smith left his car with a shotgun in his hands. The windows were rolled up and it was dark: the enraged Smith didn't care if his aim was precise or not; the .410-gauge weapon would hit everyone in its trajectory. He unloaded the gun through the window and the bulk of the payload found Bostock, splashing blood and bone everywhere. He was declared dead three hours after they reached the hospital; Barbara's wounds were relatively minor.

A police officer said later, "It'll probably come out like he was having some kind of affair with the

Lyman Bostock at bat. (*AP/Wide World.*)

woman. But it wasn't like that at all." The officer
said they'd been together "for a total of about
twenty blocks" before Bostock was shot.

Bostock's killer was arrested at his home the following day, and pleaded temporary insanity. He
was put under observation for six months and was

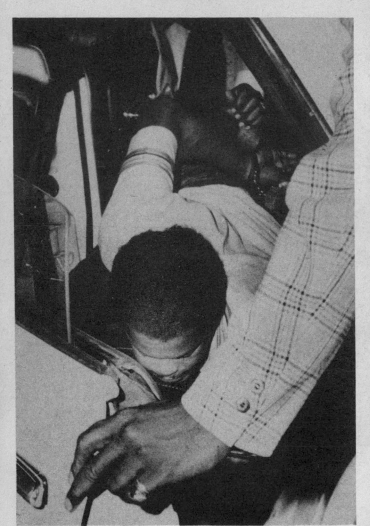

Leonard Smith on his way to the Lake County jail, where he'll be charged with the murder of Lyman Bostock. (*AP/Wide World.*)

deemed sane; because the murder had not been premeditated, Smith was released. Just like that.

Though the twenty-seven-year-old Bostock had been cut down in the prime of his life, his off-field efforts on behalf of the less fortunate were not forgotten. *The Gary Post Tribune* and People's Action Coalition and Trust established a memorial fund to provide inner-city youths with recreational and educational programs.

Some players leave behind impressive statistics, others a legacy of compassion. Bostock left both, though there's no doubt which would have been the more important to him.

Jim Brown:
"Offense and Defenestration"

Jim Brown was never accused of murder. But in his many years of off-the-field play, he's managed to score a number of firsts. In fact, for a long time the joke was, "How do you get a date in Hollywood?" The answer: "Stand under Jim Brown's window."

So he *wasn't* the gentlest boyfriend who ever lived. And, as his film career has demonstrated, his talents as an actor were equal to those of other athletes-turned-actors, Brian Bosworth and Carl Weathers. (Though he's Olivier compared to *other* athletes who have tried acting, like Roman Gabriel and Kareem Abdul-Jabbar.) But on the football field, there may never have been a better, more determined player. And those abilities were a large part of his problem.

Jim's father abandoned the family shortly after his son was born in 1936; his mother went north to find work when Jim was two, and he lived with his alcoholic grandmother in Georgia until he was eight. Moving north to be with his mother, who was working as a maid on Long Island, Brown became a high school sports star. He ended up at Syracuse, was the first round draft choice of the Cleveland Browns in 1957, and over nine seasons broke every running, rushing, and—as he puts it—"ass-kicking" record there was. For eight of those nine years, the six-foot two-inch running back led the league in yards gained rushing, and made All-Pro fullback every year he played. Since then, players like Walter Payton have broken some of his records, but when Brown was in the game he was the man to stop—and every defensive player in the league took it as a personal crusade to do just that. Brown scored in spite of being number one on the hit parade.

In 1964, Brown was asked to appear in the film *Rio Conchos,* and found that he enjoyed making movies. When he left the NFL the following year to nurture a film career—and ever since then—he has also devoted a lot of his time to women, especially those between the ages of nineteen and twenty-four, and *especially* "if she's thin and has small breasts." He also admits a fondness for threesomes with two women, and moresomes: Brown says he's had up to eight girls in his room at one time, and has had sex with four or five of them "but only if Jim Junior was feeling exceptional." More power to him and Jim Junior.

The thing is, now and then Brown is accused of having flashbacks to his playing days—imagining that the women he's with are Alex Karras or archnemesis Sam Huff.

The very year he quit football, he was charged with molesting a pair of young girls. "One dropped the charges," Brown says, "the other didn't." What came out during the highly publicized trial was that Brown had been trying to break up with the girl, Brenda, and her indignant mother "cooked up a scheme to try and get money out of me." He was found innocent and, shortly thereafter, Brenda called Brown to apologize for what she'd put him through.

But the matter didn't quite end there: a year and a half later, she hit him with a paternity suit. Dubious, he asked to see the child, a daughter; as soon as Brenda brought Shelly over, Brown says, "Her features made it perfectly clear that Shelly was mine." Though he didn't move in with Brenda, he assumed the financial responsibilities of fatherhood.

Four years after the first trial, Brown got in trouble again when neighbors called police to complain that there was a heated argument going on in his home. When the officers showed up, Brown told twenty-two-year-old model Eva Bohn-Chin that they were probably going to try to arrest him, and she should get her act together *fast*. Meanwhile, downstairs, the police were pounding on the door: as they stood there, waiting to be admitted, Eva suddenly went sailing from Brown's second-floor terrace and hit the ground, knocking herself out. The police accused Brown of having thrown her from the balcony; he says, "It didn't happen." What *did* happen, he says, was that Eva "freaked" and decided to "get the hell out of there" the quickest way possible. She climbed from the window, intending to lower herself down, and fell.

Sure, said the police. Brown was arrested and taken to the stationhouse along with the unconscious Eva; when she came to, she told the police what had happened: her story corroborated Brown's version. But the damage was done. Brown was annoyed—for in truth, he says blithely, "The toughest thing I did to Eva was slap her." Which is much better, of course; you don't ruin the flower bed that way.

In 1985, Brown really hit his stride. He had a house guest, beautiful young Carol Moses, who another friend, lesbian tennis player Margo Tiff, found very appealing. When Margo stopped by and Carol made advances, Brown asked the former to leave. The next day, the police showed up and arrested Brown: Margo had accused him and Carol of raping her. There was a trial, but after three

Jim Brown waiting in Beverly Hills municipal court for a preliminary hearing on an assault charge. (*AP/Wide World.*)

days the *prosecutor* asked for the judge to dismiss the charges, stating that he now believed the allegations to be false.

A year later, the big guy was arrested once again—this time for allegedly assaulting Debra Clark, his live-in lover, the day before they were to marry. The marriage was called off, but Debra decided to just let the matter drop. What's a scratched face and a few bruises? It's not like she was thrown from a window, or anything.

Brown does not *deny* that he occasionally still slaps women after reasoning with them fails, but he also says that the real problem isn't him, but the "cops in Los Angeles who would love to be the guy who sent me to San Quentin for 49,000 years." In their eyes, he says, "I'm big, black, and arrogant," and when they haven't got a case, or just the hint of one, he says they're content to haul him in, let the press know about it, get a front-page story, and watch him get tried in the headlines.

Though Brown reportedly showed up at at least one of Magic Johnson's notorious sex parties, he has managed to stay away from police blotters for several years now. He's joked about making a football comeback, has continued acting in movies— such as *The Running Man* (1987) with Arnold Schwarzenegger and the wonderful "blaxploitation" film parody *I'm Gonna Git You Sucka* (1988)—and is also producing films "to create opportunities for others."

Just as long as they're not windows of opportunities.

John Brisker:
"American Bullies Association"

The Anaheim Amigos.
The Memphis Sounds.
The San Diego Sails.
When the American Basketball Association played its 1967–1968 season—its first—many pundits predicted it wouldn't last. The league had no TV contracts, very little fan support (when the New York Nets played at Madison Square Garden, you could *finally* get good seats in the place!), a dearth of superstar players, some new rules that changed strategy dramatically (such as the three-pointers from outside the key, which gave little guys a shot at the hoop), bizarre halftime activities (slam-dunk contests were cool, but cow-milking contests were not), and (let's face it) a really stupid-looking red, white, and blue ball.

But the league survived—sort of. The most successful teams and rules were absorbed by the National Basketball Association after the league's ninth season. In its time, the league also produced some superstars, such as Julius Erving, Zelmo Beaty (Zel-*mo*! Zel-*mo*! was a chant that could get even a cavernously empty arena going), and Rick Barry with his crowd-pleasing underhand foul shot.

The ABA also came up with some players who brought the sport to new lows and made Jim Brown look like a wimp. For example, there was the spec-

tacle of the otherwise talented forward Warren
Armstrong (later, Warren Jabali) getting into an argument with opponent Jim Jarvis and, after Jarvis
went down, literally stomping on his head. Singer
Pat Boone, who owned the Oakland Oaks, says,
"He deliberately stepped on the guy's head, he really did. When a guy is down, you go out of your
way to avoid him, you don't step on him."

Armstrong said that that was the way he'd
played in the streets, and it just—*happened*. Perhaps. But as then-Miami Floridians PR man Rudy
Martzke put it, "The ABA had sort of this semi-
outlaw-league reputation, but Jabali was the real
thing."

The itinerant Jabali had other run-ins with players, especially those who supported the "establishment," which he perceived as the enemy; he once
tore the cotton underwear off a black rookie, snarl-
ing that their ancestors picked the stuff and ordering him to go out and buy boxers.

However, Jabali was an exceptional player and
was tolerated; besides, compared to John Brisker
he was an angel of mercy. In fact, Brisker was the
only ABA player even Jabali went out of his way
to avoid.

The six-foot five-inch Brisker played mostly with
the Pittsburgh franchise, although there are those
who think the Pipers would have traded him if
they weren't afraid of upsetting him. Guard Charlie Williams says that if you said something that
Brisker even *took* to be offensive, "You had this
feeling that John would reach into his bag, take out
a gun and shoot you." Actually, what Williams had
was more than a *feeling:* after getting into an argument during a practice once, Brisker announced
that he was going out to get his gun. The coaches
immediately called off the rest of the practice and
disbursed everyone before he got back. It got to the
point that players were offering a $500 "bounty"

on anyone who punched Brisker's clock; the only one who ever collected was Dallas Chaparrals player Lenny Chappell, who decked him during a jump ball when everyone was looking at the ball. Brisker went down, the officials didn't see it, and Chappell was a $500-richer hero. But he was the only one who ever collected the reward.

Other highlights of the Brisker career include:

• Walking up to ABA commissioner Jack Dolph after the All-Star game and demanding his $300 cut right then and there. Without hesitation, Dolph reached into his wallet and gave it to him.

• Physically assaulting rookies to make sure they didn't even *think* about going after his job.

• Going over to player Billy Knight, slugging him "for no reason," then standing there "waiting for me to do something about it." Wisely, Billy didn't.

According to Tom Nissalke, who coached Brisker when he went to the Seattle Supersonics of the NBA in 1971, Brisker "started to get into drugs" and became an extremely erratic player. He left the game and dropped out of sight: though no one knows what happened to him, the rumor is that he became a soldier of fortune and was killed while working for former Ugandan president Idi Amin.

The only people who don't snicker when they hear the rumor are the players who faced him on the court.

Muhammad Ali:
"And in this Corner . . . Uncle Sam"

Unlike Brisker and Jabali, fighter Muhammad Ali pulverized people in the ring but was a man of peace when he unlaced his gloves.

Born Cassius Marcellus Clay, Jr., in Louisville, Kentucky, in 1942, the boy began boxing at the age of twelve after his bike was stolen outside a bazaar. Reporting the theft to the police, he said he was going to whup whoever took it, and the officer, Joe Martin, told him, "You better learn how to fight before you start challenging people."

Martin gave him his first lesson, and Clay was hooked. He saw boxing as a way to "someday buy my mother and father a house and own a nice big car for myself," and worked his way up through the Kentucky Golden Gloves to the National Golden Gloves to the 1960 Olympics in Rome, where he became famous not just for winning the Gold Medal but for his habit of spouting verse to describe his abilities or predict outcomes of fights (though it wasn't Ali but cornerman Budini Brown who came up with his motto, "Float like a butterfly, sting like a bee").

Clay whupped his way to the world heavyweight title in February 1964 by upsetting the heavily favored Sonny Liston (Clay had leaked word to the

Liston camp that he was terrified, and the overconfident Liston only trained to go three rounds. Clay parried what the champ threw and after the third round shouted at him, "You big sucker; I got you now!"). At a press conference two days later, Clay surprised the public even more by declaring that for the past three years he'd been a follower of Islam: "I ain't no Christian," he said. "I can't be, when I see all the colored people fighting for forced integration get blowed up." What's more, henceforth, he said, his name was to be Muhammad Ali.

Reporters scoffed at him and Ali walked out before a friend's fight in Madison Square Garden when an official refused to introduce Ali to the crowd using his new name. He was roundly booed as he left. There were also problems due to tension among members of the Nation of Islam. After the murder of Malcolm X in February 1965—presumably by religious rivals—there were rumors that Ali, too, would be slain. Indeed, on the night of Malcolm X's murder, Ali's apartment was torched.

But Ali wasn't one to live in fear and remained in the public eye, beating Liston a second time in May, then destroying Floyd Patterson. Then, in February 1966, it wasn't religious adversaries but the U.S. government that boxed the champ into a corner.

Ali had registered with the Selective Service in 1960, and was classified 1-A. That was changed to 1-Y ("not qualified") when he did poorly on an Army IQ test. (When the failure became public, Ali declared, "I said I was the greatest, not the smartest.")

As the war in Vietnam began to escalate, however, IQ standards were lowered and Ali suddenly became eligible. Ali was reclassified 1-A, and there was a good chance that he'd be drafted. Reporters descended on Ali, and he made the mistake of telling them, "Man, I ain't got no quarrel with them

Vietcong." The comment made headlines, and those who hadn't already regarded the fighter as ungrateful and unpatriotic did so now.

Illinois found technicalities in the law to cancel the March 1966 fight between Ali and Ernie Terrell, and other states—including Kentucky—found reasons not to let Ali fight. Eventually, Terrell withdrew and Ali ended up fighting and beating Canadian heavyweight champ George Chuvalo in Toronto.

That same month, Ali went before the draft board to petition for an exemption on the grounds that he was a conscientious objector. The board turned him down, and an appeal was also rejected. In August, Ali attended a special hearing chaired by retired Kentucky State Circuit Court Judge Lawrence Grauman and presented his case. Ali said, in part, that the Qur'an taught "that we are not to participate in wars on the side of nonbelievers, and this is a Christian country." Grauman felt that Ali was "sincere in his objection on religious grounds to participation in war," and recommended that he be exempted from the draft.

Enter the Department of Justice, which presented its side to the board. Ali had been under surveillance by the FBI, and the government claimed that not only were the fighter's objections political rather than religious, but he'd said himself that he didn't oppose war but war fought for nonbelievers. These made him ineligible for exemption. (Ali later qualified what he'd said, maintaining that it was okay to fight in one's defense.)

Throughout the controversy, sportswriters nationwide had a field day with Ali. With the notable exception of Howard Cosell, virtually every member of the press crucified Ali, calling him a coward, a traitor, and the like. As much as his cause was rejected by the press, his timing was also unfortunate. We'd come through the assassination of a President and the onslaught of the Beatles; society was sick and tired of having its values questioned, especially by someone who had profited so handsomely as Ali had. You *know* values were changing when reporters went out of their way to praise Elvis Presley—who had personified rebellion just a few years before—for having done his duty in the service when he was drafted. There was a strong public outcry for Ali to be stripped of his heavyweight title.

In March 1967, the National Selective Service Presidential Appeal Board squelched the appeal, and he was told to report for induction on April 28. Ali said, "If I thought going to war would bring freedom and equality to twenty-two million of my people, they wouldn't have to draft me; I'd join tomorrow." He said when it came to choosing between "the laws of the land or the laws of Allah," there *was* no choice.

Most people thought that when the time came, Ali would change his mind and join rather than go to jail.

On the appointed date, Ali showed up at the U.S. Armed Forces Examining and Entrance Station in Houston, Texas, one of twenty-six men who were to be inducted.

When all were present, their names were called. When the induction officer called for "Cassius Marcellus Clay" to take the customary step forward, Ali didn't budge. A lieutenant told Ali to accompany him, and in a nearby office the fighter was informed that refusing to be inducted was punishable with jail and a fine. Ali told him he understood that, but couldn't oblige.

Ali was taken back to the induction room, his name was repeated, once again he refused to step forward, and this time he was told to submit a written refusal. Ali did so. He was permitted to leave, though in a prepared statement to the press the military said, "Notification of his refusal is being made to the United States Attorney, the State Director of the Selective Service System, and the local Selective Service Board for whatever action is deemed appropriate."

Ali himself distributed a prepared statement, which stated that being World Heavyweight Champion means that "the holder . . . should at all times have the courage of his convictions and carry out those convictions, not only in the ring but throughout all phases of his life." And that was what he intended to do. An hour later, Ali's boxing license was suspended by the New York State Athletic Commission, which also announced that it no longer recognized Ali as champion. The rest of the nation's athletic commissions soon followed suit, the World Boxing Association stripped him of his title, and it appeared that Ali was finished.

Those who doubted the strength of his convictions would have been surprised to learn that the government had made secret overtures to Ali. They realized that he was an influential hot potato and didn't want others following his example. Thus, the military promised that if Ali agreed to serve, he would be assigned a noncombat role. Ali rejected the plan.

Ironically, Ali might have been safer in Vietnam: even before he'd registered his in-person protest, there were death threats by the score; at one point, Ali was so concerned for his welfare that he'd taken to packing a derringer.

Ten days after he'd gone to Houston, Ali was indicted by a federal grand jury and his trial began on June 19. The next day, the all-white jury got the case and, after deliberating for 20 minutes, found Ali guilty. Conservative judge Joe Ingraham hit him with the maximum sentence: five years in prison and a $10,000 fine. It was the first defeat

Ali had ever suffered—though he didn't see it that way. As basketball star Bill Russell put it after meeting with Ali, "Philosophically, Ali was a free man."

Ali stayed out of prison while his case was appealed; his passport was revoked, however, lest he try to flee the country. He earned money by doing the college lecture circuit, of which he said, "Talking is a whole lot easier than fighting." Rather pathetically, the government watched him every step of the way—looking for *what*, it's difficult to say.

In May 1968, an appeals court refused to overturn the conviction. The court maintained that because Ali was a fighter, not a member of the clergy, he wasn't entitled to conscientious objector status. The courts also agreed that although the FBI surveillance and wiretaps may have been unjustified, they had no bearing on the case.

Believing that he was "being tested by Allah," Ali pursued the appeals process, even though his lecture fees didn't come close to covering his legal expenses. To earn some extra money, Ali became involved in a sad, sad film venture to determine the greatest heavyweight champion of all time: the woefully out-of-shape, potbellied Ali got into a ring with former heavyweight champion Rocky Marciano and filmed all kinds of blows, giving and receiving. The footage was edited based on computer projections of who would have won.

Ali lost. He may have pocketed $10,000 plus a percentage of the gross, but the freakish film further damaged his already wobbly reputation. So did a short-lived Broadway play, *Buck White*. Fortunately, he was able to get back into the ring when the NAACP Legal Defense Fund filed suit against New York State boxing authorities, maintaining that revoking Ali's license had been illegal; that, previously, more than ninety convicted criminals had been licensed to fight in the state. The District

Court agreed, the State Athletic Commission reluctantly complied with the order to reinstate Ali, and he was back fighting again, working his way toward an inevitable title fight with the man who had won the world championship in his absence, Joe Frazier. On March 8, 1971, the two undefeated athletes met in Madison Square Garden, and Frazier beat Ali.

"Joe earned it," Ali said of the victory, but at a press conference the following day, when a reporter told Ali that Frazier didn't think Ali wanted to fight him again, Ali replied with a little smile, "Oh, how wrong he is." Later on, he admitted, "I would have done anything except go against the will of Allah to get my title back again."

Meanwhile, outside the ring, the mood of the nation was turning against the war; Ted Kennedy, for one, believes that "Muhammad's actions contributed enormously to the debate." The pendulum of public opinion began to swing in his favor and, on June 28, 1971, the U.S. Supreme Court unanimously overturned Ali's conviction.

With that albatross off his neck, Ali was free to concentrate on fighting Frazier—with the "preliminaries" being held in a TV studio while the two were being interviewed by Howard Cosell. Frazier foolishly brought up the fact that he'd sent Ali to the hospital and Ali (accurately) shot back, "Everybody knows I went to the hospital for ten minutes. You were in the hospital for three weeks. You're ignorant, Joe." Frazier launched himself at Ali, and the two had to be pried apart by studio personnel. Very *brave* studio personnel.

The men were fined $5,000 by the New York State Athletic Commission, and Ali won their next two showdowns. But time and stress had taken their toll on the champion, who was only a shadow of the floating butterfly and stinging bee he'd once been. He didn't want to fight, and tried to jump-start his acting career with the unbearably bad TV miniseries *Freedom Road,* which was even worse than the 1977 theatrical biopic *The Greatest,* in which Ali starred. When that flopped, he had no choice but to go back into the ring. Finally, after taking a beating from Trevor Berbick on December 11, 1981, he hung up the gloves for good. Financially secure, he devoted himself to his faith and to talking to kids about the hazards of drugs. When he isn't traveling, he lives on his sprawling farm in Michigan. His health is good, despite occasional slurred speech and trembling due to Parkinson's syndrome, a neurological disorder that was caused—as far as his doctors can tell—by blows he took as far back as 1978 and possible adverse reaction to thyroid medication. In 1990, he began undergoing therapy to compensate for the speech problems, sessions that have clearly helped.

When he turned fifty, Ali said, "People say I had a full life, but I ain't dead yet." He's enjoying the time he's had to study and strive to achieve purity, to meet more and more people, and to talk about God and the afterlife.

"Boxing," he says, "was just to introduce me to the world. There's bigger work I got to do." A half-century old? "I'm just getting started," Ali says.

Roberto Clemente:
"Relief Effort"

So many players have been snatched from us in their prime through different kinds of tragedies. And, as with Bostock—as with so *many* people inside and outside of sport—we don't really appreciate them until they're no longer around.

This happens because we're unwilling to overlook their bad points when they're with us; when they're gone, and we don't have to suffer them anymore, our feelings soften or are supplanted by the *good* memories. We'll curse a Billy Martin while he's alive, then look back wistfully when he dies and savor his idiosyncrasies.

Other people really *are* saints, though, and we just didn't see it because we were too wrapped up in the *game*. How they were playing. What the sportswriters were saying about them. How they were getting along with teammates. Such was the case with Roberto Clemente.

Throughout his eighteen-season professional career, which began with the Brooklyn Dodgers organization in 1953—just seven years after Jackie Robinson broke the color barrier—Clemente was always battling for recognition, struggling in the shadows of contemporary sluggers Mickey Mantle, Willie Mays, and Henry Aaron. That Clemente compiled a .317 lifetime batting average while dealing with pulled muscles, tension headaches, chronic stomachaches ("spasms" he called them; "hypochondria" his doctors described them), bone chips, and insomnia, makes the accomplishment even more remarkable. And by winning four batting titles and leading the Pirates to two World Series victories, Clemente did something that both Willie Mays and Henry Aaron were unable to do in careers that spanned nearly twenty-five years.

Clemente felt that his Puerto Rican heritage caused him to be ignored for commercial endorsements, business opportunities, and even MVP awards (especially in the 1960 World Series, when shortstop Dick Groat got the honor). Many fans and players thought this was sour grapes, but they didn't understand that Clemente wasn't complaining: he was simply observing. Stating fact. He simply was not a man to wallow in self-pity or harbor bitterness. Instead, he devoted himself to playing his best during the season, and helping the less fortunate everywhere in the off-season. He was scrupulously polite and patient with fans, and was even pleasant with sportswriters—a *real* rarity.

After being voted the National League's Most Valuable Player in 1966, Clemente began to focus more on charitable work. He was compulsive about going to hospitals to visit sick kids, and devoted his time to planning a "sports city" in Puerto Rico, a large, free camp where poor youngsters could develop any athletic skills they had, learn respect for their bodies and, hopefully, avoid the lure of drugs. Teammate Willie Stargell recalls, with admiration, "Roberto was always trying to help someone."

It came as no surprise, then, that after Nicaragua was devastated by an earthquake in December 1972, Clemente took it upon himself to collect $150,000 in clothing, food, medical supplies, and other aid for victims. He had been there the previous month, coaching teams in an amateur world

Here's how Roberto Clemente earned his superstar reputation, as he miraculously steals a home run from Willie Mays in June 1968. (*AP/Wide World.*)

series, and ached for the people who were left wanting by the disaster.

Clemente's partner in the effort, TV producer Luis Vigoraux, says, "He did not just lend his name to the fund-raising activities the way some famous personalities do. He took over the entire thing, arranging for collection points, publicity, and the transportation to Nicaragua."

A four-engine DC-7 piston-powered plane was chartered to transport the supplies. The previous week, a plane had flown down and profiteers had taken the goods before they could be distributed. Although he wasn't keen on making the trip to Nicaragua—he preferred to stay at home and collect more supplies—Clemente wanted to make sure the goods got to the people who needed them. And because he was flying down, military boss Anastasio Somoza was going to meet the plane and the press would be there; no one would get near the supplies who wasn't supposed to.

On December 31, 1972, Roberto's wife, Vera, drove him to San Juan International Airport early in the evening. Vera looked at the old plane and expressed concern about the size of the cargo: even to her untrained eye, it seemed overloaded.

"Everything will be all right," her husband assured her. In fact, she was dead right: the prop plane was carrying 4,193 pounds more than its maximum permissible gross weight of 144,750.

When pilot Jerry Hill arrived—late—he didn't like the way the two right engines sounded, so the flight was delayed for three hours while engineers worked on them. Vera took that as a bad omen and said once again she wasn't happy about Roberto going.

He smiled at her. "If there is one more delay," he promised, "we'll leave this for tomorrow."

But there were no more problems, and shortly before 9 P.M. the other three passengers boarded.

After kissing his wife goodbye, Clemente climbed on. It was 9:11 P.M.

The plane took off slowly, requiring over 8,000 feet of the 10,000-foot runway to get airborne. Its ascent was also slow as it headed north over the Atlantic. After 10 minutes, the pilot radioed the tower that he was "coming around" to the southwest—but as the plane turned, instead of continuing to climb it suddenly lost altitude and, at 9:22, plowed into heavy seas a mile-and-a-half from the airport.

Coast Guard planes were dispatched at once and, using flares, tried to find the wreckage; they were unsuccessful until the following day at 5 P.M., when they located the McDonnell Douglas aircraft in 100 feet of water.

Hill's body was recovered at once, but after thirty-eight dives over four days, Navy divers were unable to locate the remains of Clemente or the other three passengers. It's presumed that they were tossed from the wreckage on impact and carried out to sea.

An investigation by the National Transportation Safety Board discovered that the aircraft could not have been in worse condition. The inboard left engine had been damaged during a taxiing accident on December 2, and had never been repaired; it failed during takeoff. Because of extensive wear, the inboard right engine could not reach full power. The plane had not been flown for four months, and the engines had been fired up irregularly during that time; the pistons were firing unevenly. There were more problems, any *one* of which might have been enough to bring the plane down.

Three days of national mourning followed the crash and Major League Baseball did something it had done only once before, in the case of the legendary Lou Gehrig: the normal five-year waiting

Before a game on April 7, 1973, Pirates board chairman John Galbreath presents Roberto's mother, Luisa, with her son's uniform. Widow Vera Clemente and son look on. (*AP/Wide World*.)

period requirement for induction into the Hall of Fame was waived, and Clemente was voted in immediately.

Clemente left behind his wife and three sons, and a legion of fans for whom perhaps one memory stands out above all: his three thousandth hit. The game against the Mets was stopped for several minutes as the thirty-eight-year-old superstar was cheered by the 13,117 fans for having reached a pinnacle only eleven other players had achieved.

The hit was special for another reason. Clemente

had expected to play for another four or five years, but his three thousandth hit was also his last—a sad but fitting finale in the career of this great ballplayer ... though not quite the end of his influence as a great humanitarian. In March 1975, in Caroline, Puerto Rico, ground was broken for Sports City, fulfilling the athlete's dream. And in that respect, at least, Roberto Clemente will never die.

Thurman Munson:
"Dogged Catcher"

Thurman Munson wasn't like Roberto Clemente.

He was a good man, say those who knew him, but he was also an intensely private one. He didn't share his beefs or his ambitions with anyone but close friends and family. He went out and played ball the best he knew how, and that was all he ever wanted us to expect of him. Back then, one's reaction to his abruptness or downright rudeness would have been something from the "Up yours" family. But then he died, and what had seemed so testy and abrasive now seemed strong and scrappy.

What's interesting about Munson is that, unlike so many athletes, he wasn't born: he was self-made. Yet, for all the acclaim that came the way of the five-foot eleven-inch 200-pound New York Yankees catcher through his storied twelve-year career with the Yankees—including being named the American League's Most Valuable Player in 1976 and the first Yankee team captain since Lou Gehrig was so-honored forty years earlier—Munson was plagued by overwhelming insecurity and a fear of failure that was sometimes palpable. When he blew up at you, it was this fear talking.

Born in Akron, Ohio, on June 7, 1947, Munson was an all-America catcher at Kent State before the Yankees selected him in the first round of the 1968 amateur draft. From the outset, Munson struck those around him as a tormented individual, plagued by what he wasn't rather than being happy with what he was.

He disdained fans, teammates, and members of the press equally. Munson himself admitted as much hours before he found out that he had won the MVP award: "You know," he said, "I'm not going to win it on popularity, so if I win it, you'll know I deserved it."

Resembling the Pillsbury Doughboy with a walrus mustache in an era when the other two leading catchers were tall and handsome Johnny Bench and Carlton Fisk, Munson grew more determined each season to prove that he was better than them, while at the same time withdrawing into a shell that closed himself off from everyone except his immediate family. Of course, certain events did contribute to Munson's distrust of people.

For example, the catcher's pride was severely wounded after the 1976 season (following the Yankees' loss to the Cincinnati Reds in the World Series, in which Munson hit a staggering .529), when Yankees owner George Steinbrenner signed Reggie Jackson at a salary higher than his—even though Steinbrenner had given Munson repeated assurances that no one on the Yankee team, other than star pitcher Catfish Hunter, would make more than him. To add insult to injury, at spring training Jackson made things worse by telling *Sport* magazine, "I'm the straw that stirs the drink. Munson thinks he can be the straw that stirs the drink, but he can only stir it bad."

Someone should have reminded Reggie what else a straw is used for. And while they were at it, someone should have reminded Steinbrenner about looking out for the men who had earned him the money to help pay Jackson. For once, the Yankee boss kept his mouth shut when he *should* have spoken up.

While deeply wounded, Munson had an even better year statistically than his MVP season the year before and helped the Yankees get into and win the World Series. The Yankees went on to successfully defend their World Series title the next season. But while his teammates for the most part enjoyed themselves, Munson grew more tense, more determined to prove his worth. Some speculated that this might have prompted an ugly, off-field incident in Minnesota that season when Munson was charged with assault for allegedly choking a twenty-two-year-old college student who had sought his autograph. ("I didn't choke him," Munson insisted. "I just had a hand on him." He had gotten a whole ten autograph requests while heading toward the clubhouse, and Munson said, "I just got sick of it." Yankee catcher Fran Healy concurs, tongue somewhat in cheek: "There wasn't enough time for Thurmon to choke him. I pulled his hand right off right away.")

When the media and Yankee management suggested to Munson that he "cool it," he became even more discourteous and nasty. He confided to his wife and his few close friends, "I can't wait for the day when I can retire." Still, Munson knew he needed to play at least ten years to be eligible for the Hall of Fame, which would give his career the stamp of validity he desperately sought.

In the meantime, to be close to his family and to have a measure of peace from New York City, which he considered to be a rat trap, Munson took up flying. As Richard Moss, Munson's longtime attorney, put it: "Thurmon was like a little boy about flying. It was just the greatest thing he'd ever done. He talked about getting up in the air alone, being with nature, able to think. And, of course, he was able to get home to his family," which consisted of wife, Diane, and three young children, all of whom lived in Canton, Ohio. He liked flying so much that he was planning to start a commercial commuter airline after he was finished with baseball.

It meant so much to Munson that before he signed his contract in 1979, he insisted that the Yankees waive the standard prohibition in Major League Baseball player contracts against piloting and flying in private planes during the regular season. They agreed; considering the salary problems they were having with him, it was the only way they could keep him from badgering them about trading him to Cleveland, which would be within driving distance of home. Munson was delighted, because it took him about an hour to fly his million-dollar, eight-seat Cessna Citation from New York to Canton.

Unfortunately, on August 1, 1979, just a month after he'd purchased his plane, the waiver proved to have tragic consequences.

The thirty-two-year-old Munson had flown in from Chicago at three in the morning. He didn't like the way the plane sounded, so he took it up the following afternoon to see if he could figure out what was wrong. He flew out from Akron-Canton Airport with two passengers on board—friends Jerry Anderson and David Hall, the latter of whom had taught Munson how to fly.

Munson did some touch-and-go take-offs and landings. The plane seemed to respond okay, and he decided that the problem he'd experienced before had simply been icing on the engine.

At 3:00, as he was approaching the airport for his third and final landing, the airplane suddenly lost altitude and began clipping the tops of trees north of the runway. Inside the cockpit, Munson struggled to bring the plane up to speed—he was just 12 miles an hour shy of stalling—but was unable to do so. Motorists on nearby Greensburg Road braked frantically and watched in horror as the jet nosed down, hit the ground 200 feet short of the runway, and ripped through a small group of trees. The right wing hit a large tree and the plane spun around, skidded several yards more, and finally came to a rest on the road. The wing caught on fire, the flames quickly sweeping closer to the fuel stored there.

When the plane hit the tree, Munson—who was not wearing his harness—was thrown forward; the impact dislocated his back and, had he survived, he would probably have been paralyzed from the neck down. His two passengers, however, were alert and unhurt. While one opened the emergency door, the other moved him from the pilot's seat toward the door. Thirty seconds after the plane came to rest, the fuel in the wing caught fire and flames swallowed the plane; despite the fact that their own clothing was burning, the men still struggled desperately to get Munson to the door. But the smoke was thick and choking, the heat was intense, and the men finally had no choice but to withdraw before they perished.

The police arrived within five minutes of the crash. Munson was dead when they reached him; death was caused by asphyxiation and a swollen voice box. Hall was taken to the Akron Regional Burn Center at Children's Hospital with burns on his arms and hands, whereas Anderson was rushed to Timken Mercy Hospital with burns on his arms, face, and neck. Both men survived.

Initially, the Federal Aviation Administration blamed Munson for the crash, and Cessna Corporation (the plane's manufacturer) saying he wasn't experienced enough for the equipment, disputed any liability. This was, they said, the first time there had been any trouble with this particular make of aircraft. The FAA concluded that the crash was Munson's fault: he'd let the plane lose speed and, thus, altitude; he'd slowed even more because he lowered the landing gear late and hadn't taken into account the increased drag; and, finally, when he found out he was too low, he

Summit County's white-haired coroner examines the wreckage of Thurman Munson's plane. (*AP/Wide World.*)

didn't know how to pull out of it quickly. Notwithstanding that, his widow filed a $42 million suit, claiming that the company had pressured her husband into buying a plane that was too sophisticated for him, and were responsible for the crash. Rather than go through a costly trial and suffer bad publicity, the company settled out of court for nearly $1.7 million.

When Munson died, there was talk that perhaps baseball's Hall of Fame would waive its five-year retirement requirement, as it had done in the case of Roberto Clemente, who also perished in a plane crash. Well, that was one waiver Munson didn't get. In fact, to this day, Munson still has not been accorded the honor he coveted most: induction into the Hall of Fame.

But that probably would not have surprised him. Stocky, sullen, and awkward at times, he never looked particularly good on the field. He didn't have "star power" like Bench or Fisk.

Thurmon Munson only got the job done.

Ron Turcotte:
"Troubled Crown"

Many people put their faith in fate. It's easier to believe that our lives are shaped by events beyond our control than it is to imagine that we're responsible for each and every thing that happens. That Clemente or Munson died because they *had* to—it was their time.

Ron Turcotte's life seemed touched by fate so often that it's possible to believe he was predestined to take his ghastly fall . . . though that doesn't make the reality of it any easier to take.

In June 1973, as Turcotte sat atop Secretariat in the winner's circle at Belmont—the first jockey to ride a horse to the Triple Crown in a quarter century—he certainly had reason to believe in destiny. Growing up in New Brunswick, Canada, where life revolved around the lumber industry, there didn't seem to be too many career options for a young man standing barely five feet tall and weighing just over 100 pounds. Turcotte wasn't sure *what* he'd do, but in the winter of 1959 fate—if you believe in it— interceded for the first time.

It was a severe winter and the lumber mill was forced to shut down. Turcotte went to visit one of his brothers, who was working as a roofer in Toronto. The seventeen-year-old liked the city and decided to stay and try to make a new life for himself.

The following spring, fate interceded for the second time. When other plans fell through, Turcotte sat and watched the Kentucky Derby on TV with the landlord at the rooming house where he lived. The landlord joked that maybe a little guy like Turcotte should give horse racing a shot. Turcotte didn't know much about horses, but he *was* the right size and it seemed like an interesting, fun way to make a living. Getting a job as an exercise boy at a local track, he quickly graduated to groom and then to breaking yearlings. Showing an innate and uncanny ability to get fractious horses to respond, Turcotte soon earned his chance to ride competitively. By 1964, he was Canada's top jockey.

Turcotte could have earned a comfortable living doing what he was doing, but he was determined to go where the competition was the greatest—the United States. Once again, Turcotte proved his mettle. He became a top rider and by 1972 had won the Kentucky Derby up on Riva Ridge. Then fate entered the picture for the third time. A huge, young colt named Secretariat needed a rider. The horse's trainer, Canadian Lucien Laurin, was the same man who had trained Riva Ridge and, naturally, Turcotte came to mind. Together, the duo made horse racing history: since 1890, only three other jockeys had ridden consecutive Derby winners (but Bobby Ussery's second crown, in 1968 on Dancer's Image, is one of those wins-with-an-asterisk, because the horse was subsequently disqualified when it was learned that it had run after being injected with the painkiller phenylbutazone).

Despite his newfound wealth and fame, Turcotte refused to deviate from the lifestyle that had helped make him successful in the first place. He kept his family life with wife Gaetane and daughter Ann private. He avoided bars, late hours, and the advances of other women. He maintained the same schedule he had for a decade, arriving at the racetrack by 6 A.M. and being at home by 6 P.M.

Turcotte has never said whether or not he believes in fate, but he certainly wasn't going to do anything to tempt it.

But just as he found the proverbial pot of gold at the end of several rainbows, Ron finally ran up against some big-time trouble on July 13, 1978. After riding in more than 22,000 races during a seventeen-year career, Turcotte was at the same Belmont Race Track where, just a little over five years before, he had known his greatest triumph. He was racing in very tight quarters when a less experienced jockey got in too close, horses went down, and Turcotte was trampled in the pileup, his back broken.

The jockey was left paralyzed from the waist down, and filed a $105 million lawsuit against various parties, including the New York State Racing Association, a fellow jockey, a horse owner, and several stewards. After protracted legal proceedings, the case was dismissed by the New York Court of Appeals on grounds that Turcotte was well aware of the inherent dangers of the sport from which he had earned his living.

To the man who had ridden arguably the greatest race horse ever and who was now confined to a wheelchair for the rest of his life, the court's decision was the equivalent of the result he always dreaded at the racetrack—finishing out of the money.

Was fate unkind to Turcotte? He doesn't think so. With his typical resolve, Turcotte settled into a new life in his home in the small town of Drummond, New Brunswick, in eastern Canada, with new goals and a surprisingly optimistic outlook.

Never a man of many words, he says, "Jockeys have died. I'm a lucky man." He still reads the *Daily Racing Form* and, more important—a seventh-grade dropout—he finished up high school across the border at Van Buren High School in Maine.

Ron Turcotte learns to walk with the help of a brace. (*AP/Wide World.*)

Willie Shoemaker:
"Busted by a Bronco"

What happened to Ron Turcotte was a tragedy, probably preventable. What happened to his fellow jockey, Willie Shoemaker, was also a tragedy—the more so because it was definitely preventable.

Despite his size, Shoe had every right to feel larger than life. By the time he'd participated in his final horse race at the age of fifty-eight, before 64,573 fans at Santa Anita Racetrack on February 3, 1990, the superjockey had ridden home an amazing 8,833 winners (1,009 stakes victories) and won purses totaling a staggering $123,375,524.

Not too bad for a man who was so small at birth that he was all but given up for dead when his mother put his tiny, blue, 2-pound body in a shoebox and placed it in a makeshift incubator—the oven.

But Shoemaker survived, the first of many lucky or miraculous breaks with which his life seemed blessed. After reaching an adult height of four feet eleven inches, he sought to escape the extreme poverty of his Texas childhood by heading to California and becoming involved in horses. Just seventeen years old, he became an exercise boy at Golden Gate Park, graduated quickly to hard-riding jockey, and on April 20, 1949, in his third professional race, won a $3,000 claiming event aboard Shafter V, a chestnut filly.

Within five years, Shoemaker had become one of the nation's leading jockeys, riding the first of his four Kentucky Derby winners, Swaps, in 1955. In the course of his storied forty-year career, Shoemaker rode such standout horses as Spectacular Bid, Damascus, John Henry, and others. At the same time, Shoemaker was also known for his share of miscues, such as standing up in the saddle just before the finish line in the 1957 Derby, costing the heavily favored Gallant Man victory, and choosing to ride Hill Rise in the 1964 Derby instead of Northern Dancer, who won.

But physically, at least, he seemed to have an angel watching over him, even when he was hit with a vicious one-two punch: being thrown from a horse in 1968 and suffering a broken leg that required a steel pin to repair it; and, a year later, being thrown again and suffering a smashed pelvis, torn bladder, and nerve damage. Yet both times he recovered from his injuries and returned to the saddle as good, if not better, than ever. His only other serious injury occurred in 1955, when a horse ran over him and his knee was crushed.

As the years went by, however, fellow jockeys and trainers began to whisper that like other legendary sports figures—Kareem Abdul-Jabbar, Willie Mays, and Muhammad Ali—Shoemaker had, perhaps, stayed on in the sport a bit too long. He still had the ability to win a big race every now and then, like the 1986 Kentucky Derby on board longshot Ferdinand, but at the age of fifty-four even *he* began to think that it was time to hang up his spurs.

Before doing so, however, he embarked on what amounted to a one-year farewell tour: in return for appearance fees, some running in the high five figures, he went to small racetracks across the United States. For their part, the racetrack operators who paid Shoemaker's fee enjoyed the substantially higher wagering the day Shoemaker appeared at the track.

He rode his final race on February 3, 1990, before 64,573 fans at Santa Anita.

Within three weeks of retiring, Shoemaker found that he just couldn't make a clean break from horse racing. So, like other jockeys before him—most notably the great Johnny Longden— Shoemaker decided to take a shot at training. After fourteen months, he had begun to achieve a measure of success, having saddled 19 winners, 19 second, and 17 third-place finishers in 147 races.

Then, Shoemaker's life changed forever. On April 8, 1991, after playing a round of golf with fellow ex-jockey turned trainer, Don Pierce, at Sierra La Verne Country Club in southern California, Shoemaker and Pierce decided to have a few beers and play liar's poker. After about 90 minutes they decided to have dinner, and made arrangements to meet at a restaurant in Arcadia.

Shoemaker felt fine as he climbed into his 1990 Ford Bronco II shortly before 8 P.M., slipped on his seat belt, and headed out to Highway 30. Traffic was moderate.

Although Shoemaker was able to hold his liquor, he'd definitely overdone it this night. Drowsy from all he'd had to drink at the country club (five beers, according to one report), he appears to have fallen asleep. His car drifted to the right side of the road, struck a beam, rolled down a 50-foot embankment, and landed upright in the middle of a transition road, used by motorists to accelerate as they head onto the FootHill Freeway.

Motorist Terry Fisher had to slam on his brakes to avoid colliding with the Bronco. His pickup truck rolled over auto parts that had been knocked from the Bronco as he screeched to a stop beside

Willie Shoemaker works out aboard Patchy Groundfog at Santa Anita Racetrack prior to his final race in February 1990. Ironically, the fifty-eight year-old said before the race, "I better get out while I can—in one piece." (*AP/Wide World.*)

it; behind him, two cars skidded and braked hard to avoid crashing into him.

"It was like a stock car race," young Fisher recalls, as cars spun in all different directions.

Finding Shoemaker pinned behind the wheel,

unconscious, his face blood-splattered from deep lacerations in his scalp, and his tongue hanging out of his mouth, Fisher reached into the broken window and moved the driver's head slightly.

"He wasn't moving or doing anything," Fisher says. "I couldn't detect that he was breathing."

While one of the other motorists called the police from a car phone, Fisher managed to open the bent door, reclined the seat, straightened Shoe's legs, and unbuckled the seat belt. After sticking his fingers into Shoemaker's mouth to clear his throat, and pressing on his chest cavity several times, Fisher got him to breathe. That done, he picked up a sweater lying on the seat and pressed it to the driver's head to stop the bleeding. Fisher had no idea whose life he'd saved.

Paramedics arrived shortly thereafter and, because Shoemaker's blood pressure was so low, they had difficulty getting intravenous fluids into his body. After a few minutes of work, however, they managed to stabilize the victim, and rushed him to Glendora Community Hospital. He had lost a great deal of blood internally, and did not regain consciousness until he was in the emergency room. His wife, Cindy, who was in Kentucky showing horses, was rushed to his side by private plane.

The doctors who first treated Shoemaker knew almost instantly that Shoemaker faced a life of permanent paralysis. In addition to a broken pelvis, he suffered a fractured back, which injured his spinal cord. A tracheostomy was performed in order to help him breathe. To add insult to injury, it was determined that Shoemaker had a blood alcohol level of .13 percent; the legal level is .08 percent, and California Highway Patrol officer Clancy Mitchell charged him with a misdemeanor of driving under the influence of alcohol and making an unsafe turning move. Obviously.

Within days, Shoemaker—alert and aware of

what had happened to him—was transferred to Centinela Hospital in Inglewood, and then to the Neuro-Trauma unit at Craig Rehabilitation Hospital in Englewood, Colorado, a facility noted for helping paraplegics adjust to life without the use of their arms and legs. With the use of computer technology, patients there learn to control wheelchairs using their head and mouth.

For a man used to having the full power of a 1,500-pound animal under his command, being completely dependent on others had to be the ultimate irony, if not the ultimate blow. But to the surprise of no one, Willie Shoemaker showed the same dogged determination in rehab that he exhibited on the racetrack. He has since returned to training horses at Santa Anita, tooling around in his wheelchair and offering his quick, familiar smile.

Perhaps Shoemaker summed it up best himself in 1987, when he went to visit Ron Turcotte.

"I saw Ron in a wheelchair," he said. "He was smiling and you would have never known that he had been in a wheelchair for many years. Jockeys have guts."

Pelle Lindbergh:
"Iced"

What's amazing about the Shoemaker accident is that he didn't know better. It's not as if there weren't precedent for getting plastered and creamed. Shoemaker read the papers. He read the sports pages. He knew about Pelle Lindbergh.

The difference between all athletes and hockey players is that the latter drink more than any other athletes. Cynics say there's nothing else to do up in Canada, but the truth is the players are an elite bunch who like to pal around, even with the guys they beat up on the ice. To them, that means drinking together. Never mind that Lindbergh was Swedish: he fit right in at the bar.

The much honored player was the team's second-round draft choice in 1979 and, in 1984, had won the prized Vezina Trophy as the leading goalie. At the close of the previous season, he'd said, "My quickness and my reflexes is my greatest strength."

But not this day. Not with a blood alcohol content of .24 percent—.14 *higher* than the legal level of drunkenness.

The twenty-six-year-old was out celebrating after a Flyers victory over the Boston Bruins. He hadn't played, but a win was a win, the Flyers were 12-2—the best record in the NHL—and this victory made it ten straight. That was reason enough to party with his triumphant teammates—and, because this was Saturday and there wasn't another game till Thursday, everyone could get as ripped as they wanted. Lindbergh, his friend Ed Parvin, and Parvin's friend Kathy McNeal packed into the goalie's fiery red Porsche 930 Turbo; Pelle's fiancée, Kerstin Pietzsch, couldn't make it. The trio headed to the sports complex in Voorhees, New Jersey, where the team practices were held; the complex includes a restaurant/bar.

The celebration broke up at 5:30 A.M. on November 10, 1985. No one was wearing a seat belt, and just 10 minutes later, Mr. Quick Reflexes was driving too fast on a curving road in Somerdale, New Jersey. Unable to hold the turn—the skid marks went on forever, suggesting just how fast he was going—he left the asphalt and plowed into a 3½-foot-high concrete wall in front of an elementary school. The two passengers received relatively minor injuries—but not Pelle. He suffered serious brain and spinal cord injuries, broke his skull and both legs; before paramedics could arrive, he'd gone without oxygen for 15 minutes.

Lindbergh was taken to John F. Kennedy Memorial Hospital in neighboring Stratford, where there was enough of him left to save using life support. However, he was declared brain dead after a quick examination; he was kept alive until his father, Sigge, could arrive from Sweden on Monday; Pelle's mother, Anna, was already in the United States on a visit. The next day, the young man's parents authorized the removal of their son's organs for transplant, after which he was permitted to die. Officially, death came from an intracerebral hemorrhage. His remains were returned to Sweden and he was buried in Stockholm on Wednesday, November 20.

Team members skated through that week's practices in a daze; tears flowed freely in every corner of the locker room. Generously, the Edmonton Oil-

Pelle Linbergh's car. It's amazing *anyone* survived the wreck. (*AP/Wide World.*)

ers offered to postpone Thursday's game: Coach Mike Keenan and general manager Bob Clarke declined, Clarke thanking them but saying, "We have to play sooner or later. It's better to get on with it." However, an hour-long tribute to Pelle was planned and held before the game. Moreover, in the kind of tribute you've *got* to respect, the Flyers honored the player's $1.5 million contract in full.

The team's other goalie, Bob Froese, was injured in a practice and, with the help of minor leaguer Darren Jensen, the Flyers won 5-3. Watching the game, Sigge leaped from his seat and cheered when the Flyers scored the first goal of the game.

It was all so stupid and pointless. As the team

physician, Dr. Edward Viner, put it, "He wasn't a drinker. He had had a fair amount to drink, but Pelle was not a drunk." Just careless. Unfortunately that, in combination with the same speed and excitement he showed on the ice, proved a deadly combination. In a strange way, what happened to Pelle underscores how amazing it is that more athletes don't end up like him.

As Froese, puts it—his eyes tearing, still, as he thinks of his teammate—"A lot of times athletes think they are invincible. We don't realize who holds the trump cards."

Billy Martin:
"Billy's Club"

Billy Martin's alcohol-related death was probably the least surprising of any in the annals of sport, yet in many ways it was the most shocking. He seemed too flinty to ever die.

It's ironic that Billy Martin is so closely identified with baseball's flagship franchise, the New York Yankees. Throughout much of their fabled history, the Yankees—baseball's dominant team, with more than 20 World Series victories to their credit—have symbolized the buttoned-down traditions of the 1920s, straitlaced and conservative.

Perhaps that's why it meant so much to Billy Martin to wear the Yankee pinstripes. If a player didn't have the right pedigree but made it with the club anyway, then no one could question his talent.

Alfred Manuel Martin was born in Berkeley, California, on May 16, 1928. He was raised by his mother and got the name "Billy" from his grandmother, who called him "Belli"—Italian for "pretty." Although he would grow to be five feet eleven inches and weigh 165 pounds, Martin was a small child with a large nose that gave his face a ferretlike appearance. Growing up in an extremely poor neighborhood with a diverse ethnic mix, Billy had to fight just to be given the chance to play in baseball games at the local park. Billy also fought to fend off the cruel taunts of other kids about his father, who abandoned him and his mother when he was only a year old. It wouldn't be a reach to say that Billy's later love/hate relationship with Yankee manager Casey Stengel and Yankee owner George Steinbrenner stemmed from his search for and conflict with a surrogate father.

In high school, the fiercely competitive Martin caught the eye of a Yankee scout. In 1950, the scrappy second baseman made it to the majors where, often as a late-inning defensive substitute, he played a pivotal role for the Yankee teams of the early fifties, playing on five World Series winners between 1950 and 1956. In fact, the Yankees were able to beat the Brooklyn Dodgers in 1952 thanks to Martin's spectacular running catch in game seven and again in 1953, behind Martin's record-setting 12 hits and torrid .500 batting average.

Just as important as his statistics, however, Martin kept the Yankee team loose, fitting in with superstars like Mickey Mantle, Yogi Berra, and Whitey Ford, while making sure no one took themselves too seriously, qualities that would serve him later as a manager. In fact, by 1957, Martin felt so much a part of the team that it came as a complete shock to him that the Yankees would trade him after a celebrated brawl at the trendy Copacabana nightclub involving himself and several teammates, including Mantle and Berra. For the rest of his life, Martin always felt that had Yankee Manager Casey Stengel gone to bat for him with management, he would not have been exiled to Kansas City.

Martin moved from team to team during the next few years, a bitter and angry man. There were regular fisticuffs among teammates and opponents, and in 1960, while playing for the Cincinnati Reds, he punched Chicago Cub pitcher Jim Brewer and broke his jaw, eventually paying Brewer $10,000 to settle a lawsuit.

Martin retired after the 1961 season, drifting on

the outskirts of baseball for many years. In fact, if not for his close friendship with Mickey Mantle, Martin might have severed his ties with the game altogether. Talking with Mantle kept him current, interested, passionate about the game. Then, out of the blue, the Minnesota Twins hired Martin to manage their languishing Denver Triple A farm team in 1968. Martin was surprised at how glad he was to be back, and turned the club around. Miraculously, he found himself named the Twins' manager for the 1969 season.

Mantle says today that Billy "wasn't the most graceful infielder you ever saw. But he would always find a way to beat you. Which is why he became a great manager."

Taking a blend of veterans, including Harmon Killebrew and Tony Oliva, and young players like Rod Carew, Martin displayed the competitiveness and compassion that would become a hallmark of his tenure as manager for five different major league teams. And, as was to become his managerial legacy, Martin produced results immediately, piloting the Twins to a 97-65 record and an American League Western Division Title—this, after a seventh-place finish the year before. However, as was also to become a recurring theme in Martin's career as a manager, he soon ran into trouble due to alcohol and fisticuffs.

Martin's victim was not someone from another team but one of his own players, star pitcher Dave Boswell who, it turned out, had been arguing in a Detroit bar with another Twins player. Rather than letting the two settle the problem between themselves, Martin got between them and—in his inimitable way—managed to tick Boswell off. Fists flew and Martin put his pitcher on the disabled list with two badly swollen black eyes, making him unavailable for the league championship series against Baltimore. Although there were jokes about the incident—like an "Enter at your own risk" sign posted on the clubhouse door—owner Calvin Griffith wasn't amused, and Martin found himself out of work that winter. Twins fans definitely were *not* happy: more than 10,000 "Bring Billy Back!" bumper stickers were sold. But Griffith stood firm and hired Bill Rigney, the veteran Angels coach who had been dumped by the team he'd managed since the American League expansion in 1961.

Martin busied himself with private projects for two years, when he was hired by the Detroit Tigers, a veteran team that just three years before had stunned defending World Champion St. Louis by winning the World Series. The first season with Martin at the helm, the Tigers finished second, but the next year they captured the Eastern Division crown, battling the eventual World Series champion Oakland Athletics in a hard-fought League playoff. The following season, however, Martin's magic wore off. Players had grown tired of his ways. Some claimed he played favorites; several, primarily pitchers, went behind Martin's back to team management and complained that his whimsical use or nonuse of them was ruining their careers. Once again, Martin found himself out of a job. But he quickly hooked up with the lowly Texas Rangers and, in less than a year, transformed them into a winning ball club.

Throughout his time at the helm of the Twins, Tigers, and Rangers, Martin could have been likened to the boy who leaves home and tries to prove to his parents that he can make it on his own—his parents being the New York Yankees. Ironically, in the intervening decade, the Yankees had gone from a team that routinely made the World Series to a struggling, last-place club. Things got so bad that in 1973, CBS—which had purchased the franchise from millionaire Del Webb in the late 1960s—unloaded the team for just $12 million, less than it had paid, to George Steinbrenner, a Cleveland shipbuilder, and his minority partners.

A college athlete and coach before turning his attention to business in his early twenties, Steinbrenner was first and foremost a businessman. On the other hand, many of his baseball counterparts were the sons of "old money" men, like Peter O'Malley of the Dodgers, Rudy Carpenter of the Phillies, and Augie Busch of the Cardinals, who, although they didn't regard owning a baseball team as a hobby, were wealthy men who simply weren't as "bottom-line" oriented as Steinbrenner.

Moreover, Steinbrenner had to contend with the popularity of the crosstown rival New York Mets, who not only had stolen many of the Yankees' fans in 1969 with their amazing World Series triumph over heavily favored Baltimore, but captured the National League pennant in 1973 by beating the mighty Cincinnati Reds, then battled the Oakland A's in seven hard-fought, dramatic games before losing the World Series. They were young, brash contenders and they were pulling in the young baseball fans. The kind of fans who would stick around for decades.

While many would later look at Billy Martin and George Steinbrenner as an "odd couple," the men actually had a strong common bond: making the Yankees champions. Steinbrenner wanted to attract fans, and Martin wanted to prove himself largely out of resentment over the circumstances surrounding his departure from the Yankees. Before hiring Martin, however, Steinbrenner made overtures to former Yankee star Mantle who, even though he didn't want the job himself, apparently put in the final good word that Martin needed with Steinbrenner. The rest, as they say, is history—albeit a checkered one unparalleled in all of sport.

In 1976, Martin's first full year at the helm, the amazin' Yankees reached the World Series. Though they lost to champion Cincinnati, Martin and Steinbrenner were the toast of the town. Both resolved to put the Yankees over the top the next year.

Steinbrenner did his part in the off-season, signing former Oakland A slugger Reggie Jackson to what was then the game's biggest free-agent contract. Just as quickly, Jackson incurred the ire of several teammates—most notably, All-Star catcher Thurman Munson—by making some tactless comments to reporters about his teammates' skills. When the season got underway, the slugger quickly found himself in Martin's doghouse due to inconsistent hitting and defense. The two even had to be separated in the dugout in Chicago after Jackson ignored Martin's signal to bunt, struck out, and cost the Yankees a game in the heat of the pennant race.

But Jackson delivered for the Yankees in September and October, when it counted most, including hitting a spectacular three straight home runs in game six of the World Series, to lead the Yankees to a victory over the Dodgers.

Unlike the previous season, Martin found he couldn't enjoy the accomplishment, feeling incredible—largely self-imposed—pressure to deliver a World Series victory the following year. This deeply concerned Mickey Mantle, because for all Billy's intensity on the field, Mickey knew him to be a good-hearted, fun-loving man. Billy was not that anymore, and his fondness for drink was quickly growing into something more insidious.

By July 1978, Martin had the drawn, hollow look of a man on the verge of a breakdown. The Yankees were 14 games behind division leading Boston, seemingly finished for the year. Reggie Jackson was struggling and George Steinbrenner was calling the dugout regularly from his owner's box, offering suggestions—in his inimitable "do this or it's your job" style. And although Martin's heavy drinking did not appear to directly affect any of his managerial decisions, it certainly was impacting his relationship with his players and coaches. There were more arguments than before, more nose-to-nose confrontations, and finally Martin himself brought things to a head when he suspended the mercurial Jackson, in effect telling Steinbrenner to choose between the superstar or himself.

Steinbrenner chose Jackson.

Martin didn't go down without getting in the last word, however. As he tearfully told reporters at Chicago's O'Hare Airport, "The two of them [Jackson and Steinbrenner] deserve each other. One's a born liar; the other's convicted."

Unhappily for Martin, the Yankees really cooked under new manager Bob Lemon, catching the Red Sox and then defeating them in a dramatic one-game playoff, then subsequently vanquishing the Dodgers in the World Series. Within the league, it was generally perceived that it had been Martin's manner that had been holding the team back, inspiring resentment in his players that affected their game. As soon as he was gone, the talent rose to the "insurmountable" challenge.

By mid-1979, however, history repeated itself: this time Lemon found himself on Steinbrenner's hot seat. The Yankees weren't performing again and, hoping to light a fire under his world-class talent, Steinbrenner relieved Lemon and reinstalled Martin . . . who was only too happy to come back and try to prove himself again. The owner's only caveat was that Martin not pick fights with the players or anyone else—a reasonable enough request.

Despite playing .573 ball under Martin, the Yankees couldn't catch Baltimore. Never mind, a somewhat calmer Martin told the club: we'll do it next year. Unfortunately, Martin wasn't around for the race. He provoked a fight with a marshmallow salesman and, fearing similar blowups ahead, Steinbrenner once again fired Martin. Almost immediately, the Oakland A's hired him, and in 1981 Martin saw revenge on the horizon: he led the team to the league playoffs, where they faced the Yankees. Yankees fans were torn: they didn't know whether to root for their team or cheer for Martin because they hated Steinbrenner. Fortunately, they didn't have long to wrestle with their torn loyalties: the Yankees swept the A's in three straight games. And when the A's faltered in 1982, many blamed the team's decline on Martin's overuse of his young pitching staff. When he refused to change his way of doing things, he found himself unemployed once again.

Meanwhile, in New York, George Steinbrenner was frustrated: Lemon's Yankees had lost to Lasorda's Dodgers in the 1981 World Series—blowing a 2-games-to-none lead—and didn't even make it to the Series in 1982. Looking to inspire and/or manhandle his players, Steinbrenner once again turned to Martin—something he was to do twice again in the 1980s, and which he might have done more than that if not for Billy's heated skirmish in a hotel room in 1985 with one of his pitchers, Ed Whitson, who broke Martin's arm, and a brawl with strangers in 1988 in the restroom of a Texas topless bar, a fight that ended with Martin hospitalized for several days.

Like a married couple who can't live together and can't live apart, the Martin/Steinbrenner relationship endured whether or not Billy was at the helm of the Yankees. Every time Martin was relieved of his duties, Steinbrenner told the press that he was doing it out of concern for Billy's health; whenever Steinbrenner made an offhanded comment to the effect that Billy was feeling better, reporters knew the fiery Italian's return as field general was imminent. The men even appeared in beer commercials together, which played off their volatile relationship.

Billy spent the 1989 season as a special consultant to Steinbrenner—a win-win situation for the boss. He got to pick Billy's brains without putting up with his on-field antics. When the Yankees struggled to a dismal below-.500 finish under Bucky Dent, however, rumors abounded that Billy would return. Billy did nothing to dissuade those rumors: more than anything, he had a burning ambition to lead the Yankees to one more world title.

Tragically, he would never get the chance.

In the closing weeks of 1989, Martin seemed to have the weight of the world on his shoulders. His mother had died after a long illness, he managed to fight with every relative he had at the funeral, and spurned the efforts of his devoted fourth wife, Jill, to comfort him; he had even confided to friends that he was thinking of leaving her so he could start his life over.

The sixty-one-year-old Martin spent December 25 drinking, much of the day, inside and outside his 148-acre farm in Fenton, New York. He was spending the day with William Reedy, a longtime friend and bar owner from Detroit; late in the morning, the two went out to pick up some groceries, and on the way back stopped at a restaurant just 6 miles from the farm. They ate, drank, and left around 5:40 P.M. in Martin's pickup truck, neither man wearing his seat belt.

As they headed along icy Potter Hill Road, just beside Billy's property, they came to a turn that was nearly a right angle. The truck went into the turn too quickly, left the road, skidded down a 300-foot embankment, and came to a crashing halt against a concrete culvert at the foot of Martin's driveway. Martin was thrown through the windshield and Reedy was flung across the seat. He was conscious; Martin was not.

Witnesses called the police, and the men were rushed to nearby Wilson Memorial Hospital in Johnson City, where Martin was pronounced dead; he had suffered a broken neck, compressed spinal column, and massive chest, abdominal, and head

Billy Martin, eyes puffy after his Texas bar brawl in 1988. (*AP/Wide World.*)

Superstar Mickey Mantle fights back tears at the funeral of dear friend Billy Martin. (*AP/Wide World.*)

injuries. Reedy remained in the hospital for several
days with a broken hip and ribs.

At the request of Martin's widow, no autopsy
was performed.

Initial reports had listed Martin as the passenger

and Reedy as the driver of the vehicle, but in the next few days it became clear that Martin was almost certainly driving. At Reedy's September 1990 trial for driving while intoxicated, he said that he lied and told police he was driving "to protect Billy": he didn't know that Martin had died, and didn't want people saying that his long history of alcohol abuse was to blame for the accident. Reedy later reiterated Martin's "guilt" to the press, claiming that not only was Martin behind the wheel, but as the pickup spun out of control, he told Reedy, "Hang on! Look out!"—sadly appropriate last words for Martin.

However, the state continued its prosecution of Reedy and there were those who suspected that that, too, was to protect Martin. Shortly after Martin's death, it was disclosed that his estate was worth less than $100,000—not much in the way of assets for Martin's widow and two grown children from previous marriages. If it had been determined that Martin were legally responsible for the crash, Reedy could have sued the estate. So despite his testimony, and despite the fact that his blood alcohol level was not over the 0.10 drunkenness limit, Reedy was found guilty of driving with a blood-alcohol content above legal limits. (Not that that saved Jill Martin from her creditors: just one day after her husband's death, the Internal Revenue Service filed three liens against the estate, in an effort to recover $86,137 in back taxes.)

There's no question that Billy Martin put people off with his abrasive ways and fierce loyalties and hatreds. Yet in death, he was eulogized for those things. More than 6,500 people, including former President Richard Nixon and former and current Yankee stars, jammed into New York's St. Patrick's Cathedral, while another 3,500 stood outside on a brutally cold winter day to honor Martin's memory. They knew what many would come to realize later: that without Billy, the Yankees would never be the same.

Lenny Dykstra:
"Tough as Nails"

One would think that after the highly publicized deaths of Martin and the others that people would learn. If not ordinary folks, at least baseball folks—those who had known Billy.

But it doesn't always work that way. One of the tragedies of drinking and driving is that so many victims feel that the rules don't apply to *them*.

When he played for the New York Mets from 1985 through 1989, Dykstra—whose nickname is "Nails"—was a star in the outfield, at the plate, and base-stealing. Many fans booed when he was traded to the Philadelphia Phillies, but you've got to wonder if the Mets knew something the rest of us didn't. Not long after the trade, Dykstra was summoned to court in Oxford, Mississippi, to testify in the matter of one Herbert Kelso, who had been charged with running serious-money poker games, laundering money, and committing perjury.

In one of those ironies that is enough to shake one's faith in truth, justice, and the American way, Kelso got off while Dykstra got into trouble for testifying that he had incurred $78,000 in poker losses while playing at Kelso's house from 1988 to 1990.

Did Dykstra break the law? No. And despite the sensitivity Major League Baseball had for players consorting with gamblers, he got off with one year's probation.

The second time he tempted fate, Dykstra wasn't as lucky—though things weren't as bad as they could have been.

In the small hours of May 6, 1991, Dykstra and catcher Darren Daulton left a bachelor party for teammate John Kruk. On the way home through suburban Radnor, Pennsylvania, Dykstra lost control of his spanking-new red Mercedes 500SL and plowed into not one tree but two. Both men were rushed to Bryn Mawr Hospital.

Though the passenger's side took the brunt of the hit, flattened from fender to trunk, and Daulton had his heart bruised and an eye socket shattered, Dykstra was the more seriously hurt of the two. He suffered a punctured lung, bruised heart, and broken collarbone and cheekbone, among other lesser fractures. Dykstra was subsequently charged with drunk driving.

Fortunately, the twenty-seven-year-old star was in excellent shape and just eight weeks later he was back in his uniform . . . not quite ready to play, but able to take batting practice.

As he told reporters after the gambling incident, Dykstra told reporters he'd learned his lesson about drinking and driving.

One hopes so: it takes a long time to grow a tree.

Doug Harvey:
"Played Hard and Played Hard"

Not everyone who drinks kills themselves in a car, or even right away. But eventually, the damn stuff does catch up with you.

Professional hockey has never received the kind of media attention other sports have enjoyed in America. Unlike football, where there are set plays, or baseball, which tends to be nice and orderly, hockey has an air of improvisation. Basketball has that too, but at least you can always *see* the ball during play. Hockey fans spend a lot of time squinting to find the puck.

So it is that a player like Doug Harvey, who entered the game in 1947 after playing semiprofessionally, and revolutionized the defensive man's position in hockey and was the cornerstone of the Montreal Canadiens five consecutive Stanley Cup Championships from 1956 through 1960, remains unknown to sports fans who are very familiar with names like Mickey Mantle or Bill Russell. In 19 NHL seasons, Harvey was named a first-team all-star ten times, despite scoring only 88 goals: he willingly sacrificed offensive opportunities to concentrate on preventing opponents from scoring. Today, players who make those kinds of sacrifices are relatively rare. Today, too many salaries are determined by personal, offensive stats.

Harvey also wasn't as big and imposing as other

players of the time—though, when necessary, he wasn't afraid to stand his ground and fight. Quite the contrary, in fact, and that occasional flash of stubbornness involved him in one of the sport's more ghastly brawls when, in 1956, he used his stick to spear New York Ranger center Red Sullivan, rupturing his spleen and nearly killing him.

Harvey was a rugged individualist who heeded an inner voice rather than followed the crowd. This sense of self-confidence and trailblazing also explains his participation in the founding of the NHL Player's Association over the strong objection of NHL owners. And that difficult, uphill battle may explain, in turn, why Harvey too often turned to alcohol for comfort.

While it was no secret to teammates or opponents that Harvey had a drinking problem, it didn't affect his play. Still, the NHL didn't approve, and when Harvey first became eligible for election to the NHL Hall of Fame in 1972, he was cold-shouldered—hockey's way of saying that despite all he'd done for the sport, it found his behavior socially inappropriate. (It *was,* but that wasn't the issue, any more than gambling is with Pete Rose or any other blackballees.)

Harvey didn't take the snub lying down: when informed that he'd basically been blackballed, he huffed, "I don't care what the rest of the world thinks. It's my life." He added that the NHL was way out of line for "telling me they won't put me in because I'm not averse to sampling the nectar of the gods now and then," and he vowed that he would not change his lifestyle: "When they drop this body into the ground," he said, "it won't rot for a long time. It's got its own embalming fluid."

Only after a strong public outcry did the NHL relent and induct the 20-year veteran a year later. Ironically, that year he went to work as a scout and assistant coach for the Houston Aeros of the rival World Hockey Association.

Unfortunately, the years of drinking had taken their toll on Harvey—one "decision" that couldn't be reversed. In fact, after leaving the game that he loved so much and having investments fail to live up to expectations, Harvey began to drink in increasing quantities and developed cirrhosis of the liver, succumbing to the condition in a Montreal hospital on December 26, 1989. He was fifty-six.

Willie Galimore
and John Farrington:
"Speed Kills"

Meanwhile, not every athlete killed in a car is drunk.

Where automobiles and professional athletes are concerned, the real surprise is that more have not perished. Michael Jordan's kamikaze-type driving was chronicled in the book *The Jordan Rules,* and Wilt Chamberlain has boasted publicly on many occasions that one of his proudest accomplishments was setting and holding for many years the record for driving cross-country from New York to Los Angeles in the shortest period of time. It's as if athletes want to prove that the rules of the road—indeed, the rules of life—don't apply to them.

There's also another factor at work. In sport, "speed" wins. Athletes don't seem able to grasp the fact that in life, just the opposite can happen—as demonstrated by the fate of Willie Galimore and John Farrington, members of the Chicago Bears 1963 world championship team. These two weren't drunk, they weren't high, they weren't anything but in a hurry—but the results were tragic all the same.

The season before, Galimore had gained 321 yards on 85 carries; he shared the Chicago team record of 4 touchdowns in one game. Farrington held the team record for the longest pass reception, 98 yards, and had caught 21 passes for 335 yards and 2 touchdowns in 1963.

Returning to training camp following an afternoon round of golf in Wisconsin, Galimore and Farrington were in a rush. The Bears had an 11 P.M. curfew and the pair was eager to avoid being fined and/or punished by having to do extra drills the next day in the summer heat. Chicago Bears owner, coach, and legendary disciplinarian, George Halas, was not a forgiving man.

It was 10:25 and they were not far from Rensselaer, Indiana. They could still make it if they hurried. Traveling 55 mph as it approached a curve on Bunkum Road, Galimore's Volkswagen spun out of control and went off the road. The rear wheel buckled and collapsed, Galimore and Farrington were thrown from the top of the car, and then the vehicle rolled over on the pair, crushing them.

A farming couple heard the crash and hurried over. They called the police and an ambulance; the men were pronounced dead at the Jasper County Hospital, the cause of death listed as a combination of multiple skull fractures and internal injuries. State Trooper Ivan Finch said from the scene, "If they'd had seat belts, they might have survived." Tragically, the curve was not that severe: Deputy Yayne Calloway said that if they'd been more familiar with it, they would have had no trouble holding it at an even higher speed. They could have reached training camp with time to spare.

(Alas, the Bears weren't the only team touched by tragedy in 1964. Just a few months earlier, Terry Dillon, a halfback for the Minnesota Vikings, drowned in Montana, just months before that, Don Fleming, a Cleveland Browns back, was electrocuted in Florida. In all, not one of pro football's finest years.)

Joe Delaney:
"Kansas City Superchief"

The death of Joe Delaney is unique among the tragic ends in sports.

Athletes have many reasons for giving their all on the field: pride, ambition, even greed. What Delaney did off the football field, however, resonates more than anything anyone has ever done during the course of a game.

A first-round draft choice from Northwestern State, the halfback gained 1,121 yards in his first season with the Kansas City Chiefs, won AFC rookie of the year honors, and seemed destined for a great career in professional football. The twenty-four-year-old had a wife, Carolyn, and three children.

On June 29, 1983, he and his family were visiting a park in Monroe, Louisiana, not far from their home. Renovations were underway at the public facility, and there was a big construction ditch that had filled with rainwater.

Delaney noticed three kids swimming in the pit and shouted for them to get out. They didn't listen—or couldn't. Moments later, they began screaming for help. Apparently, they'd been wading in a shallow end, the soft ground had given way, and they found themselves in water over their head.

Delaney couldn't swim, but that didn't matter to

him. He bolted toward the ditch and jumped in, reaching down to try and grab an arm, trousers, hair, anything that would allow him to pull the boys up. Unfortunately, the murky water was obviously deeper than Delaney had imagined and he, too, went down.

One of the boys managed to reach the edge of the pit and pull himself up. The other three were lost in the waters, and it remained for a team of divers to arrive and pull up the others. One of the boys was still alive when they found him, but died shortly after. Delaney was dead.

Coach John Mackovic was understandably distraught, "I think Joe Delaney was a hero before today," he said. "I think people ... could always point to him and say, 'You can be like him.'" Vice President George Bush presented the Presidential Citizen's Medal to Delaney's widow.

When you look at the people who squandered their lives on drugs and drink, you've got to admire a man like Delaney even more, who died for others. Of course that doesn't bring him back. But by appreciating who and what he was, it insures that he didn't die in vain.

Darryl Stingley:
"Jack Hammered"

When a senseless tragedy touches someone, that's bad enough. But it's even more painful when you sit there asking yourself, *Could this possibly have been prevented?*

What if Ron Turcotte had been riding a little faster or a little slower and hadn't gotten caught in a jam? What if Paret had tagged Griffith just a few seconds earlier in round six?

In sports, critics are constantly asking questions like these, but there's another twist: the idea that a lot of the bad things that happen are not only preventable, they're intentional. Did the fighter really need to deliver that additional punch to finish off a beaten foe, did the angry pitcher throw the fastball right at a batter's head, did the irate hockey player use his stick to slash an aggressive opponent?

People *will* lose their cool in the heat of competition, but the fine line that separates hard-hitting play and a deliberate desire to maim an opponent has never been called into question more painfully than in the case of the encounter that occurred on a football field on August 12, 1978, between twenty-six-year-old Darryl Stingley of the New England Patriots and twenty-nine-year-old Jack "Assassin" Tatum of the Oakland Raiders.

Just reaching his prime as a football player,

247

Stingley was a talented, swift football player who, at six feet, 195 pounds, was recognized as one of the most skilled wide receivers in the game. Indeed, throughout his athletic career—first as a high school football player in Chicago and later at Purdue—Stingley was always a standout.

Stingley's defensive counterpart, Jack Tatum, at five-foot-eleven, 205 pounds, was widely recognized as one of the fiercest, hardest-hitting defensive players in the game. Even the famed Woody Hayes, his coach at Ohio State, said, "Without a doubt, Jack Tatum was the hardest hitter I ever coached or saw play the game of football." More than one NFL team had complained to the league office about the Raiders' secondary and, in particular, Tatum's aggressive style of play. In the game before his fateful encounter with Stingley, a pair of Chicago Bears had to be carted off the field after being decked by Tatum.

The Patriots were driving for a touchdown in a meaningless exhibition game—the kind of game in which teams iron out the kinks without pressing too hard on each other (except for the superstars who have been targeted by the opposition for elimination before the regular season). Stingley's assignment on the play called by quarterback Steve Grogan, 94 slant, was to run an 8- to 10-yard slant pattern, which would leave him open for a second or two if he could get between one of the Raider linebackers and the cornerback.

The instant the ball was hiked, Stingley broke past Raider cornerback Lester Hayes and turned his head back to look for the football. It came in his direction later than he expected and was too high for him to catch. He leaped for it anyway.

"I was on my way back to earth," he later said, "when, in a flash, I saw number 32 of the Raiders, Jack Tatum, all 205 pounds of him barreling toward me. I looked Tatum dead in the eye, and I saw his look. It was vicious."

Tatum puts a somewhat different spin on what he describes as "a rather dangerous pattern." He says that when he saw what was coming down, "I could not possibly have intercepted, so . . . I automatically reacted to the situation by going for an intimidating hit. It was a fairly good hit, but nothing exceptional."

Tatum *was* coming fast, his forearm cocked, and Stingley ducked his head in an effort to get under the arm before collision. He didn't make it. Both men went down, and Tatum recalls that he didn't think anything unusual had happened: "I got up and started back toward our huddle. But Darryl didn't get up and walk away." And with good reason: his neck was broken between the fourth and fifth vertebrae.

At the hospital later, the only way to keep Stingley alive was to immobilize his head and neck using an 80-pound weight, a "halo" screwed into his head, and tubes stuck down his throat and up his nose. After several terrifying near-death episodes—including one where a frantic Raider coach John Madden had to summon a nurse when a machine suctioning phlegm from Stingley's mouth malfunctioned—the former athlete had to come to terms with the fact that he would never walk again.

There was no false bravado, no *I'll-beat-this* determination. Stingley was devastated. Like so many athletes, he hadn't developed much sense of self-esteem outside the game; he was angry and ashamed of what he'd become. "I didn't like myself," he says. "I could take losing football. But what about me? What about the physical me?" He quickly lost 40 pounds; where his arms and legs once rippled with sinew, now the muscles were withered and useless. He had lost control of his bladder and bowels. At first, the only way he could

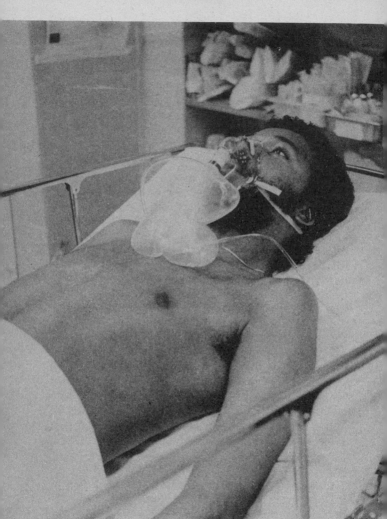

Paralyzed pro footballer Darryl Stingley in his hospital bed. (*AP/Wide World.*)

communicate was by blinking when someone pointed to the correct letter, on a large alphabet card, of the word he was trying to spell.

Sadly, one of the things that kept Stingley going were the strong feelings he harbored toward Tatum—who, incredibly, never came to visit during Stingley's long hospitalization.

"I had not caught the ball," Stingley says, incredulous still. "He could have stopped short of hitting me. And he certainly didn't have to nail me across the head with a blow that ... left me unable to move."

Which is not to say that Tatum came off the field unscathed: he says he was "shattered" by what had happened, that it "was constantly on my mind and tearing at my insides," that he spent "hours talking with the doctors about Darryl's condition." To this day, he still feels "hollow" inside when he thinks back to that day.

It took many long months of reflection coupled with intensive physical and mental therapy before Stingley was able to begin to come to terms with his anger. With the help of the staff at the Rehabilitation Institute of Chicago (which was located near his parents' home), Stingley regained very limited use of his right hand. Perhaps more important, he learned how to channel the sense of self-worth he had as an athlete into a positive feeling about himself as a human being.

Stingley was discharged in April 1979. Except for the ability to push buttons on his wheelchair with that right hand, he was paralyzed.

A year after his injury, Stingley was flown to Foxboro, Massachusetts, to attend a nationally televised *Monday Night Football* game, pitting his former teammates against the Oakland Raiders. The return couldn't have been sweeter: the Patriots won in the closing minutes and Stingley was awarded the game ball.

There was more pain ahead for Stingley: his wife, Tina's, decision to leave him, along with their two young boys (whom he sees frequently, however), and his continuing bitterness toward Tatum, who continued to play yet "has not contacted me, not even a postcard." He added, "Sitting in my wheelchair, I'm taller than he is." (Tatum claims he tried to phone Stingley but never got through.)

Yet, Stingley has managed to make his life a happy and productive one. He took a position with the Patriots as a Director of Player Personnel, which allowed him to remain close to the game he could no longer play. Unlike many who are left paralyzed by accidents, Stingley also came away from the incident on a somewhat stable financial footing. NFL insurance paid the vast majority of his medical bills and he was awarded a $2,000 per month lifetime disability pension from the league, along with Social Security and Workers' Compensation benefits.

Football players know the risks of their profession. Stingley knew. So did others, like Green Bay cornerback Tim Lewis, who sustained a career-ending neck injury after tackling then Chicago Bears wide receiver Willie Gault during a game in 1986. Or like safety Jeff Fuller of the San Francisco 49ers, whose career was cut short when he collided helmet-to-helmet with New England Patriot running back John Stephens on October 22, 1989. But that doesn't mean the crippling injuries are unavoidable.

As a way to prevent others from being injured by unnecessary roughness, Stingley recently proposed that players judged guilty of excessive violence be fined and forced to miss games. "Then you would see coaches clamp down, and you would see the players stop it, too, if it was going to cost them two or three paychecks."

For his part, Tatum—who went to the Houston

Oilers and hung up his helmet in 1980—doesn't blame the players but the management for the violence in football. He says that most rule changes are instituted *not* to protect players, but to add to the excitement of the game, which "means higher risks for the players." As an example, he cites the kickoff return. When the ball was kicked from the 40 yard line, it usually went out of the end zone and play automatically began on the 20 yard line. So, he says, "Some whiz who sits behind a desk in an office" decided to move the kicking team to the 35 yard line to make a kickoff return more likely than not. Tatum adds, "The very first injury I ever sustained came on the kickoff team."

Pro football players talk about the courage wide receivers show when they run pass patterns over the middle. (Tatum just snorts and calls them "dangerous.") In his playing days, Darryl Stingley never hesitated to enter the breach. But that is dwarfed by the bravery he has shown in confronting his physical limitations. Hired to work as executive director of player personnel for the Patriots, Stingley took correspondence courses and in May 1992 earned a diploma from Purdue University.

"It means a great deal to me," he said. "I look at my graduation as a message to others to not give up."

More than any athlete today, Darryl Stingley is truly a role model.

Mike Utley:
"Turf War"

Unlike the sad saga of Darryl Stingley, there are two stories in what happened to the Detroit Lions' Mike Utley. One is the unfortunate but unavoidable fact that football is a game where people can get hurt. The other is more insidious: the fact that artificial turf, which has been in use since 1965, isn't a fit surface for players.

Just about all that Mike Utley dreamed about while growing up was playing pro football. And when you hit six feet six inches and weigh 290 pounds, and are smart, strong, and agile, you have a chance to make the dream a reality.

As a "top-flight" player while a collegian at Washington State, and then as a third-year guard for the Detroit Lions during the 1991 season, Mike Utley stood on the verge of a long and rewarding pro career. Moreover, by late November, the Lions had regrouped from a 45-0 season-opening drubbing at the hands of the Washington Redskins and were in the midst of a five-game winning streak, as well as contending for their first division title in nearly thirty-five years.

Everything seemed to be clicking for Utley and the Lions as they took on the Los Angeles Rams on November 18, 1991. Late in the game at the Pontiac Silverdome, with the Lions leading and driving toward another score, Utley set up to pass block

Rams tackle David Rocker as Lions quarterback
Eric Kramer searched for an open receiver. Just as
Kramer found Robert Clark in the end zone for
an 11-yard touchdown completion, Utley lost his
balance. At the same time, Rocker jumped in the
air in an attempt to block the pass and fell on
Utley. The lineman's head was driven into the artificial turf, which covers the hard cement floor of
the Silverdome complex. There was no give in the
surface—not a fraction of an inch. The only thing
that gave was Utley's neck.

The perfectly legal but unfortunate collision
caused Utley to suffer a severe spinal column injury. Ironically, Rocker had just signed with the
Rams the week before.

The game was stopped as the young player lay
there, unmoving; the players watched in reflective
silence as Utley was taken off the field. Later, after
hearing from team orthopedist David J. Collon that
"we don't expect him to regain any mobility,"
Lions coach Wayne Fontes said, "It was just one of
those freak things that happen on the football
field." Players and coaches on both teams went out
of their way to make sure Rocker knew that he
wasn't to blame. As Ram defensive line coach John
Teerlink put it, "It wasn't a cheap shot. It was just
a play. Boy, you don't want a guy carrying that
around with him for the rest of his life."

The Lions won the remainder of their regular
season games that year and blew out the Dallas
Cowboys in the first round of the NFL playoffs
before losing to eventual Super Bowl winner, the
Washington Redskins, in the NFC Championship
Game. As a gesture toward a stricken comrade, the
Redskins made it a point to dedicate their efforts
in Super Bowl XXVI to Utley, who watched the
game from a hospital bed in the Craig Rehabilitation Institute in Denver.

Although diagnosed as a paraplegic for life by

Detroit Lions coach Wayne Fontes, right, watches as offensive lineman Mike Utley is examined by trainers. (*AP/Wide World.*)

his doctors, he has maintained high spirits and is determined that his rehabilitation efforts will prove the medical experts wrong.

"I'm not going to let this beat me," he said at the time and, true to his word, in January 1992, he took a proverbial step in the right direction when he opened a pop-top can for the first time since the accident. By February, he was moving both arms again and by March he was able to swim, drive a specially outfitted car, and was undergoing rehabilitation as an outpatient.

"I've got a long way to go yet," he says today, "but give me a little time and I'll be able to do a helluva lot more. The goal I have is to talk again. Everything I do is one more step toward that."

Despite what happened, artificial turf isn't going anywhere—even though it's never been popular among players. As Ram guard Tom Newberry said, commenting about Utley's accident: "Grass tends to tear away on your helmet, and you'll slip more and you don't seem to get such severe injuries." At the end of the 1991 season, there was some indication that as part of the players' efforts to negotiate a new collective bargaining agreement with NFL owners, they would demand that all games be played on natural versus artificial surfaces. But the owners remain intransigent: though injuries are unfortunate, the stuff is easier to maintain. They may not remain so adamant for long, however: on March 13, 1992, Utley's attorney, Kenneth Silver, wrote to Pontiac's Stadium Building Authority, blaming his client's disability on the "dangerous and defective condition" that exists at the Silverdome—that is, the artificial turf. The letter smelled very much like a prelude to a whopping big lawsuit.

But for now, money still talks . . . and Utley doesn't walk.

Ray Chapman:
"Struck Out"

Football's a tough sport, and enthusiasts tend to look down their noses a little at baseball. Chubby players like Ruth or even smokers like DiMaggio and Mantle can still be superstars, games are called if the weather's on the inclement side, and players rarely suffer the kinds of injuries endured by Stingley or Utley.

But "rarely" isn't "never," and critics tend to forget that batters get up in front of balls coming at them faster than a speeding locomotive. And pitchers face line drives traveling just as fast. And when the twain meet, disaster may follow.

It was August 16, 1920—just a few weeks before baseball would nearly be undone by revelations about gambling in the sport. The Cleveland Indians were in a pennant race with the New York Yankees and the Chicago White Sox, the team that had thrown the previous year's World Series (see entry). Jovial Indians shortstop Ray Chapman— "Chappie" to his teammates—was a nine-year veteran of the game, and one of its most likable players. Chappie had gotten married earlier in the year and was planning to retire and go into business at the end of the season.

Over in New York, the Yankees had recently acquired slugger Babe Ruth and pitcher Carl Mays. In contrast to Chappie, Mays was an abrasive, often

abusive player. He openly criticized fellow teammates when they weren't performing at the peak
of their form, and he had no patience for fans, especially noisy ones; once, during a road game, he hit
one with a ball for making noise. The only reason
no charges were pressed was because Mays had
hurried out of town ahead of the team.

Despite his failings as a human being, the six-
year veteran was an amazing pitcher with a remarkable degree of control. He had a tendency to
throw the ball inside, and it's difficult to say
whether this was just his style or whether it was
a vendetta: he resented batters who stood too close
to the plate, looking to hit the pitches that ordinarily might be a little outside. As Mays once told
a teammate, "I'm not going to change what I do to
make it more comfortable for the batter. One way
or another, my job is to get them out."

In other words, hug the plate and you take your
chances.

Despite having said that, Mays was sobered early
in the 1920 season when teammate Chick Fewster
was knocked out after being struck with a fastball
thrown by Brooklyn Dodger Jeff Pfeffer. Fewster
was sidelined for a month, unable to speak. After
that, Mays was overly cautious for nearly two
months—and his won/loss record suffered.

As he closed in on his one-hundredth win, however, he regained his poise and sizzle, especially as
the pennant race tightened up. By August, Mays
was at the top of his form and on the sixteenth,
the Yankees were just a half-game behind Cleveland and playing before an enthusiastic home
crowd.

The score that day was three-zip, Cleveland. It
was the top of the fifth and Chappie was at the
plate. There was no one on base, no outs, and Mays
threw a one-one fastball. The pitch was high and
inside, but for some reason Chappie didn't move:

he just stared at it. Maybe he expected the ball to sink or curve; maybe he just didn't react soon enough. In any case, the ball hit him in his left temple with such force that it rolled all the way *back* to the mound, where Mays—unsure whether or not the ball had hit the bat—took the precaution of flipping it to first.

Chappie, meanwhile, lurched several steps toward first before his legs simply folded under him. The umpire was the first to see blood gushing from Chappie's ear, and began screaming toward the grandstand for a doctor to come forward.

Meanwhile, on-deck batter Tris Speaker had run over and was joined by most of the Yankees and Indians—though not Mays, who remained on the mound, his face very pale.

Surrounded by players, Chappie managed to get to his feet and apparently tried to tell them he was all right. But while his lips were moving, nothing was coming out. Under his own steam, he started walking slowly off the field—then fell again, still conscious but unable to get up. His teammates carried him to the clubhouse.

"Tell Mays not to worry," he finally managed to say, and that was communicated to the pitcher. If he was relieved, Mays didn't show it: there was fire in his arm as he retired the Indians one after another for three innings. Though the Yankees managed to rally, it wasn't enough and they lost 4-3.

In the clubhouse, Chappie managed to say a few words—he asked for trainer Percy Smallwood to give him back his wedding ring, which had been removed—then passed out. An ambulance was called and he was taken to the hospital, where he underwent surgery; as soon as doctors opened him up, they knew he was in serious trouble. Not only was there brain damage where the ball had struck him, but the right side of the brain had been crushed where it was pushed into his skull.

Chappie died at 4:40 A.M., before his pregnant wife, Kathleen, could arrive by train from Cleveland. He was the first baseball player to die because of injuries received during a game.

The New York district attorney headed up an inquiry, and Mays was found to be blameless of intentional malice. As if to prove that he still "had it" after the tragedy, the pitcher was sharper than ever. He went 26-11 for the season, though many cynics claimed that he had an advantage because batters tended to get a little wobbly in the knees whenever they had to face him. Sadly, despite having posted better career statistics than a slew of Hall of Fame pitchers—including more than 200 victories—Mays was never voted into that august body.

The tragedy didn't end there, however. Kathleen gave birth to a daughter six months after her husband's death; the little girl contracted measles and died a year later. Her mother never recovered from the loss of her family and took her own life in 1928.

As for the Indians, they slumped for a while after Chappie's death, then pulled it together to win the pennant and the World Series for "the gipper."

Mays lived for another half-century, bitter about how the press and fans had treated him, but unbowed.

In a strange way, though, Chappie was lucky: his ordeal ended in just a few hours. The next pitch-that-killed took far longer to do the deed.

Tony Conigliaro:
"C as in Comeback"

Of all the stories of athletes who have been hit with debilitating injuries, there may not be a sadder or more moving story than the long, difficult road traveled by Tony Conigliaro. He fought so long and so hard and with so much class that he deserved better than he got.

A local boy with a matinee idol's good looks and an athlete's sculpted build, Tony C, as Boston Red Sox fans adoringly called him, turned the very first pitch thrown to him in his first major league game at Fenway Park into a home run. The year was 1964. The product of a working-class family, the twenty-year-old Conigliaro became, in 1965, the youngest ballplayer ever to win the American League home run crown. By 1967, largely behind the bats of Conigliaro and Carl Yastremzski, the Red Sox had gone from cellar dwellers to contenders for the league pennant.

Ominously, in all three of those seasons he'd endured injuries caused by pitched balls. In 1964 he suffered a fractured arm, had his wrist cracked the following season, and picked up a hairline arm fracture during spring training in 1967.

But all of that was forgotten on August 18, 1967. In the heat of the race, the Red Sox were at home in Fenway Park against the California Angels—a team that had seen so many of its own players succumb to misfortune, such as Donnie Moore and Lyman Bostock. Conigliaro already had hit 20 home runs and had 65 RBIs that season as he faced hard-throwing veteran righthander Jack Hamilton.

Hitting in the fourth inning of a scoreless tie, Conigliaro momentarily lost track of a high inside fastball. He failed to get out of the way, and the baseball smashed into his left temple; he went down, unconscious. Second baseman Mike Andrews remembers, "I'll never forget that beaning; when we got out to home plate, his left eye was already closed." Tony C was carried by stretcher to the clubhouse, where he regained consciousness and was taken by ambulance to the hospital.

The pitch had shattered Conigliaro's cheekbone, caused a severe nasal hemorrhage, dislocated his jaw, and damaged his left retina. Although doctors were initially optimistic and estimated that Conigliaro would be out of the lineup for just three weeks, his injuries, especially to his eye, were more severe than they'd initially thought; the Red Sox were forced to play in the World Series without him, losing a heartbreaking seven-game series to the St. Louis Cardinals. To this day, Boston fans are convinced their team would have won its first title in nearly fifty years with Conigliaro's bat in the lineup.

But Conigliaro's problems didn't end with the lost Series. During the off-season, he suffered vision and balance problems that forced him to sit out the 1968 season. Conigliaro was determined to come back though and in 1969 he did, socking 20 home runs; the next season he smacked out 36 home runs and drove in 116 runs. Then, when it appeared as if all were right with the world, things soured.

Early 1971, something was different and both Conigliaro and the Red Sox knew it. There were physical problems: the vision in his left eye was clouded, and he was suffering from increasingly

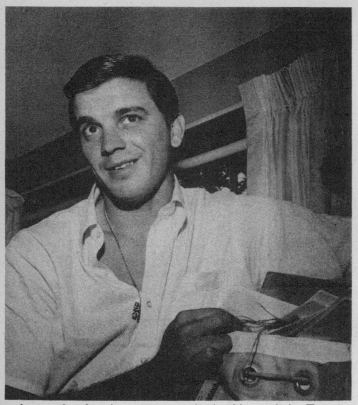

A month after he was smacked with a pitch, Tony Conigliaro was in spirits almost as high as the fan mail in his Swampscott, Massachusetts, home. He had hopes of rejoining the team "shortly." (*AP/Wide World.*)

frequent headaches. Rather than let his hometown fans down, Conigliaro agreed that he should be traded—ironically, to the California Angels. There, his vision worsened, limiting his productivity to four home runs. He retired gracefully in midseason, July 1971.

Life away from baseball held little allure for Conigliaro. Working on modifying his stance to compensate for his impaired vision, Conigliaro staged another comeback with the Red Sox in 1975, but was forced to quit again after managing just seven hits in 57 at bats for an anemic .123 batting average.

Everyone who knew Tony C was saddened when he hung it up for good. Mike Andrews, a second baseman on the 1967 Red Sox, expressed the sentiments of fellow ballplayers when he said, "If it hadn't been for the beaning, without a doubt Tony was destined for the Hall of Fame and would have been among the top five all-time home run hitters."

Yet, Tony wasn't about to wallow in self-pity. In 1976 he became a TV sportscaster and was quite successful at it until 1981, when a succession of management changes suddenly left him without a job. Tony applied for unemployment, but California cut him off when they learned he had a part interest in a health food store (records show that it was losing a bundle at the time); the state even tried to get back the $270 in benefits they'd paid out.

In serious financial straits, Tony went back to the batting cage to try for yet another comeback: miraculously, by late 1981 he was once again hitting 90 mph fastballs with ease. With his thirty-seventh birthday fast approaching, Tony Conigliaro was bent on having one last chance to claim the glory that he believed should have been his all along.

"I know I can do it," he told his brother, Billy, who was also a professional ballplayer and remains one of Tony's biggest boosters. However, this comeback was not to be.

In order to pay his bills, Tony flew from Los Angeles to Boston to audition for a job doing broadcasts for the Red Sox. It seemed like a natural progression, and he felt good about the way the interview had gone. But while Billy was driving him to Logan Airport on the morning of January 9, 1982, he recalls, "We were talking. Tony said something and I glanced over at him and he seemed to be making a face." In fact, Tony was having a massive heart attack.

Maybe it was genetic; maybe it was triggered by the fastball that jarred his brain; maybe it was induced by the pressure he put on himself to come back. None of that seemed to matter just then, as Tony winced and reached for his chest. Billy spun the car around and, with Massachusetts General Hospital just in sight, he remembers that Tony just "slumped over and his eyes rolled up." By the time they reached the hospital and the medics got to him, Tony C had no pulse.

Though the emergency room team was able to restart his heart, the fact that he'd been without oxygen for more than five minutes had caused brain damage. Tony slipped into a coma and had to be fed through a tube that carried fluids directly to his stomach and given air through a respirator. His feet had become twisted due to brain damage, and even if he came out of the coma he would need corrective surgery before he could walk again.

Then, after five months, beyond the expectations of his doctors, the fighter, the comeback kid, opened his eyes. Though initially unable to speak, he could understand what was being said to him; then, one day, when his mother made her daily visit, he looked up at her and said, "Hi, Mom." Tearfully, she phoned his father and, weakly, Tony said, "Hi, Dad," into the phone.

Though a battle was won, the war continued. The weakened athlete caught pneumonia and had to have part of his left lung removed. He came through it. He continued to speak, managing slurred but understandable sentences. And when

Months later, Conigliaro was still on the sidelines. (*AP/Wide World.*)

his medical insurance was about to run out, there were benefits to help cover his weekly expenses of $3,000 to $4,000—Frank Sinatra, Dionne Warwick, and a slew of ballplayers at Symphony Hall, a Red Sox game where the net proceeds (more than

$100,000) went to Tony, a celebrity golf tournament in California, and more.

"It's great the way everybody has tried to help," a visibly moved Billy Conigliaro said at the time. But while Tony C had defied overwhelming odds in making his many comebacks, the ultimate victory was not to be his. Subsequent seizures and heart attacks left him in a vegetative state and, in 1990, death finally claimed him.

There were numerous tributes to the heroic ballplayer, but nothing can be as meaningful as what Tony C himself accomplished in his short life, and the stirring legacy of courage he left behind.

Dave Winfield:
"Fowl Ball"

In light of what happened to Ray Chapman and Tony Conigliaro, it might, at first glance, seem disrespectful to mention the following. Yet, for a few hours, the beanball incident that occurred during an August 4, 1983, game between the New York Yankees and the Toronto Blue Jays, threatened to become far, far more incendiary than it should have been.

Superstar Dave Winfield has had his share of attention, from the day he signed his ten-year, $20 million contract with the Yankees in 1980 and, before that, with the San Diego Padres.

There were charges of gambling—which, incredibly, were never investigated à la the allegations of Pete Rose and *his* gambling. (Maybe because the mob was reportedly involved?)

There were rumors that moneys given to the David M. Winfield Foundation for needy kids was being misused.

Ruth Roper, the mother of actress Robin Givens—the ex-wife of Mike Tyson—claimed that the athlete had given her a sexually transmitted disease; the matter was settled out of court.

Another woman, Sandra Renfro, sued Winfield for palimony and was awarded $1.6 million in court.

However, perhaps *nothing* Dauntless Dave has done attracted as much universal condemnation as when the Yankees took the field in the fifth inning, and the center fielder threw a few warm-up balls to left fielder Don Baylor. Now, one thing Toronto's Exhibition Stadium has plenty of are sea gulls: sometimes, there are more of the birds in the stands than fans.

One bird in particular was being a bit bold that afternoon, touching down here and there before finally alighting—apparently settling in for a long stay—in right center field. Winfield skidded a ball in its direction to frighten it off; taking an unexpected hop on the artificial turf, the ball hit the gull in the head, killing it instantly.

Jogging over, Winfield saw that the bird was dead and thoughtfully stood by it until it could be scooped up and carried away. He shrugged at booing fans, but said to the ball boy who came to collect it, "I feel awful."

. Toronto lost the game 3-1—thanks to a pair of Winfield RBIs—and as the players exited the field, the Blue Jay fans began throwing trash and baseballs at the Yankees. The logic that it's okay to endanger a human life on purpose, but not to hit a bird by accident, is elusive at best.

After doing a radio interview, Winfield went to the clubhouse where a bigger surprise awaited him: Toronto police had come to arrest him for cruelty to animals.

"Dillinger" Dave went to the stationhouse, where third baseman Graig Nettles comments to a reporter probably didn't help his case: "I think Winfield should have been given a medal for killing the damn thing."

It took several hours for investigators to decide that the beaning *had* been an accident, that no malice had been intended, and the charges were dropped. Winfield wasn't *quite* finished with the law, however: he needed a police escort the following day to enable him to get back into the stadium.

Emile Griffith
and Benny "Kid" Paret:
"Blood Feud"

Death comes in other forms as well, especially when athletes participate in a sport where the very object is to destroy an opponent physically.

Unlike baseball or football players who get knocked down and *may* suffer injuries, boxers are paid to beat a person's brains out. And when they do that too well or outside the ring, they're castigated. (If these guys were bright enough to realize the difference, would they be doing this for a living?)

They're also paid to take punishment, and it can be argued that that kind of brass gives them an unwarranted sense of invincibility. The key word there is *unwarranted.*

Not the first death, but certainly the most notorious in the history of boxing, was that of heavyweight Ernie Schaaf—notorious because he had no business being in the ring. Schaaf died at the hands of Primo Carnera in February 1933. The thirteenth-round left jab wasn't a hard one, but the fighter went down and died four days later of a hemorrhage; many writers of the time felt that Schaaf shouldn't have been fighting *anyone,* let alone the six-foot five-and-a-half-inch Carnera. In June 1932, Schaaf had been severely battered in a furious bout with Tony Galento, and in August he had to be carried from the ring after a ten rounder with powerful Max Baer. Carnera's blow was simply the last straw. Schaaf was twenty-four when he died.

Welterweight Jimmy Doyle's death in 1947 was also predictable—doubly so. In March 1946, fifteen months before he fought Sugar Ray Robinson, the twenty-two-year-old suffered a serious concussion in a fight with middleweight Artie Levine. After that, his manner was considerably subdued, his reflexes slowed. Nonetheless, he climbed into the ring with the up-and-coming Robinson—who, the night before, had had a vivid dream in which he killed his opponent in the ring. That was not an unusual dream to have, given the circumstances, but Robinson's handlers report that he was unusually disturbed by it.

Robinson clocked Doyle with a modest left hook in the eighth round; the fighter went down and died 17 hours later. Robinson was so distraught he nearly gave up fighting.

For fight fans raised on TV, however, there has never been—and, hopefully, never will be again—a bout to rival the awful March 24, 1962, encounter between Benny "Kid" Paret and Emile Griffith.

The two welterweights hated each other, and the title bopped back and forth between them for two years. Benny held it from 1960 to 1961, Griffith held it in 1961, then it was Benny's again in 1961 to 1962—thanks to a questionable decision—and then they met once more. At the weigh-in, the Cuban Paret called his foe a *marecon* ("faggot"), and Griffith promised to make him eat his words.

Their rematch, in New York, was aired on ABC's *Gillette Fight of the Week,* and it was a tough one from the opening bell. The bout went Griffith's way for the first five rounds, though Paret managed to get in some serious licks of his own. In round six, he bided his time and caught Griffith with a right, knocking him to the canvas where he would have stayed were it not for the bell. Griffith came back fighting in the seventh and took command, though Paret held on until the twelfth, when Griffith backed him against the ropes and hammered him with blow after blow—nearly 30 in all. To referee Ruby Goldstein, it *appeared* that Paret was still standing; the truth was, he was dead on his feet but couldn't fall because of the way he was propped up on the ropes. Griffith wasn't even aware that Paret was limp: all he saw was the smug fighter who'd insulted him at the weigh-in, and he kept hammering away.

When Goldstein finally stopped the fight, Paret slumped to the floor. He was taken to Roosevelt Hospital where he underwent surgery to relieve the pressure on his brain; after clinging to life for just over a week, the comatose fighter died of pneumonia on April 3.

The repercussions were to be expected. Goldstein insisted he'd done nothing wrong, pointing out (as observers could see) that Paret "wasn't down; his feet were firmly on the ground. The first time I saw him sit on the middle strand of the ropes, I stepped in and stopped it." Though the New York State Athletic Commission found him blameless for any wrongdoing, and said that he'd "acted in good judgment," Goldstein decided never to ref again.

The match, along with the ring death of Davey Moore in a lightweight title match the same year in Los Angeles, nearly killed boxing as well. Legislators in various states moved to ban the sport, and Massachusetts came within nine votes of doing so. Sponsors withdrew from broadcasts, and the networks cut back dramatically on their coverage. If it weren't for the first Clay/Liston fight in February 1964, and the subsequent publicity Clay received,

Referee Ruby Goldstein finally steps in as Paret goes down, after having taken one of the most savage punishments in ring history. (*AP/Wide World.*)

Paret is viewed in his casket by his mother Maximo Crespo (right) and widow Lucy. Even the morticians couldn't fix his face after the battering it took. (*AP/Wide World.*)

the sport might have found itself down for the count.

As for Griffith, he expressed heartfelt sorrow over the death of his rival. "After the fight, I knew I won my title back, but I couldn't feel good about it," he said. "I never had a headache in my life, but that night my head pounded and it lasted for two days." He adds, though, "In a case like Paret, who used to act like he was hurt, it was hard to tell. I thought maybe he was faking, but still all I knew was that, once I had him, it was my business to keep punching because that's what fighting is all about."

Griffith got back in the ring ("What else could I do?" he asked at the time), lost the title to Luis Rodriguez in 1963, then won it back that year and held on to it until he joined the middleweight ranks in 1966. Griffith held that title from 1966 to 1967, and again from 1967 to 1968 (losing to Nino Benvenuti in between and then in 1968). Throughout that period, Griffith never again fought with the fire that had earned him his tragic victory over Paret. After retiring from the ring, he worked training fighters, which he still enjoys doing and in 1990, was enshrined in the International Boxing Hall of Fame—not entirely vindicated, perhaps, but reportedly "at peace with himself."

Ironically, while working part-time as a bouncer at a midtown Manhattan restaurant during the summer of 1992, Griffith reportedly was attacked and severely beaten by a band of youths on a "wilding" spree. The proud, exchamp disputed this version of events to authorities from his bed in the intensive care unit of Queens Hospital Center, claiming the kidney failure which forced his hospitalization resulted from his taking a bad fall at home.

Ray "Boom Boom" Mancini: "Dead Duk"

Ray Mancini was never a boxer of exceptional skills, but the straight-ahead fighter had heart: his father, Lenny, had been a fighter, but had to abandon his quest for a title when he went to fight in World War II. When Ray entered the fight game, he wanted to win a title for his dad. He even took his father's nickname, "Boom Boom" as a tribute to the elder Mancini.

Likable and good-looking, the Ohio-born Mancini picked his way to the lightweight championship fight in 1982, defeating Art Frias for the title. Some sportswriters complained (not without justification) that Mancini had been given the path of least resistance to the title, boxing's masters feeling that the appealing white kid would get them TV ratings—which he did.

In November of that year, Mancini was set to defend his title against South Korean fighter Duk Koo Kim, a man with four years experience, in which he scored 17 victories, 8 of them knockouts, in 20 bouts. None of those foes had been as experienced as Mancini, however, making Kim a perfect patsy, in the eyes of many cynics. Still, the twenty-three-year-old Kim regarded the fight as his *Rocky*-esque chance to become an international star, and surprised Mancini in their Las Vegas showdown by

Duk Koo Kim takes an uppercut from Ray Mancini in their title fight. (*AP/Wide World.*)

lasting 14 rounds of a 15 rounder. Frias had gone down in the first.

The fight was a brutal one, each man seeming to be in control at different points. However, it was Mancini who took control for the last time with an atom bomb of a right that dropped Kim instantly: the unconscious fighter was carried from the ring and brought to a hospital, where a blood clot was surgically removed from his head. Kim was brain dead, but was kept alive on life support until his mother could be flown in from South Korea. Upon her arrival, the machines were disconnected and Kim was allowed to die. His mother committed suicide several weeks later.

Ironically, like the Griffith/Paret fight, the Mancini/Kim bloodbath was seen by a huge TV audience. To forestall possible public outrage and legislative calls for a banning of the sport, the World Boxing Council took steps of its own to make the sport safer—limiting championship fights to 12 rounds, instituting more comprehensive prefight physicals, more balanced pairings, not so much in terms of size but experience.

Mancini considered hanging up his gloves, but decided against it; he held onto his title until June 1984, when Livingstone Bramble knocked him out—ironically, in the fourteenth round. Bramble defended his title against Mancini the following February.

Mancini turned to acting, and then, in February 1992, at the age of thirty, announced that he was returning to the ring "to see how I stand with the top fighters right now." The answer came when he faced tough Greg Haugen on April 3 for the North American Boxing Federation's junior welterweight title: the thirty-one-year-old Haugen creamed him.

Back to acting for Boom Boom.

Joe Harris:
"King of the Gypsies"

At least Ray Mancini was given the opportunity to try and make a comeback. Emile Griffith continued to fight despite what happened to Paret. But Gypsy Joe Harris—a canny fighter, a crowd-pleaser, a speed demon, and a championship contender—got a strange and unfortunate break that not only destroyed his career but helped to end his life at the age of forty-four.

When the welterweight broke into the pros in 1964, he, like his heavyweight contemporary Cassius Clay, zipped out of harm's way. Or sometimes he'd just *stroll* away, leaving behind him a surprised foe who he'd suddenly turn on and drop with a jackhammer blow.

The North Philadelphia native was never predictable, never boring—he was known to wear bells on his shoes in the ring—and, for a long time, was never defeated.

Gypsy labored in the lower rankings for two years, finally becoming a serious contender by beating the tar out of Stanley "Kitten" Hayward, the number-one ranked contender. He chewed up several other opponents on his way to a fight with champ Texan Curtis Cokes—whom he demolished in their first meeting. Unfortunately, it wasn't an official title fight, so Gypsy didn't get the belt and

Cokes got to see what kind of an opponent he'd be up against when it was "for real."

As splendid an athlete as Gypsy was, he was also an undisciplined one. He preferred pool to boxing, and spent more time with a cue in his hand than with a fist in a sparring partner's face. He would train for a few days before a bout—though "train" is a something of an overstatement. He'd get in the ring with heavier fighters, beat them up, and *voilà!* Gypsy Joe was ready to rock and roll.

He also liked the good life as far as food and drink was concerned, and after three years he was a junior middleweight with a visible paunch. Nonetheless, he still had fists like pistons, and though he never got to fight Cokes again—a fight was arranged, but these were the days when boxing was still dominated by guys who were *overtly* crooked, and the promotors were thrown in prison for counterfeiting—he fought other major boxers like Miguel Barretto and Dick DiVeronica.

It was Emile Griffith who gave Gypsy his one defeat in 25 professional fights, but Gypsy was pragmatic about his loss ("Emile took me fair"), and looked forward to other fights and an eventual rematch.

But it was not in the cards.

In 1968, a fight with Manuel Gonzalez had to be canceled when Gypsy tipped the scales in middleweight territory. He went on a diet, ran, got in shape, and showed up for the rematch—only to fail the prefight physical. Amazingly, the doctor discovered something no one had noticed before; something that explained the way Gypsy fought, with his head always facing an opponent dead *on;* something that caused his boxing license to be revoked permanently.

Gypsy could only see out of one eye.

As a child, he'd been hit with a brick by another kid in an argument over candy, and he'd lost his vision. He'd been able to get this far for one reason and one reason only: bribes had apparently been paid in order to keep the popular fighter in the ring. When he became too difficult to control because of his hedonistic ways, his boosters simply pulled the plug on him.

Gypsy got a lawyer to try and have his license reinstated, but a member of the Pennsylvania Athletic Commission also happened to have only one good eye, and this little Ulysses didn't see any way that, in good conscience, they could allow Gypsy to continue fighting. If he were ever hurt because of his handicap, the outcry would be enormous.

What the Commission failed to take into consideration, however (or were they being punitive, given Gypsy's irreverent ways?), was the fact that the boxer had nothing else in life. No skills, no savings, nothing to fall back on. He turned to drink and then to drugs of all kind, accepting welfare, borrowing, stealing, hustling at pool, and doing whatever he had to pay for them. His marriage to his devoted wife, Gladys, fell apart. After half a decade of dissolution, of becoming a strangely puffy but haggard-eyed figure, he went to a hospital and begged for help.

He was put into a drug rehabilitation program and, after nearly a year, managed to kick his habit—but he still couldn't hold down the odd jobs he landed, and spent more time on welfare than off. In 1988, he suffered a heart attack; between then and 1990, he had three more. He died on March 6, a shattered man who had managed to overcome his handicap and his opponents before being kayoed by the system.

Akeem Anifowoshe:
"Down for a Very Long Count"

Despite the new measures instituted to protect fighters, there are still accidents, still crippling injuries. On June 15, 1991, twenty-two-year-old Nigerian immigrant Akeem Anifowoshe—"Kid" Akeem—faced junior bantamweight champion Robert Quiroga in a title fight in San Antonio. After the 12-round fight of which Quiroga was declared the victor—and during which Akeem had taken a staggering 400 blows to the head—the loser suddenly dropped to one knee and began throwing up blood on the canvas. He fell unconscious and was rushed to the Baptist Medical Center, where doctors drilled a hole in his head to relieve the pressure on his brain, and it was determined that he has only a 30 percent chance of recovering fully. Today, he is able to move his legs and arms, but that movement is limited and walking is extremely difficult. The father of two sons, Akeem says he's told Quiroga, "Robert, you know I won the fight. We must do it again." Quiroga, says Akeem, just looked at him and said, " 'You're crazy.' "

Ironically, to look at the two of them right after the fight, you'd have thought Akeem won: Quiroga's face was a raw, swollen mess. In fact, if the bout hadn't been held in the champ's hometown, where pride was a factor, chances are good it would've been stopped and Akeem declared the victor. Akeem's face was unmarked, and he had actually done better than Quiroga in the last round.

Boxing authorities in Texas and elsewhere charged, quite correctly, that the IBF might be partly to blame for the tragedy, having made the fighters wear thin 6-ounce gloves; in his previous 23 fights (all wins), Akeem had fought with more heavily padded 8 ouncers. IBF president Bob Lee said that the heavier gloves might well cause smaller fighters to tire before the fight was over—which may be true, but the 115-pound Akeem never had that problem despite having worn 8-ounce gloves in all his fights ... except this one. What the heavier gloves would *really* do is make fights less interesting and cause them to end quicker, decreasing revenues.

And so boxing continues as it always has, just as the patently dangerous artificial turf continues to be used in football: because there's a lot of money to be made in the way things are done *now*. And the gladiators who fight do what gladiators have always done—risk lives and limbs for the maximum entertainment of the crowd.

Ted Green:
"Maki-avellian Defeat"

Boxing may be the sport where athletes intentionally pummel each another, but it's probably a less violent sport overall than hockey.

Back in the days of yesteryear, when men were men and only sissies wore helmets or masks, when there were fewer teams and rivalries were far more intense, when TV cameras weren't there to record your every crime, players weren't namby-pamby about violence the way they are today. If someone went after a guy, the unspoken objective wasn't to put him on the bench but in the hospital. At the very *least* in the hospital. Retirement due to injuries was nice, too.

The most insidious example of this attitude occurred on September 21, 1969, when the St. Louis Blues were playing an exhibition game against the Boston Bruins, home of Bobby Orr and Phil Esposito—a team described as tough by their fiercely loyal fans, as scum or monsters by just about everyone else. ("Derek eats shit" was a popular chant in New York's Madison Square Garden whenever Bruin star Derek Sanderson took the ice there. But that's another story . . .)

Ted Green was a star player for the Bruins and, after a minor run-in with Maki, the two traded harsh words. No big deal—until Green decided that Maki didn't deserve to be standing, and proceeded to knock him down. Scrambling to his feet, Maki went after Green and made like one of the protohumans from *2001: A Space Odyssey:* with both hands wrapped low around his stick, he raised it up then brought it down hard on Green's head. The Bruin went down and was rushed to the hospital; there, a pair of operations and the insertion of a metal plate were necessary to repair the damage to his shattered skull.

Both players were benched for 30 days (which didn't affect Green) and fined $300 (which did). But the matter didn't end there. The game had been played in Ottawa, and Canadian officials didn't take kindly to what had happened (because the teams were from the United States, maybe?) Criminal charges were filed against the two, and the case went to trial—a show trial, really, because most people seemed to realize that if these two weren't acquitted, the courts would have ended up entertaining more hockey players than criminals during the season.

In any case, when the wound healed, Green resumed his hockey-playing career, hockey survived, and fights continue—albeit with far less damage to the well-protected (and expensive) players. The incident did produce one "positive" result—the NHL decreed that all players, except certain veterans, had to wear protective helmets.

Rudy Tomjanovich:
"Blasted Are the Peacemakers"

Unlike hockey, basketball isn't known for interne-
cine combat. The foul system does a pretty good
job of keeping players out of each others' faces,
ribs, and guts.

But not always.

On December 9, 1972, six-foot eight-inch Los
Angeles Lakers forward Kermit Washington got
into a dispute with Kevin Kunnert of the Houston
Rockets. The two got into a clinch and Lakers center Kareem Abdul-Jabbar came over to break it up,
grabbing Washington's left arm in the process.

Houston's Rudy Tomjanovich also came over to
see if he could help, but in his blind fury Washington thought it was *another* Laker coming to grab his
right arm. Launching a preemptive strike, Washington swung a hard right at the newcomer.

"I had no idea who it was," Washington said
later. "It was an honest, unfortunate mistake."

Maybe. But the blow drove in Tomjanovich's
nose a solid inch, also cracking his skull and jaw.
"Rocket" Rudy dropped to the court and lay there,
totally out, for several minutes.

But that wasn't the worst part. It took numerous
operations and several *years* before Tomjanovich's
face could be completely reconstructed—though even
then, it didn't look the same as it had before the
blow.

Washington received a 60-day suspension and a $10,000 fine, but it took Tomjanovich six years to return to the court, at which time he never played without a mask that covered his nose and forehead.

Because of his lost years (and lost income), Tomjanovich sued for damages and was awarded a whopping $3.1 million. Even though that's more than he would have made on the court, no one begrudged Tomjanovich the money. For his part, Tomjanovich, who ironically was hired to coach the Rockets in 1992, summed it all up articulately when he said, "I'd rather have been playing basketball."

J. R. Richard:
"Second Opinion"

The fate of boxer Ernie Schaff shows how absurd it is for athletes to try and conduct business-as-usual when they're not in tiptop condition. Yet, not only is this done—in some circles, it's expected. Fashionable, even. The idea of "playing hurt," especially in a big game, is a macho badge of honor.

Sometimes, this can have a galvanizing effect on a team. Perhaps the outstanding example was in 1970, when hobbled New York Knicks center Willis Reed literally dragged himself around the court, like the Mummy, helping to defeat the Los Angeles Lakers in one of the greatest playoff series of all-time. (At least, it was if you were a New York fan.)

At other times, however, athletes push themselves beyond the limits of their bodies. Occasionally, there are warnings, but they ignore them. That, in a nutshell, is the James Rodney Richard story.

Richard was already at a disadvantage when he began playing professional ball. Ask any physical giant among men in the sports world—Wilt Chamberlain, William "The Refrigerator" Perry, Darryl Strawberry—and they'll all tell you the same thing: being big can be a pain. No matter how many points you score, how many tackles you make, or how many home runs you wallop, it's never enough. Everyone expect you to perform at a higher level. Just as unrealistically, fans think it's impossible for you to hurt yourself. You're so big, after all. You can absorb more punishment.

In 1980, no Houston Astros fan could understand how a man standing six feet eight inches, weighing 250 pounds, and capable of throwing a baseball 100 miles per hour could fail to complete every game he started, especially after striking out more than 300 batters two years in a row—a remarkable achievement. Not only that, but J. R. got the reputation for being a hypochondriac. Once, he asked to be taken out of one game because he had a stomach ache. In the heat of a pennant race in July 1980, J. R. falsely told reporters that noted sports medicine specialist, Dr. Frank Jobe, had advised him to take a month off. Then he made matters worse by adding, "I'm going fishing." *This* was a guy serious about the game? This was a heroic athlete? Houston scribes responded with columns entitled, "As the Stomach Turns" and "Who Shot J. R.'s Arm?" And the more that people gossiped, the more J. R. retreated.

Naturally, by keeping his distance, J. R. left fellow players, team management, reporters, and fans to speculate that J. R.'s problems might be worse than mental: that they were calculated, that he was jealous of Nolan Ryan, his white teammate, who was making $200,000 more than he was even though Ryan had won five games and lost eight compared to J. R.'s 10-4 record and 1.89 ERA. These statistics had earned J.R. the starting-pitcher slot for the National League in that season's All-Star Game.

Ryan tried to put a charitable spin on the situation, saying "J. R. is a loner." But the truth was, despite what he felt were legitimate ailments, and despite having signed a four-year, $3.2 million contract just the year before, J. R. *did* feel that because he was black he would never get his due.

"No matter how much money I make, no matter how many records I set, no matter how many guys I strike out, someone's going to remind me I'm black," J. R. complained to a reporter. Despite his agent's efforts to downplay J. R.'s image as a racial activist, J. R.'s words made the task difficult. "I try not to watch too much TV," the pitcher said in another interview. "Like those car commercials, always a white girl sitting on the car. Why not a black girl?"

Whether or not J.R.'s feelings were valid, all the talk about him being a malingerer or hypochondriac came to a tragic halt on July 30, 1980.

Richard and former Astro teammate and close friend Wilbur Howard had gone to the Astrodome to work out. Just four days before, Richard had been released from Houston Methodist Hospital after learning for the first time that his complaints had some diagnosable physical basis: doctors had determined that a blood clot had formed in an artery leading to his right arm. However, the doctors advised Richard that they considered the blockage stable and of no danger.

Play hurt.

The way Richard was feeling at the time, he didn't want to create a bigger stir by "crying wolf," as it were. So he continued to play, even though his wife, Carolyn, was worried about the idea of him having a blood clot. Both knew where it could lead.

After pitching to Howard for a little over 10 minutes, throwing gradually harder as the session progressed, Richard gleefully told Jim Ewell, a former Astros trainer who happened to be at the Astrodome that day, that he never felt better. Howard noticed, however, that J. R. was sweating profusely, so he suggested they go to the dugout to rest.

Suddenly, Richard grabbed Howard's forearm. "Feel this," he said.

The pitcher's hand was cold as ice.

After a few minutes, Richard decided he wanted to do some more throwing, get the blood flowing, so he and Howard returned to the field. After catching one of J. R.'s tosses, Howard saw the huge man weave, taking steps this way and that "like a person who was drunk," then suddenly drop to his hands and knees. After a moment, he dropped over onto his left side. Ewell and Howard were beside him in seconds.

"I got a headache," Richard told them as he lay there. "My head hurts."

Howard said, "Is that all? Are you all right?"

"Just let me lay here," J. R. said, as he repeatedly closed and opened his eyes, squeezing them hard as though trying to clear his vision. He complained of a ringing in his ears, and when he tried to talk again his speech was slurred.

With each passing second, Howard and Ewell grew more alarmed. After turning Richard so he was lying facedown—and wouldn't choke on his tongue if he fell unconscious—Ewell ran to call an ambulance. Howard remained with his stricken teammate, agonized by the fact that there was nothing he could do to help

"J. R. was drooling," he remembers. "His eyes were red. It was like he got stuck in both eyes by a stick."

An ambulance arrived and J. R. was rushed to Houston Methodist Hospital, where emergency surgery was performed to remove a blockage in his neck. When he woke up, he was paralyzed on his left side and unable to speak. He had to write notes to communicate. Ironically, his first was to his agent, Tom Reich. It read: "Black walnut ice cream. One quart."

After the fact, J. R. wondered whether the

Astros' doctors really had his or the team's interests at heart when they told him he could play. He wondered if maybe the doctors had believed press accounts that his problems were psychosomatic.

Dr. Harold Brelsford strongly denied such suggestions when he pointedly told reporters, "I've known J. R. since he came up as a rookie and truthfully, I can say after going over this and discussing it with at least fifty other doctors, we couldn't find anything different we could have done in his case."

Despite Brelsford's assurances to J. R. and the public that J. R. would recover fully, just two months later, Richards was suddenly and unexpectedly forced to endure an 18-hour operation to remove additional blood clots from his shoulder and rebuild his vascular system through the use of arterial grafts and Dacron tubing. This prompted Richards to file a lawsuit against Brelsford and Houston Methodist Hospital, claiming that they had been negligent in treating him before and immediately following his stroke.

Richards struggled valiantly to come back but, not surprisingly, he never regained the form that had made him a leading candidate for the Cy Young Award in 1980 and had enabled him to win 107 games in only eight seasons with the Astros. When J. R. finally accepted the inevitable and retired, some sensed that he was still bitter.

But if he was, who can blame him? He had played hurt and paid the consequences. And, as with Roberto Clemente, it was only after tragedy struck that those around J. R. Richard acknowledged that they had never given him his due. The best pitcher in baseball, some were calling him now. He might have become the best pitcher ever, said others.

There was only one consolation in all of it: folks finally knew he hadn't been faking all those ailments. Tragically, J. R. was vindicated.

Chuck Hughes:
"Lion Down"

J. R. Richard suffered because he didn't want to cause trouble. He heard his body talking, but made the fatal decision of keeping the conversation private. Twenty-eight-year-old Chuck Hughes, on the other hand, never heard a peep—though he, too, paid the ultimate price for playing hurt.

The date was October 24, 1971. A backup wide receiver for the Lions, Hughes had entered the game against the tough Chicago Bears late in the fourth quarter, replacing injured starter Larry Walton.

In short order, the six foot, 180-pound Texas native caught a 32-yard pass from quarterback Greg Landry and was immediately tackled by two Chicago Bear defenders. It was Hughes's first catch of the season, and although the tackle was a hard one, Hughes leaped to his feet, happy as can be. In fact, to many observers, the play seemed to "pump up" the always high-spirited Hughes even more.

The next two plays transpired without incident. As he returned to the huddle, however, after running a pass pattern, he suddenly clawed at his chest and fell face-forward onto the field, like a marionette whose strings had been cut.

Dick Butkus, one of the fiercest competitors in the history of football, was near Hughes when he fell; sensing that something was wrong, the middle linebacker stopped what he was doing and rushed over. No sooner had Butkus dropped to his knees than he began waving frantically to the Lion coaches on the sidelines.

Hughes had fallen so suddenly that several players and coaches thought he was faking an injury to stop the clock. As soon as Butkus started shouting to them, they knew it was real. The doctors ran out and massaged Hughes's chest; the stadium was so quiet that you could hear them pounding on his chest way across the field. When that failed, they administered mouth-to-mouth resuscitation, after which he was carried off on a stretcher. But before he even reached the hospital, Chuck Hughes, the father of a twenty-three-month-old son, was dead.

The game resumed but the life had gone out of the team; Chicago defeated them easily. In the locker room, there was a prayer for Hughes; teammate Charlie Sanders was so upset that no sooner had he dressed then he collapsed and had to be carried to a car and driven home.

Initially, doctors felt that Hughes had been killed because of a ruptured artery, possibly received during the tackle. To everyone's astonishment, however, the autopsy revealed that Hughes had suffered a heart attack due to advanced atherosclerosis: clogged arteries. Seventy percent of Hughes's blood flow was severely restricted.

Tragically, doctors had missed the problem during two earlier "warnings." The first occurred when Hughes was hospitalized with abdominal pains following an exhibition game the summer before. He was X-rayed and given an electrocardiogram, but doctors found nothing. Of course, they weren't looking for an "old person's" disease.

Then, on the eve of playing against the New England Patriots on September 26, Hughes was hurting again and was examined again. Once more, doctors saw nothing unusual, and Hughes lamented to a reporter, "I don't know what's wrong. I've had sharp pains in my stomach and in my chest and they've made all sorts of tests but nobody seems to be able to figure them out."

He shrugged. "I want to play, though. They aren't that bad."

To the contrary: they were bad enough to kill him, Had doctors known, they might have advised him against playing; at the very least, they'd have have put him on a low-fat diet and given him blood thinners and/or vascular dilators. Instead, they inadvertently let him go out there and die.

(Rather pathetically, a handful of commentators did the same, dumb "What's the point of staying fit?" song-and-dance that also rose up like swamp gas when running guru Jim Fixx dropped dead due to heart problems. This rationale for sofa spudship would simply be moronic rather than contemptible if these people didn't actually *believe* it.)

Hughes's widow received a $20,000 lump sum life insurance payment and a meager monthly payment for life, or until she remarried, under the terms of the NFL Players' Association pension contract. Not much in the way of compensation—certainly not in view of today's mega-buck settlements for injuries and/or malpractice—but then, Hughes was just a "grunt," not a legend.

On the other hand, at least Hughes died with his boots on, doing what he loved. The same can't be said for other victims of injuries.

Travis Williams:
"From the 40-Yard Line
to the Bread Line"

There's another side to sports-related injuries: the athlete who is stopped from playing because of an injury, but is not debilitated by it. The life of Travis Williams is a poignant reminder of what can happen to an athlete who thinks he's going to play forever and has no skills to fall back on once the playing stops.

Travis liked to tell his fellow students at Arizona State that he didn't have to go to class, that all he had to do to stay in school was show up for practice and the games. An education? What did he need that for? He'd make a lot of money in the pros and invest it wisely. At least, that was the game plan.

In the pros, at Green Bay, even legendary coach Vince Lombardi, a gruff disciplinarian who was never one for coddling or spoiling athletes, applied a different set of rules where Williams was concerned. The reason: his blazing speed. Friends and foes alike called him the Road Runner—he was *that* fast.

Williams made his deal with the devil, went pro for the big money without having anything remotely resembling an education. During his rookie season, in 1967, there was no disputing his ability: he helped the Green Bay Packers win the Super

Bowl by setting an NFL kickoff return record (which still stands) of 41.1 yards per return, as well as taking back kicks 85, 87, 93, and 104 yards for touchdowns. In his wake was a field littered with Wile E. Coyotes.

No one could have maintained the momentum with which Williams began his career and, sure enough, just a little more than five years and several knee injuries later, the good times came to a crashing halt when his new team, the Los Angeles Rams, released the hobbled player. By then, the twenty-six-year-old had eight children to support and no skills or job training to help him. All he knew was football, and now that was gone.

For a while, Williams did whatever he could to put food on the table. He drove a truck. He worked as a security guard, and then as a bouncer in bars. He opened a videogame arcade, but the height of the *Pac-Man* craze had passed and that, too, went bust. He even lost his Super Bowl ring, which was stolen from his mother's house.

Depressed that the glory was gone and the future looked grim, he began drinking. Incredibly, within the span of three months in 1985, his wife—also a street person—mother, and sister all died of natural causes, and that sent him over the edge. Too young to be eligible for his NFL pension, he lost his house and, knowing he couldn't care for or support his kids, Williams just gave up. He became a street person, sleeping in friends' homes when they'd let him, or in any car he found with the door unlocked.

Williams continued to try to bury his miseries with alcohol until liver and kidney damage forced him to stop. Anyone seeing the bearded, filthy, nearly toothless black man standing on a Richmond, California, street corner in 1989 would never have believed that this was the same, muscular, six-foot titan who once boasted, "As long as I've got a ball on my fingertips, I've got the world there too."

But that year, Williams also seemed to realize that he *still* had a reason to live. By the same force of will he used to muster to gain him those few extra yards, he stopped drinking, got training so he could work as a word processor, found a job during the day, and devoted himself to helping the homeless at night. He even made his way to the "Housing Now" rally in Washington D.C., going up to California Senator Alan Cranston's office and refusing to leave until he saw the lawmaker. Williams was arrested; it was one of the proudest moments of his life.

Unfortunately, too many years of living in the streets had taken their toll on the once-magnificent athlete: on February 17, 1991, at the age of forty-five, he died of heart failure.

At Williams's funeral, longtime friend Susan Prather summed up the reality and tragedy of Williams's life when she said, "Travis lived in a world people only dream about. He died in a world nobody wants to acknowledge."

Bruce Gardner:
"Potential Disaster"

And then there are the unseen wounds that athletes suffer. Not the physical ones, but the mental agonies.

According to statistics, of the nearly 100 baseball players who have killed themselves during the sport's long history, nearly half have been pitchers. Like quarterbacks, they're regarded as the caretakers of the ball, the symbols of the game, but not all of them handle that responsibility as well as they should. Indeed, psychiatrists tell us that professional athletes are already at a disadvantage when it comes to handling problems: their profession extends adolescence and, as a result, many players do not develop the normal coping mechanisms that most young people do as they mature.

Like Bruce Gardner.

An All-America pitcher for the powerhouse USC Trojan baseball team in Los Angeles, coached by the legendary Rod Dedeaux, Gardner signed with the Dodgers in 1960, filled with dreams of becoming the local boy who'd make good. And as he worked his way through the Dodger's minor league organization to the Triple A level, the hard throwing left-hander seemed well on his way, drawing favorable comparisons to Dodger ace Sandy Koufax, whom he greatly admired.

Unfortunately, Gardner's progress started to

slow as he was beset by arm problems, which effectively ended his hopes of ever reaching the major leagues. Gardner hung on, hoping for a miracle that never happened, and eventually he was given his unconditional release.

Like many other athletes, Gardner found it difficult to make the transition from being the star athlete, the proverbial "big man on campus" envied by everyone, to being just another young man, in his early twenties, struggling to come to terms with what he was going to do with the rest of his life.

A series of failed business ventures and personal relationships followed quickly. Even after Gardner became a high school baseball coach a few years later, he still felt he was a failure, haunted by thoughts of what might have been, increasingly convinced that nothing and no one could ever give him the sense of self-worth he'd have had with a major league baseball career.

Finally, one night in 1971, Gardner climbed the fence of the locked college baseball field where he had been a star, walked slowly to the pitcher's mound, put a gun to his head, and pulled the trigger. Police discovered a plaintive suicide note near Gardner's bloody remains:

"I saw life going downhill every day and it shaped my attitude toward everything and everybody. Everything and every feeling that I visualized with my earned and rightful start in baseball was the focal point of continuous failure. No pride of accomplishment, no money, no home, no sense of fulfillment, no attraction. A bitter past, blocking any accomplishment of a future except age.

"I brought it to a halt tonight at thirty-two."

Nor was he the last frustrated pitcher to choose this sobering option.

Donnie Moore:
"The Pitch That Cost More Than a Pennant"

Who hasn't wished for the chance to relive one moment in their past, do something differently? In sports, certainly, that feeling is commonplace.

Wouldn't Dodger catcher, Mickey Owen, like another chance to catch the third strike that got past him and led to a Yankee victory in the 1941 World Series? Or how about Ralph Branca who threw the famous gopher ball to Bobby Thompson, which propelled the Giants to a heart-stopping playoff win over the Brooklyn Dodgers in 1951? Does anyone doubt that Bill Buckner would like a second chance to field the ground ball that rolled through his legs in the 1986 World Series and let the Mets stage a remarkable come-from-behind victory?

Then there was the sad case of Cincinnati Reds catcher Willard Hershberger who took the "sins" of the entire team on his shoulders. A likable Indiana farm boy, Hershberger replaced the Reds' regular catcher, future Hall of Famer Ernie Lombardi, in 1939, and was instrumental in the Reds reaching the World Series that year. As the 1940 season wore on, the pressure of *wanting* to win began to take its toll on Hershberger and in August, in the midst of a tight pennant race, he took personal responsibility for the Reds' loss of the second game of a critical doubleheader.

"I'm going to go back to my room, order in dinner, and get to sleep early," he told teammates after the game. Then he returned to his hotel room where, over the bathtub, so as not to make a mess for hotel housekeeping, he slit his throat and slowly and silently watched his life go down the drain.

Though players are understandably haunted by the memory of errors or simple miscalculations, most do not go the Hershberger route. They realize they're only human and learn to cope. Sadly, Donnie Moore was an exception. The fireball relief pitcher made one errant toss in an otherwise solid career, and no matter how hard he tried—and he *did* try—he could never look at what happened to him that fateful Sunday in game five of the 1986 League championship series as just another pitch in another game.

The California Angels—the long-in-the-cellar team owned by former cowboy singer and Hollywood movie star Gene Autry—were one pitch away from winning their first American League pennant . . . and their first trip to the World Series. But then Dave Henderson hit Donnie Moore's two-strike pitch into the left centerfield stands, and the dream evaporated. It didn't matter that the Angels rallied to tie the game in the bottom of the ninth, or had two more games to beat Boston to make it to the World Series—chances blown by the team as a whole. Moore was never the same.

His wife, Tonya, reveals, "He'd come home and burst into tears."

Dave Pinter, Moore's longtime agent, says, "Donnie couldn't live with himself. He kept blaming himself. Everything revolved around one pitch . . . the guy was just not the same after that."

Following the 1986 season, Moore was plagued by injuries, overshadowing the two previous seasons when he had been hailed as the top relievers in the game and earned himself a three-year, $3 million contract—at the time, one of the must lucrative contracts ever signed by a free agent pitcher. But rib and arm injuries, as well as a painful bone spur in his lower back that led the Angels to release him after the 1987 season when his contract expired, and Moore signed with the Kansas City Royals' Triple A minor league team in Omaha. On top of the injuries, his heart just wasn't in the game, and after compiling a 1-2 record, no saves, and a 6.39 ERA, he was released on June 12, 1989.

It only got worse after that. Moore began toying with the idea of playing in Puerto Rico in the winter leagues; the Houston Astros talked with him about playing for their Triple A team, perhaps as early as September. But his mind and heart weren't on the game. Concurrent with being released by the Royals, Moore was released by Tonya, who moved out.

Financial pressures mounted. Moore owed $6,000 a month on his $850,000 Anaheim Hills home, where the family had been living for nearly four years; Moore's agent filed a grievance claiming he was owed $75,000 in past commissions. Early in July, the pitcher reluctantly contacted a real estate agent and said he wanted to sell the house, fast. He was a mess. As his seventeen-year-old daughter, Demetria, put it, "He was really depressed. First of all, when he got cut from Kansas, he'd been really depressed about that ... and then he comes back to home and the marriage, the family is all destroyed. I mean, what else does he have left?"

On Tuesday, July 18, 1988, early in the afternoon, Tonya went to the house to show it to a realtor; Donnie met her and the kids there. The realtor never showed, and the couple began talking about where the family would move when the house was sold: Texas, they agreed, which is where they had both grown up. They also talked about reconciling if Donnie would seek professional help—which was when things got ugly. The couple began to quarrel, as they had frequently since the previous fall. Sometime during the argument, Moore hit his wife. She ran from the house, stopped outside where the boys were playing, told them their father had hit her, then went back in.

She found Donnie in the kitchen, and they started arguing again. This time, Moore left—only when he returned, he was carrying a .45 caliber semiautomatic his wife had given him as a gift the previous Christmas. The argument resumed and, without warning, he opened fire on his wife. The first shot went through her neck, but she managed to run from the room. He fired two more times, striking her in the torso as she staggered through the laundry room toward the garage. She hit the ground near her car.

The Moore children rushed in. Demetria dragged her bleeding, still-conscious mother to the backseat and sped to Kaiser Permanente Foundation Hospital, leaving Moore, shellshocked, alone with his seven-year-old son, Ronnie, and his ten-year-old-son, Donnie Jr. Suddenly, with a whimper, the troubled thirty-five-year-old pitcher put the gun to his head and, with a single squeeze of the trigger, forever erased the all-consuming memory of Dave Henderson's two-run homer. One of the boys ran to the phone and called the police.

"I think insanity set in," says Pinter. But Brian Downing, one of Moore's Angels teammates, put a different spin on it. After learning about the shooting, he said, "It's not a game, it's our life." In the case of Donnie Moore, that was clearly an understatement.

Sadly, his death was just one more in a series of tragedies and misfortunes that struck the franchise—some deadly, some career-ending—which date back to April 1961, the first month of the first season the team was in existence. That was when

Johnny James, a highly touted pitching prospect the Angels had just acquired from the defending world champion New York Yankees, felt a bone snap in his arm when he threw a curve ball. He never pitched again.

In April 1962, Ken Hunt, who had hit 25 home runs for the Angels the year before, broke his collarbone while flexing his back by arching a bat behind his head while waiting to hit in the on-deck circle. He, too, never played a full season in the major leagues again.

In August 1962, in the heat of the pennant race, the Angels' best relief pitcher, Art Fowler, was hit by a line drive during batting practice before a game in Boston. Fowler lost the vision in his left eye and never regained his pitching form.

In the spring of 1964, Ken McBride who, together with Dean Chance, had been the ace of the Angels' pitching staff, suffered neck and back injuries in an automobile accident. He only won four more games in his short major league career.

In the summer of 1964, the Angels drafted outfielder Rich Reichardt from the University of Wisconsin, and high school catcher, Tom Egan, and gave each a $300,000 signing bonus. A few years later, after Reichardt began to suffer severe headaches, tests disclosed a rare blood disorder and he had to have a kidney removed. Reichardt never regained his promise and retired, a journeyman.

Egan, who became the Angels' starting catcher, was hit in the face by a pitch thrown by Detroit's Earl Wilson in 1969 and suffered a broken jaw and impaired vision in his left eye. He was forced to retire prematurely.

In 1968 alone, Angel relief ace, Minnie Rojas, was left permanently paralyzed by an automobile accident that took the lives of his wife and two of his three children; first baseman Don Mincher, who had hit 25 home runs the year before, was beaned by Cleveland's Sam McDowell, ending his career; and third baseman Paul Schaal had his jaw broken by a pitch. He became a frequently traded utility player whose career potential was never fulfilled.

In 1972, utility infielder Chico Ruiz was killed in a car accident; the following year, outfielder and future Texas Ranger manager Bobby Valentine broke his leg when he crashed into the tarpaulin-covered chain-link centerfield fence at Anaheim Stadium while pursuing a fly ball. Although Valentine attempted a comeback, his speed was greatly reduced and he never again played on a regular basis!

In 1975, former Angel pitcher Jim McGlothlin, who had been a consistent winner during five seasons with the Angels, died of cancer after being traded to the Cincinnati Reds. And then there was poor Lyman Bostock.

In 1992, the Angel team bus crashed into an embankment on a New Jersey turnpike, flipping over and settling in a gulley twenty feet below the road. Several players were badly injured; team manager Buck Rogers was hurt so badly he was hospitalized for two weeks, then forced to convalesce in bed at his Anaheim, California, home for nearly three months afterward.

All of this, of course, is just coincidence.

On the other hand, maybe the players—or fate—simply took the team's name a bit too literally.

Don Wilson:
"No-Hitter Missed"

And then there are some pitchers whose fate we will never fully understand. Did Don Wilson mean to do himself in, or was what happened just an awful accident?

In the winter following the 1957 season, after he had led the New York Yankees to their third straight World Series appearance, batted .365, and was named the American League MVP for the second year in a row, Mickey Mantle expected a pay increase. Instead, the Yankees tried to *cut* his salary from $70,000 to $65,000. Recently, Mantle, like Joe DiMaggio and other sports greats of yesteryear, joked that if he had a season like that today, where $5 million salaries are common, the Yankees would have had to make him a co-owner before he'd agree to play for them.

Unfortunately for many athletes, the same muse that blesses them with their incredible athletic gifts does not always have a sense of timing. This is true of Mantle and DiMaggio, but also in the case of a lesser known star, Houston Astros righthanded pitcher Don Wilson. In his case, timing—ten years, perhaps—might have made the difference between life and death.

Signed by the Houston Astros as a free agent straight out of Compton Junior College, California, in 1964, the powerful, six-foot-three-inch Wilson was a marvel. Grady Hatton, his first manager at Houston, says that the pitcher had "a great arm . . . a high-riding fastball and a short, hard slider. He won ten games for us when he didn't know what it was all about." In 1967, he pitched a no-hitter against the Atlanta Braves and a second no-hitter two years later against the Cincinnati Reds—this, when the team's fielding was, to put it charitably, not among the best in the league. He might have pitched a second no-hitter against the Reds that year, but the Astros were down 2-1 and manager Preston Gomez pulled him in the eighth inning to put in a pinch hitter. The relief pitcher gave up a hit in the ninth, but Wilson said, "I respect Preston Gomez. When people start putting personal goals ahead of the team, you'll never have a winner."

You've got to like a guy who can say that. Never mind if he believed it or not: he had the class to take the heat off Gomez and *say* it.

Amazingly, Wilson compiled a career record of 104 wins and 93 losses while toiling for eighth- and ninth-place teams. Today, such numbers would surely entitle Wilson to a multiyear, multimillion dollar contract. Back then, Wilson earned approximately $40,000 per season—far less than other people with less talent.

But he didn't complain. He never blamed his earnings on the fact that he was black—or, if he did, he never said so in public. "I like to think we're past all of that," he once told a reporter.

He *was* worried about money, however, about being able to provide for his family after his playing career came to an end. At the age of twenty-nine, he had nine seasons under his belt, all of them with the Astros, and was talking with other players about enterprises they might get into to provide a second income—and a second career when the time came. He liked the idea of opening a baseball camp or clinic for kids.

In any case, these thoughts preoccupied him in the off-season. He told friends and coworkers that he was really looking forward to spring training so he could concentrate on baseball—though he was worried because the previous season he'd gone 11-13. He couldn't help but wonder if he were losing it.

In January, his mind was definitely on money and on the future. He had a wife, Bernice, and two children, nine-year-old daughter Denise, and five-year-old son Alexander: he had to be able to provide for them, and the new year had brought home to him the fact that time was passing.

On the night of Saturday, January 4, 1975, he went out drinking; later reports revealed a blood alcohol content of .167—.067 higher than the legal limit for intoxication. He pulled into his garage at approximately 1 A.M. the following morning, used the automatic garage door closer to shut the door, then slid over to the passenger's seat, leaned back, and sat there thinking. He left the car running, apparently to keep the heater on. At some point, he dozed off.

Around 1 P.M., the twenty-nine-year-old Bernice was still asleep when she heard one of the children cry out. Surprised at the hour, she went to their rooms. They were cool, so she wiped their faces with a damp washcloth then carried her son to the master bedroom. She lay him on the bed and covered him to the waist with a blanket, intending to lie down beside him. But she wondered where her husband was and went searching. (She later said she heard the engine running in the garage, which was below the master bedroom; in fact, the engine had died sometime during the morning.)

Bernice found him in the 1972 Thunderbird, his arms at his sides, his head tilted back on the seat, his legs crossed—as though he were resting. Going to the car and calling his name, she couldn't rouse him. She rapped on the window, then tried to open the doors but couldn't because they were locked.

Running inside—slipping and hitting her jaw, she says, leaving it badly bruised—Bernice frantically phoned a neighbor who was a nurse. When she told her what she'd found, the woman told Bernice to check for a pulse. She said she couldn't because the doors were locked; the neighbor told her to call an ambulance.

At 1:24 P.M., the Houston Fire Department received a call from Bernice Wilson. At the time, calls for ambulances in Houston were automatically reported to the Houston Police Department; in just over five minutes, firemen and policemen arrived at the Wilson home. They broke into the car, found Wilson dead, and hurried into the house. Alexander had also died of the carbon monoxide fumes that had seeped into the house, and Denise was in a coma.

Bernice had to be sedated, and was taken to Southwest Memorial Hospital. Denise was rushed to the Texas Children's Hospital, where she recovered slowly but fully from carbon monoxide poisoning.

Understandably, the police had some questions about the whole affair. They wondered whether there had, in fact, been a fight on Saturday night—if Wilson had struck his wife, giving her the bruised jaw, then gone out drinking. Or if she'd found him asleep in the car and turned it on. But the trauma induced amnesia in Bernice, and she literally has no idea what happened the night before. Moreover, there was no hint of any previous domestic discord, nor was Wilson a violent man. Quite the contrary, in fact. As former teammate J. C. Hartman put it at the memorial service, "I'll remember Don for several reasons, and number one is that he never did get too important for other people." That was especially true where his wife and beloved children were concerned.

The coroner and police are both satisfied that the whole thing was a tragic accident, and pitcher Dave Roberts says that any thoughts to the contrary are absurd. "Don had everything going for him," Roberts says, adding that he was one of the few players who really "had it all together."

In an interesting postscript, today some fans chalk Wilson's death up to an Astros "curse" (or maybe it's just teams that start with the letter "A"?), for it wasn't the first time disaster had struck the team—or, for that matter, one of the team's pitchers. In 1964, the year Wilson joined the team, thirty-three-year-old pitcher Jim Umbright died of cancer. In 1973, another pitcher, Larry Dierker, struck and killed a pedestrian while driving a car near Cocoa Beach, Florida; he was later cleared, but the shadow of disaster remained. That same year, Caesar Cedeno, the Astros' All-Star outfielder, was charged with involuntary manslaughter after he shot a woman in the Dominican Republic. He received a $100 fine. In 1967, outfielder Walt Bon died of leukemia at the age of twenty-nine, and in 1970, another outfielder, Jimmy Wynn, was stabbed during a domestic quarrel. He recovered, but wisely, got a divorce.

Some people get a second chance. Unfortunately, Wilson wasn't one of them.

Ricky Berry:
"Young Man with a Gun"

Of all the senseless suicides in sports, however, there may not be one as disturbing as that of rising basketball star, Ricky Berry. He was just a kid, one faced with problems that, in the long run, would have proved to be minor. Unfortunately, he didn't realize that—and he simply wasn't equipped to deal with them.

Hardly anyone who ever met or knew the six-foot eight-inch guard-forward suspected he was anything but perfectly well-adjusted. From an early age, he seemed to be one of the lucky few destined for the type of charmed life about which others only dream. Blessed with an agile body and mind, Ricky had the added benefit of a basketball coach for a father: Bill Berry honed his son's game and made sure he didn't succumb to the pressures and pitfalls that could throw his athletic future off course.

In fact, things went so smoothly for Ricky that the biggest problem he faced growing up was deciding to transfer from nationally ranked Oregon State after completing his freshman year in 1984, to play for his father at San Jose State. There was gossip that Bill would favor his son over the other players, make sure Ricky racked up the type of stats and got the type of press coverage to insure being a top NBA draft choice.

But just the opposite happened. Bill was *harder* on his son than he was on the other players, which makes all the more remarkable the fact that Ricky became San Jose State's all-time leading scorer—which includes a 24-point-a-game average his senior year and being selected for the U.S. team that won the silver medal in the Pan American Games in 1987. However, the ultimate reward for Ricky was when the Sacramento Kings made him their first-round pick in the 1988 NBA draft.

For someone who had once been the ball boy for Magic Johnson's Michigan State team when his father had served as an assistant to head coach Jud Heathcote, the prospect of playing in the same league with his boyhood idol was both intimidating and exhilarating.

Ricky rose to the challenge, averaging 11 points a game, but he still felt there was room for improvement. Unlike many of his fellow NBA players who didn't so much as touch a basketball during the summer, he remained in the Sacramento area with his new wife, Valerie, practicing each day to improve every facet of his game. Ever civic-minded, Ricky also found the time to participate in basketball clinics for inner-city youths.

While on the surface, Ricky Berry's life appeared filled with promise and purpose, something "dark" was lurking underneath—something that was troubling him deeply. On Sunday, August 13, 1989, four friends had come to the couple's suburban home in Carmichael—a home they'd moved into just two weeks before. The six of them chatted, played Nintendo games, then had some pizza, after which the visitors left and Ricky and Valerie had a fight. The two had been married for fifteen months, having known each other just a few weeks before deciding to wed, and fights were reportedly common; this one had been about the friends whom Ricky had invited over without having asked her.

Ricky Berry stuffs one as Russ Schoene of the Seattle SuperSonics looks on helplessly. (*AP/Wide World.*)

After a few minutes, Valerie left the house and drove off to stay with a friend. Alone in the family room, the twenty-four-year-old Berry apparently sat and brooded for two hours. Sometime during that period, he wrote a note to his wife and parents apologizing for what he was about to do—but complaining that he couldn't live because his wife didn't love him anymore and was just using him. When he was finished, Berry went and got a 9mm semiautomatic he used for target practice, put it to his head, and fired. None of the neighbors heard a sound.

Valerie Berry discovered her husband's corpse when she returned home Monday morning. Sacramento Chief Deputy Coroner Bob Bowers performed an autopsy, and concluded that Ricky was in perfect health; nothing about his body condition or chemistry revealed an emotional or physical state conducive to suicide. There were no drugs in his system, no alcohol, no diseases. The Sacramento Sheriff's Department initially suspected that the couple's quarrel was to blame for pushing him over the edge, but no one could understand what had brought him that *close* to the precipice. Eric Saulny, his former San Jose State assistant coach, said they might never know, because Berry had been "such a poker-faced player, nobody really knew what was inside him."

That's true—and it's apparent that there was more than one factor that drove the young star to take his life. On the one hand, there's evidence that Berry was very upset about an aborted affair with a local sixteen-year-old he'd met at one of his basketball clinics. He had been phoning her at home, trying to see her on the side; he was motivated not by lust alone, but because he was himself somewhat immature and felt *comfortable* with younger people.

Berry would have succeeded in seeing the girl,

too, if her mother hadn't picked up an extension during a conversation and told Berry to stay away or she'd have him arrested. Unhappy in his marriage and unsuccessful with this one stab outside of it, Berry just wasn't equipped to deal with what seemed to him an unbearably empty life.

Then too, Berry appears always to have had a desperate fear of disappointing his strict father or upstanding mother. He had been happy at Oregon State: assistant sports information director Mike Corwin recalls him as "Carefree—that's why it was a surprise when he left." But he didn't just up and leave: he debated about it until just weeks before his sophomore year, apparently succumbing to pressure from the elder Berry. He obviously felt that the shame of a dissolving marriage would have subjected him to their scorn—something he just couldn't bear.

To top things off, his father had been fired by San Jose State the previous season after team members resigned to protest his coaching methods, which have been generously described as "strict." After failing to find another job, Bill Berry went to work as a scout for the Kings. It's quite possible that Ricky felt there would be added pressure for him to perform, what with his father watching from the front office, as well as criticism from the press that he'd used pull to get his father a job.

Regardless of the degree to which each of these contributed to his sudden depression, together with his own self-described habit of being "impulsive," it's clear Berry simply wasn't equipped to cope with life outside the court; growing up, he'd had so little opportunity to learn how.

The news of Berry's death rocked everyone who knew him. Kings coach Jerry Reynolds dissolved into tears at a brief press conference the team held to announce the tragic news. Others present cried openly. To those who knew him only as a friend—

not as a son or husband—it just didn't make sense that a kind, sensitive, generous, and energetic young man should feel that death was the only way out.

Teammate Vinny Del Negro, who came to the Kings the same year as Ricky, remains mystified by what happened.

"Ricky was a very competitive player with a bright future," he says. "He always enjoyed himself. He seemed to enjoy life a lot." Vinny has no idea what drove him to suicide, and refuses to speculate.

However, perhaps Vinny unwittingly revealed a great deal when he said, "I hope his family can find some peace of mind."

The Black Sox and "Shoeless" Joe Jackson: "Series Business"

Of all the sports tragedies, the mildest would seem to be the victimless ones: gambling. Gamblers have destroyed many a career, and in none of the most famous instances have the participants taken their lives. They've lived with their shame. And that, in a way, makes them some of the most pathetic figures of all.

Today, most people know "Shoeless" Joe Jackson from the movie *Field of Dreams* (1989), which was inspired by author William P. Kinsella's sentimental, highly romanticized 1982 book *Shoeless Joe,* in which a mysterious voice tells Iowa farmer Ray Kinsella, "If you build it, he will come"—"it" being a baseball diamond, and "he" being "Shoeless" Joe Jackson, the Chicago White Sox leftfielder.

It isn't surprising that Kinsella chose Jackson as the personification of the ill-fated team. The illiterate son of a poor South Carolina plantation owner, Jackson began playing baseball at the mill where he went to work when he was thirteen. Though he played without shoes just once due to sore feet, a fan for the opposition called him a "shoeless bastard" after he hammered a hit, and the name stuck. Part of it, anyway. A great fielder and an extraordinary batter, Joe was scouted by the majors and ended up playing for Charles Comiskey's Chicago White Sox. With the money he earned, Jackson bought a large house in Savannah for himself and his loving wife, Katie; he also lost a lot of his earnings on lousy business deals.

But money didn't matter as much as baseball, and he was devoted to improving his performance. His ability and perfectionism were particularly important in the 1919 season, the first since our boys, our "way" had triumphed in World War I. Through hard work, Jackson had used the all-American sport to realize the American dream; he was the embodiment of what we'd fought for and what we'd won. Indeed, sports figures were the only incorruptible heroes we had left: the likes of "Boss" Tweed had shown us how corrupt our political system could become; out in Hollywood, movie favorites were beginning to fall from grace, as popular director D. W. Griffith made heroes of the Ku Klux Klan in *Birth of a Nation,* and beloved comedian "Fatty" Arbuckle went on trial for rape and murder. Even our victorious soldiers were frowned upon by many because of the loose morals they'd picked up in Europe and brought back to Small Town U.S.A.

But not our ballplayers. They were clean of body and spirit. And the 1919 World Series was the epitome of what those qualities could achieve: it was a matchup between the powerhouse Chicago White Sox and a Cinderella team, the Cincinnati Reds. A team of seasoned giants vs. hungry upstarts. Though few people felt the Reds had a prayer, no one had expected them to get *this* far, either. The game was attracting more attention than any of fifteen previous annual showdowns.

The White Sox. People talk about this Yankees team or that Yankees team, but the argument could be made that this was the finest team ever to take the field, with the thirty-year-old Jackson as the heavy-hitting linchpin. In ten years of professional play, he had averaged an amazing .356.

His other world-class teammates included dynamic knuckle-ball pitcher Eddie Cicotte, who was coming off a staggering 29 and 7 season; the "dancing" third baseman George "Buck" Weaver; fast, powerful shortstop Charles "Swede" Risberg; strong, scrappy catcher Ray Schalk; miraculous second baseman Eddie Collins; centerfielder Oscar "Happy" Felsch, who never seemed to miss the ball; rightfielder "Shano" Collins; and huge first baseman "Chick" Gandil.

Even the folks in Cincinnati figured that the White Sox were going to show the upstart Reds how the game was played. And that was okay: Ohio loved baseball, and while they were rooting for the home team, they understood the beauty of the Chicago team.

Then the incredible happened: Cincinnati won the best-of-nine series, five games to three. Or rather, as it turned out, Chicago lost. On purpose.

The seeds for this still-heartbreaking betrayal of the fans, the sport, and the nation itself had actually been sown the year before. Because of the war, attendance was down and players' salaries had been stripped to the bare bones. The players on the hot Sox were disgruntled, none more so than fourteen-year veteran Cicotte and the intinerant Gandil, who had joined the team in 1910, was traded to the Washington Senators and then to Cleveland, then returned to Chicago.

During Gandil's brief tenure in Washington, glad-handing Boston gambler Joseph "Sport" Sullivan had befriended the ballplayer, skillfully pumping him for information about how this batter was swinging in practice, how this pitcher was throwing, what the lineup might be—tips he could use to his advantage in his bookmaking operation, especially if none of the other gamblers had them. Gan-

Shoeless Joe Jackson. (*AP/Wide World.*)

dil didn't realize he was being used at first, and when he finally caught on he was already Sullivan's friend and was glad to help him out. No one was being hurt; a pal was able to make some money on this game or that, was all.

In September, just weeks before the Series, Gandil contacted Sullivan, and the big, heavyset gambler came to see him in his hotel room. The ballplayer and several of his teammates were disgusted with tight-fisted owner Charles Comiskey. They were angry about their salaries, about their meager meal allowance when they were on the road, (which was 25 percent less than some of the *worst* players in the sport received), about their bonus for an incredible season (a case of flat champagne). Gandil shared teammate Cicotte's outrage for a promise Comiskey had made to pay him a $10,000 bonus if he won 30 games: just shy of that, Comiskey benched the pitcher to avoid paying.

What Gandil told Sullivan in the hotel room was something he'd been mulling over since July: if the gambler could come up with $80,000, Gandil felt he could pay off enough of his fellow players to get them to throw the Series, which they were sure to be in. Though Gandil's motive was largely the money, it was also the only way he could think of to strike back at Comiskey—by shaming him with a very public loss.

Sullivan wasn't a big money type, and eighty grand was big money. But he saw the value of what was being offered; as the only one who would be aware of what was to happen, he would clean up. Sullivan said he'd get the money, and Gandil promised he'd get the players.

At that time, Gandil had actually broached the subject with a few of his teammates and had three men in his pocket. Cicotte was earning $6,000 a year and, when Gandil had first proposed the idea, the bitter pitcher agreed to go along for $10,000 in cash, up front. Number-two pitcher, Claude "Lefty" Williams, was initially opposed to the scheme, but came aboard when he heard Cicotte was in. The otherwise dispensible infielder Fred McMullin had to be made a part of it when he overheard Gandil discussing it with Risberg—who also said he'd be interested in joining, though he hadn't actually committed.

In order to make the fix work, Gandil felt that in addition to the men he'd landed, he had to bring in the three key hitters—Weaver, Felsch, and Jackson. He met with them in a hotel room on September 21—ten days before the Series would begin in Cincinnati. The players listened to the proposition and, despite their frustration, they agreed to nothing; Jackson, in particular, felt ashamed by what they were contemplating.

Meanwhile, Sullivan had scored on his end. He'd gotten millionaire gambler Abe Rothstein involved, and Gandil was told the money had been raised—including additional money for Jackson, who decided he'd join the others for $20,000. Gandil assured his crooked sponsors that everything was set—though that wasn't true. Even when they arrived in Cincinnati for the Series, nothing concrete had been decided. Some players were waffling. Others wanted the money. Jackson couldn't even bring himself to attend a meeting in Cincinnati's Hotel Sinton, where the players sat down with Abe Attell, a former featherweight boxing champion who'd been suspended for fixes and now worked with Rothstein.

The persuasive Attell said the money would be paid in pieces: $20,000 for each game they threw. Without their hearts being in it (and without the money in hand . . . only Attell's promises) the players were swept along with the tide, and by Gandil's enthusiasm for the scheme (a front: he was having his own doubts). They talked about the order in which they'd throw the games, though it was decided that Cicotte would be allowed to win at least one so he'd have some leverage for renegotiating his contract the following year.

Even when everything had been decided, the players *still* weren't sure they could go through with it. Gandil had received $10,000—half what he was supposed to get before the first game—and had given it all to Cicotte, who refused to throw anything but his best pitches unless he was paid.

So the money wasn't there as promised and, worse, gossip was floating around as word of the fix spread through gambling circles and the odds began to shift in favor of the woefully outclassed Reds. On the day of the game, Jackson and several of the other players were worried not about ethics or where their money was: they feared being found out. They talked among each other quietly at the hotel and, later, at the ballpark. Most of them could still look forward to up to decade more in the sport, with an eventual loosening of the purse strings. And there was the winner's share of the Series gate to consider. The thing wasn't making financial sense anymore.

Then there was their reputations to consider. Now that the anger that had brought them here gave way to the cold reality of what they were planning, they realized that if the fix were ever exposed, their greatness would be a footnote to their tragic dishonesty.

There was a huge network of gamblers and a fortune riding on the game. Jackson didn't care. He was thinking of sitting out the Series—which would have been tantamount to a confession for the healthy player. He was told by Gandil—who heard it from an anonymous phone caller that it might be unhealthy for players and their loved ones if Jackson didn't play. According to Bernie Michaelson, a New York cop who knew Rothstein, "Once you got in bed with him, you didn't get out until he got what he wanted. And if he didn't get what he wanted, you didn't get out of bed at all." Gandil reminded him and the others that, like it or not, they were *already* in: the fact that they'd been involved with Sullivan, Attell, and Rothstein just talking about throwing the game would ruin them if it ever got out.

There was no choice but to follow through what they'd started, and when the game ended the score was an improbable 9-1.

Rumors of a fix were stronger than before, and Comiskey was fiercely concerned about it. He was like the movie moguls who controlled their stars, their salaries, and their films, but loved to make motion pictures. Generous Comiskey wasn't, but he lived for baseball and the thought of the Series being thrown by anyone, let alone his team, was unbearable. Unfortunately, though he knew in his gut something was wrong, neither he nor his aides could find out what.

The next day, many of the players were sick over what they'd done—and didn't feel any better when Attell hedged about the money he owed them. It was coming, he told Gandil. And what about the money for the second game? That was coming too, he said. The Sox went out and threw the game: Attell paid them $10,000 for their efforts.

By this time, Gandil knew they were cooked. The gamblers had no intention of paying anything near the full amount, yet there was nothing to do but take whatever was offered: if Attell and his pals squealed, they were dead. Ironically, a fix wasn't even necessary by this point: few of the guys were sleeping well enough to play a really decent game.

The Series went to Chicago, where the White Sox were allowed to win the third game. They took the Reds and felt a flush of their old pride: if they wanted it, they could still win the Series. There was talk of screwing the gamblers and playing for themselves.

That feeling grew by the fourth game, and only Gandil seemed to realize two things: first, that the gamblers meant what they said about sticking to the game plan, and second, that only money could bring the players back in line. He explained the situation to Sullivan, who got them another $20,000 and *swore* they'd have another $20,000 before the fifth game. The cash did the trick, and the Sox threw the fourth and fifth games, after which the Series returned to Cincinnati. The funds stopped again, and the angry Sox went to the ballpark and beat Cincinnati the next two games, bringing the Series to 4-3. They could beat the Reds another two games in a row, no sweat.

Rothstein was alarmed and, through Sullivan, got word to Williams—who was pitching, and who had a wife he loved very much—to make sure the eighth game was the final one. It was no longer a question of money: the players knew they wouldn't see another nickel. It was a matter of survival. Heartsick, Williams went to the ball field and let the Reds score three runs in the first inning. They scored another off the relief pitcher, Bill James. When the inning ended, so, for all purposes, did the Series.

Though he still suspected a fix, Comiskey knew that a scandal would destroy his team, and perhaps professional baseball as well. He would not have that. He'd been a manager, had founded the White Stockings in 1901, and had grown wealthy from them: he had to protect them and, publicly, denied that anything untoward had taken place: "These yarns are manufactured out of whole cloth and grow out of bitterness due to losing wagers," he told the press. He added sanctimoniously, "I would be the first to want information to the contrary," and, underscoring his confidence in his players, he offered $20,000 to anyone for "unearthing any information" about a fix. You've got to wonder if any of the eight players thought of collecting the reward.

Not for the money but for conscience, Jackson tried to tell Comiskey in person, then by letter, that the Series had been thrown. Comiskey refused to listen. However, he had a private eye check up on his players to see who was spending more than usual. Most were, especially Gandil, who had bought a house and car and made various other investments. Comiskey did nothing—except to spitefully withhold the loser's share of the World Series gate from eight of his players. He still didn't understand what it was that had made these brilliant players turn on him. For their part, the players complained, but not too loudly. They didn't want an investigation any more than Comiskey did.

A year passed, and the rumors quieted. The White Sox played well the next season, but they were still under the thumb of gamblers (and on the payroll, with cash coming in regularly now), and blew key games as ordered: the object was to keep the race with the Cleveland Indians tight, sustaining interest and generating bets. There wasn't a more crooked outfit in the league, yet it wasn't anything the White Sox did in 1920 that caused things to become unraveled.

An August 31 game had been fixed between the Chicago Cubs and the Philadelphia Phillies, and the press got wind of it. A grand jury was convened in Cook County, Illinois, and Judge Charles Mac-Donald ordered an investigation of that particular game. And while they were at it, he also wanted them to look into those lingering allegations surrounding the 1919 World Series.

When the grand jury convened on September 7, and baseball figures were subpoenaed, the White

Sox began to sweat—none more than Cicotte, who was tired of keeping his awful secret, tired of the stranglehold the gamblers had on him and his teammates, and tired of baseball. He finally went to Comiskey, and when the pitcher told him what had gone on, his boss was literally unable to listen. After ordering the player to tell the grand jury what he knew, Comiskey told him to get out.

Looking for absolution, the young pitcher went before the grand jury and spilled his guts—let them know who was involved, how the money was delivered, what he did with it, and how he threw the games—easy pitches, errors, relaying the ball slowly or badly. He wept throughout most of his over two-hour testimony, and concluded by saying that one of the worst things about what he did was that, "My friends all bet on the Sox. I knew it, but I couldn't tell them. I had to double-cross them."

Independently, the miserable Jackson had also decided to testify—even though Risberg had said he'd kill him if he did. Jackson either didn't take Risberg seriously or didn't care, or both. He knew in his heart that he was an honest man; in a perverse way, the Series had proved it. Even though he was only paid $5,000 of what he was promised, he still went ahead and threw the games. In any case, there were legitimate reasons why this mess had come about, and he was sure the jury would understand them. Regardless, he had to get it off his chest.

Jackson's testimony was heartfelt though at times incoherent, and he felt great and confident upon leaving the Criminal Courts Building. Sadly, his happiness was short lived: largely for political reasons, Illinois State's Attorney Maclay Hoyne wanted the eight players to stand trial. So did other influential politicians as well as many owners. An example had to be made of these men whom the press had dubbed the Black Sox.

Meanwhile, to the surprise of no one but Jackson and a few of his teammates—who thought that the act of confessing had exonerated them—Comiskey suspended the conspirators, informing them by telegram, "If you are innocent of any wrongdoing, you and each of you will be reinstated; if you are guilty, you will be retired from organized baseball for the rest of your lives if I can accomplish it."

Other owners rallied in support of his action, the New York Yankees part-owner Colonel Jacob Ruppert going so far as to wire him, "In order that you may play out your schedule, and, if necessary, the World Series, our entire club is at your disposal"—a nice gesture, though it was in violation of the rules of the game.

Other testimony was heard, and on October 22, 1920, the eight players, five gamblers—including Attell and Sullivan, but not the influential Rothstein—and Hal Chase, a crooked member of the New York Giants, were indicted on nine counts of conspiracy, among other charges. The participants were brought to trial on June 27, 1921; having sat on the sidelines for so long, and having gone through emotions ranging from remorse to outrage, they were all eager for the chance to be heard in public.

The trial was a fiery one but, to a man, the players expected to be acquitted, not because they hadn't done anything wrong but because they knew the jury would understand why they'd been forced into their deal with the devil, and how they were then manipulated by the gamblers. Their defense attorneys worked hard to show that even the law hadn't been on their side: the players who had gone before the grand jury didn't have attorneys; Jackson couldn't even *read* the document he was compelled to sign, waiving immunity.

The case went to the jury for deliberation on August 2; their decision was returned just over two hours later. The players may have thrown the games, but their *intent* was not to defraud the public. They were found not guilty.

The eight players went wild, believing that they could finally put the Series behind them. But there was a catch. Between the time the scandal had broken and the trial, the press, the public, and the owners all realized that the structure of organized baseball was as much at fault as the eight players. Before things got out of hand—Congress was threatening to intervene with laws and its own investigations—the club owners got together and formed a new commission to oversee the sport. After considering several prominent Americans to head the commission—including General John "Blackjack" Pershing, who had commanded the victorious American Expeditionary Forces in the war—they gave the position to tough, conservative judge Kenesaw Mountain Landis.

Despite the findings of the courts, Landis told the press that baseball could not tolerate players "associating with gamblers and crooks," and he refused to allow them back in the game. Angry and despondent, the players left Chicago for good, and all ended with short, unsatisfying careers in semiprofessional baseball, hoping for reprieves that never came. Eventually, they drifted off into other professions. Risberg became a dairy farmer and died in 1975, Gandil became a plumber and died in 1970, Cicotte took a job as a game warden and died in 1969, Felsch became a bartender and died in 1964, Williams went into gardening and gardening supplies and died in 1959, and Weaver opened a drugstore and died in 1956.

Jackson went into the dry-cleaning business, then managed a liquor store. He took the banishment harder than anyone, not just because he wasn't being allowed to play but because he believed he was innocent of wrongdoing. And as he

Jackson in 1935, managing a rare smile. Though he had achieved a lifetime batting average of .356 during his career (1908–1920), all he ever talked about was his bitterness over the way he was treated by Commissioner Landis. (*AP/Wide World.*)

grew older, he became more and more fervent in his desire to clear his name. Unfortunately, in 1951, because the movement to do so was finally picking up steam, he suffered a series of heart attacks and he died in December of that year.

What happened to him—to all the players—was the antithesis of what should happen to a hero. But while Jackson may have been the best ever at what he did, that talent carried a responsibility that he failed to understand. Ironically, though Jackson never earned the kind of money he deserved, his signature recently sold at an autograph auction for $23,000. Even in death, others were making money off Shoeless Joe.

Pete Rose: "Red Faced"

Children often are raised to pursue the dreams their parents couldn't obtain. Although that hardly accounts for every stage mother or Little League coach, it's rare that a sports star achieves fame without significant encouragement from his or her parents.

Baseball legend Pete Rose is no exception. In fact, his amazing career achievements and his humiliating exile from the game can be laid directly at the feet of his demanding father.

To say that Pete Rose idolized his father, Harry, is an understatement. After Rose smacked Eric Show's two-ball, one-strike pitch into center field on September 11, 1985, at Cincinnati's Riverfront Stadium to break Ty Cobb's all-time major league hit record, Rose tearfully told the media that he had called time out so he could gaze at the evening sky where he claimed to see his father and Ty Cobb standing side by side, applauding his achievement.

There is no question that in his own right Harry Rose was a talented athlete, widely recognized as a skilled amateur boxer, an accomplished softball and baseball player and, most of all, a talented semipro football player. His approach to each sport was to give no quarter, and he instilled this unyielding spirit in his young son.

But Harry Rose had the misfortune of growing

up during the height of the Great Depression, saddled with the difficult responsibility of supporting a wife and raising a family. Professional athletics was never really an option for Harry, who worked as a bank clerk.

Still "what might have been" was not lost on the intensely competitive elder Rose. He was willing to overlook his son's mediocre performance in school so long as young Pete demonstrated athletic progress. Unfortunately, Harry's son was hardly an imposing specimen: in his senior year of high school, Pete stood just five-feet nine-inches and barely tipped the scales at 140 pounds. Despite Pete's willingness to do whatever it took to improve his game, most of the major league scouts who attended Western Hills High School games were drawn to Rose's teammate, Eddie Brinkman, a pitcher and shortstop who would reach the major leagues two years before Rose and received a $75,000 signing bonus from the Washington Senators. By most accounts, Rose was, at best, no more than the fourth or fifth best prospect on the team and his uncle, a part-time scout for the hometown Cincinnati Reds, had to plead with the club to sign him.

Although Rose would continue to grow, finally reaching six feet, his barrel-chested body filling out to 200 pounds, he showed very little immediate promise, and the Reds left him unprotected after he completed his first minor league season: any other team in baseball could have drafted the man who would become Baseball's all-time hit leader. Remarkably, in retrospect, no one did!

Rose had two seemingly contradictory things working for him. First, there was his father-instilled sense of self-confidence, even when nothing he did on the field seemed to support his swagger. Second, and more important, he had a nearly overwhelming fear of disappointing his father.

After minor league stops at places like Geneva, New York, Tampa, Florida, and Macon, Georgia, Rose was invited to attend the Reds' spring training in 1963. The team was composed primarily of veteran players such as Frank Robinson, Vada Pinson, and Milt Pappas, who had played in the 1961 World Series against the New York Yankees, and then the following year finished in third place just 3½ games behind the San Francisco Giants.

No one tried to make things easy for the eager-to-please rookie, who was perceived to be a "hot dog" because of his habit of running to first base on a walk. Superstar Mickey Mantle was so amused at the sight of Rose running out a walk that he derisively pinned the name "Charlie Hustle" on him—and it stuck. Rose was overjoyed to receive any recognition from a superstar like Mantle, and later said he felt as if he had been knighted.

Though eight-year veteran Don Blasingame seemed a lock at second base, Rose's power and enthusiasm appealed to the Reds' gruff, no-nonsense manager and veteran baseball man Fred Hutchinson. Against all odds, not only did Rose make the squad, he took away the aging Blasingame's job in the starting lineup—which *definitely* didn't endear him to many of his teammates, particularly "old-timers" like Bob Purkey, Eddie Kasko, and Gene Freese. In retaliation, Rose hung around with Frank Robinson and Vada Pinson—black players who understood what it was like to be ostracized. (In fact, Robinson had been jailed in 1961 for pulling a gun on someone who'd made racial slurs in a restaurant.) Robinson later said, "Nobody had to show Pete how to hit, but they wouldn't even show him how to be a major leaguer. So we did."

Rose went on to hit .273 that year, earning National League Rookie of the Year honors.

Rose had a slight sophomore slump the next year,

hitting only .269, then in 1965 he cracked .300 for the first time—something he would in do fourteen of the next fifteen seasons. By 1970, he became the first "singles" hitter to crack the then-magic $100,000 salary barrier.

And Rose had the last laugh against the veterans who'd turned on him. Under the guiding hand of General Manager Bob Howsan, the Reds were transformed from an aging team to a group of young, talented upstarts who would dominate National League play for nearly a decade and be known to fans and foes alike as "The Big Red Machine." In addition to Rose, there were Johnny Bench, Joe Morgan, Tony Perez, and George Foster: it was an awesome array of offensive talent, and from 1970 to 1977 the Reds won five Western Division Titles and played in four World Series, winning back-to-back titles in 1975 and 1976. While "golden boy" catcher Bench and speedy second baseman Morgan received most of the credit, no one could ignore Rose's versatility, switching positions and learning new ones as the need arose, becoming the only player in baseball history to make the All-Star team at four different positions: second base, third base, left field, and right field.

It's ironic that in the twilight of his career, many would criticize Rose because of all the attention being paid to his individual achievements. The fact is, he was the consummate team player, willing to make whatever sacrifice it took to win, whether that meant giving himself up at the plate or on the base paths. It wasn't Rose's fault that his name found its way into the record books, nor did he mind: that was, after all, the way to fulfill his ultimate ambition, which was to be inducted into baseball's Hall of Fame.

Throughout the 1970s, Rose regularly racked up 200 hit seasons, earning progressively larger salaries and national recognition in the process, includ-

ing winning the 1973 National League MVP award
and being named the MVP of the 1975 World Series when Cincinnati bested the Boston Red Sox in
seven close and classic games.

In the free-agent era of today, owners gladly pay
the most surly and foul-tempered players a king's
ransom as long as the player's statistics merit it.
But back in the reserve-clause days of the 1960s
and early 1970s, this wasn't the case. Rose knew
that what little negotiating leverage he had with
the Reds depended not just on good playing but
good press. No team would want to lose a player
whom the papers painted as a hero.

To that end, Rose cannily nurtured good relationships with reporters—which helped when he
found himself in trouble in 1970 and again in 1973.

The first incident involved Rose's home plate
collision with Cleveland Indian catcher Ray Fosse
in the twelfth inning of that year's All-Star
Game—which, ironically, was played before Rose's
hometown fans in Cincinnati. Though he was safe,
and the play produced a dramatic ending to what
ordinarily is a boring game, Rose's body-slam slide,
which leveled Fosse and separated his shoulder,
was regarded by many as a case of "Charlie Hustle" grandstanding. Although players in both
leagues took the annual contest seriously, everyone
was smart enough to realize that there was no sense
risking permanent injury by doing things one might
do only in a game that counted in the standings.
As far as players were concerned, Rose had clearly
violated the "unwritten rule" to play to win, but
not to get hurt.

Yet there was little media criticism of Rose, even
after it became clear that Fosse's promising career
would be shortened.

In 1973, history repeated itself when Rose slid
hard into New York Mets shortstop Bud Harrelson
in game three of the league championship series.

The two men sprawled in the dirt—but as Rose rose, his elbow hit Harrelson in the nose. Hard. Harrelson swore at Rose, and Rose ignored him. Harrelson then yelled, "You tried to elbow me!"

Rose said over his shoulder, "What're you talking about?"

Instead of answering, the scrappy Harrelson pushed Rose, Rose pushed back, then pushed him again, and the two men ended up slugging it out in the dirt. This ignited a bench-clearing brawl—perhaps the messiest, most savage until the infamous Perez/Wiggins bout. When play was finally resumed and Rose headed for left field, the fans pelted him with garbage. It stopped only when they were informed that the Mets, who were ahead 9-2, would have to forfeit if play did not resume.

Later, the perception in the Mets' clubhouse and in the New York press was that Rose was being something more than just a hard-nosed, play-to-win competitor. He had 3 inches and 50 pounds on the smaller Harrelson, and they accused the mop-haired Red of trying to take Buddy out.

He denied the charge, vigorously: "I play hard, but I don't play dirty. If I was a dirty player, I could've leveled him."

New York may have been down on Pete, but the rest of the nation's press let him off. However, the ultimate proof that Rose could do no wrong, media-wise, occurred in 1978 when his first wife, Karolyn, divorced him, accusing him, among other things, of having had affairs with numerous women and being an absentee father. Rose put his own unique spin on the matter, cattily pointing out to reporters how tough it was to continue being able to hit .320 while going through a very public and messy marital breakup.

Yeah, they echoed. It must be.

Then, in 1979, the media gave Rose a forum when he was hit with a paternity suit by the sultry

Terri Rubio, whom he'd met in 1976; the two had
had a long-lived affair *and* had a daughter, Morgan.
The press was gentle, pointing out that, gosh, he *had*
sent Terri child-support checks for more than a year.
Worse, they let him put an outrageous spin on the
matter: "If a guy doesn't like women, he's queer,"
he said. "I'm not queer." Only Pete Rose and his
loyal press could have turned infidelity into an
asset.

But although he presented a cool front, Rose *was*
frustrated, and channeled his anger into whacking
the ball—though not for the Reds. After the 1978
season—in which he had put together a 44-game
hitting streak, the longest in the game since Joe
DiMaggio's record-setting 56-game streak nearly
forty years earlier—Rose left the Reds to sign a
four-year, multimillion-dollar contract with the
Philadelphia Phillies. Through friends in the press,
in Cincinnati and Philly both, Rose once again put
his own spin on things, making it appear as though
the moralistic Reds had driven him out of town.
Rose managed to paint himself as not just another
money-hungry ballplayer, but an orphan forced to
look for a new home.

But whatever his dubious tactics with the press,
Rose delivered on the field, getting the Phillies into
the World Series twice and winning in 1980, something the team had been unable to do despite having captured three consecutive National League
Eastern Division titles in the mid-1970s. Despite a
subsequent decline in productivity, Rose proved to
be a steadying influence in the Philly clubhouse
and, as always, a leader on the field. More important, Rose was laying the groundwork for his challenge to Ty Cobb's all-time base hit record and the
transition he hoped to make to manager when his
playing career ended.

After his contract with the Phillies expired, Rose
signed with the Montreal Expos. Cynics believed

Not only did Pete Rose have the audacity to pose for this picture, he had no compunctions about signing it! (*Author's collection.*)

it was simply a marriage of convenience: money for Rose and an increased gate for the Expos. That much wasn't true. He'd had a bad year in Philadelphia and, for the first time in his years he really *needed* to deliver. He did weights (which he'd never done before) and got himself into the best shape of his career. Unfortunately, though he slapped his four-thousandth hit while in Montreal, he languished at the plate: he *was*, after all, forty-two. There was a real possibility that Rose would suffer the humiliation of being released by the Expos, depriving him of his chance to better Ty Cobb's career mark; luckily, the Reds were having problems, and a trade was worked out allowing Rose to return to his hometown as a player/manager. The club realized that even if the team continued to do poorly, Rose's historic quest, in addition to his outgoing nature and popularity with the sportswriters, would put fans in the seats. As for Rose, he was happy to return; despite his sluggish years away, he was perceived as a conquering hero.

The next few years saw Rose put the cap on his career, breaking Cobb's record and, at the same time, developing into a proficient manager, as the Reds improved to the point where they were once again contenders in the National League West. Rose's personal life seemed to be at a high-water mark too, with his marriage to beautiful ex-Philadelphia Eagles cheerleader Carol Woliung in 1984, and the birth of a baby boy named—what else?—Ty.

Then things started to unravel for the surefire Hall of Famer.

In a carefully worded statement released by the office of the baseball commissioner, it was revealed that on March 20, 1989, the league was launching a full inquiry into serious allegations about Rose's gambling activities.

For years it had been an open secret that Pete Rose liked to gamble, the way Chicagoans like to vote on Election Day: early and often. College basketball, pro football, and horse racing were reputed to be his sports of choice. Significantly, however, there was not now, nor had there ever been, any suggestion that Rose had wagered on Major League Baseball and, more specifically, on games in which he had participated either as a player or manager.

This side of Rose's life had received little publicity before 1989, due to the coddling of the press and the fact that baseball in the 1980s reflected the

Pete Rose. Notice the "good conscience/bad conscience" angels (ball players) on his shoulders. (*Author's collection.*)

economic values of the country itself: there was nothing wrong with making money. Commissioner Peter Ueberroth, who had been responsible for commercializing the 1984 Summer Olympics in Los Angeles and ushering baseball into a new era of prosperity by negotiating landmark TV contracts, consistently took the big view where the game was concerned: people like Pete Rose, who were immensely popular, who weren't known to drink or do drugs, were good for the game. They were the reason people went to the ballpark.

Bart Giamatti, Ueberroth's successor, and the man who would preside over Rose's investigation, took a very different view. To the scholarly former president of Yale University, baseball wasn't a business, or even a sport: it was a pseudo-poetic endeavor with drama that at times bordered on Greek tragedy.

Even if Pete Rose and Bart Giamatti were adrift in the ocean in the same lifeboat, they would still have had nothing in common. Rose had been in the trenches from the bush leagues to the big leagues for more than a quarter of a century, playing with aches and pains, knowing if he didn't make it as a ballplayer—or worse, suffered a career-ending injury at any point along the line—life would hold little possibility of fulfillment for him. Giamatti, on the other hand, with his Vandyke beard and detached, academic air, struck many as having a vision of the game that bore no reality to the sport major leaguers played.

Through chief investigator John M. Dowd, a trial lawyer with the high-powered Washington law firm of Heron, Burchette, Ruckert & Rothwell, the commissioner's office assembled compelling evidence that Rose was less than a model citizen, having wagered heavily and lost large sums of money gambling. Dowd also found evidence that Rose had raised large sums of cash by hocking his baseball memorabilia. So far, big deal: Rose hadn't committed a crime. But

Dowd finally discovered evidence that Rose had bet on Major League Baseball, including Reds games while managing them—and *that* was not only a crime, but a betrayal of the public trust.

Rose vehemently denied the charges, noting that his accusers included two convicted felons, Ron Peters and Paul Janszen, and a self-described professional gambler, Tommy Gioiosa. Rose further contended that Dowd was determined to get him, pointing out that the supposedly impartial fact-finder had arranged for Giamatti to write a favorable letter to the Federal District Court judge in Cincinnati who was to sentence one of his accusers. Rose was also offended—and not without some justification—that baseball's investigation was not subject to any constitutional due process standard. Bart Giamatti was prosecutor, judge, and jury.

The battle dragged on for most of the 1989 season, baseball and Rose waging war first in the media and then in the courts, as Rose's advisers determined that their only hope of saving him was to bring a lawsuit challenging the commissioner's powers and possibly raising the specter of a larger challenge to baseball's exemption from antitrust laws, a prospect that might prompt baseball's owners to intercede and encourage Giamatti to work out some type of settlement with Rose.

In the end, Rose simply ran out of the money necessary to continue his fight. On August 24, 1989, Giamatti hastily called a press conference to announce that Major League Baseball and Rose had reached an agreement, the effect on which would be to impose a lifetime suspension on Rose, while simultaneously giving him the right to apply for reinstatement after one year. In many quarters, Rose's acceptance of such terms amounted to unconditional surrender and an acknowledgment of guilt, despite the document's language: "Nothing in this agreement shall be deemed either an admission or denial by Peter Edward Rose of the allegation that he bet on any Major League Baseball game." For his part, Giamatti made a point of telling reporters that despite what the document said, there was no question in his mind that Rose had, in fact, bet on baseball.

With the suspension, Rose's dream of becoming the first player to be unanimously selected for induction into Baseball's Hall of Fame all but evaporated. In 1990, baseball writers, under intense pressure from Fay Vincent—who succeeded Giamatti's as baseball commissioner—voted, obviously with Rose in mind, that any player on the commissioner's suspended list was ineligible for induction into the Hall.

The final indignity for Rose came when the Internal Revenue Service brought charges of tax evasion against him. On April 20, 1990, seemingly having lost his will to fight, and sensing what politicians have long known—that contriteness goes a long way toward rehabilitating one's public image—Rose pleaded guilty to two felony charges of concealing income on his 1985 and 1987 federal tax returns. In addition to paying nearly $500,000 in back taxes, Rose served five months in prison, then three months in a Cincinnati halfway house. He did his time without incident or complaint.

For some time after his release, Rose maintained a low profile. Then, gently putting his toe back in the sporting waters, he signed to host a radio show, *Talk Sports with Pete Rose,* which originated in West Palm Beach, Florida, and debuted on March 9, 1992.

Other than admitting publicly that he was receiving counseling for his gambling problem, he never admitted that he had ever wagered on Major League Baseball.

As of this writing, the chances seem remote for Rose to get into Baseball's Hall of Fame or have his lifetime suspension lifted, although with Fay Vincent's Bart Giamatti's good friend's, resignation as commissioner in September, 1992, Charlie Hustle's odds improved. Ironically, just eight days after Rose agreed to his lifetime ban with the possibility of reinstatement, Bart Giamatti, who had spent more than $1 million pursuing baseball's investigation of Rose, dropped dead in his New York summer home, the victim of a massive coronary. Though Rose said all the right things at the time, and for that matter has never publicly criticized Giamatti, many in baseball's establishment seem to have formed the judgment that Rose was largely to blame for the Commissioner's death—even though Giamatti's autopsy revealed what anyone who has spent an hour with the man would have concluded: that as an overweight man who liked to eat rich foods, high in cholesterol and smoke several packs of cigarettes a day, he was a heart attack waiting to happen.

There's no question that Pete Rose will persist in his efforts to get back in Major League Baseball in some capacity in the same way that he never gave up on the field, no matter the score, no matter the inning, and no matter whether the game had a bearing on the pennant race.

Frankly, in spite of all his flaws, we wish Charlie Hustle luck. Unlike most of the figures in *Sports Babylon*, he's still got a chance of realizing his dream.

Michael Jordan:
"Bulls Hit"

In sports today, if there's a more insidious scourge than cocaine it's gambling. From the Black Sox to Pete Rose, it seems to go with sports like ham goes with eggs. And you've got to ask yourself *why?* Why, for example, would a player making more than $20 million a year in endorsements, and $40,000 *per game* get tied up with gamblers?

Ask Michael Jordan.

In March 1992, checks from the athlete totaling $165,000 were discovered among the papers of a murdered bondsman and suspected money launderer. The checks were used to settle gambling debts that Jordan had incurred at his Hilton Head, South Carolina, home in October of the previous year, betting on golf and cards with the dead man and two others—one, a convicted cocaine dealer, the other the owner of an illegal gambling and after-hours establishment.

Upon learning of the checks, NBA Commissioner David Stern looked into the matter and, after a brief investigation, decided, "There appears to be no reason for the NBA to take action against Michael," since Jordan wasn't being investigated by any law enforcement agencies, and, in any case, didn't bet on basketball games and wasn't involved in point-shaving. Stern added that Jordan "understands the gravity of the situation (*it had to be pointed out to him?*) and that if he is not more careful about his associations, it can reflect adversely on his fellow players and the entire NBA. He has assured us that he will be more careful about those associations in the future."

After he had had his wrist lightly slapped and the wind taken from his sails, Jordan sat in the Bulls' locker room before a game and said softly, "I was very shocked about the information I received regarding the background of those individuals. From my standpoint, I made a very critical mistake about the people I deal with. I was very naive about that. I let myself down as well as my family and friends."

So Jordan was in the clear as far as the NBA was concerned, and the affair blew over faster than you can say "Joe Jackson." The only question remains why would a man with so much riding on his image do anything even to *suggest* impropriety? Unless they limited their chats to the NBA and the weather, he had to see that these men weren't on the level. He's not blind or naive.

Jordan gives an unsatisfactory, aw-shucks answer as to why he got involved with them. "I'm the biggest sucker around when it comes to golf," he says.

More likely, he's so set for life he needed a little risk to make things exciting. Or else living in the rarified air of the NBA's upper echelon made him feel invincible. Or both.

In any case, Jordan was lucky: he got caught by a commissioner who doesn't subscribe to the scorched-earth policies of Kenesaw Mountain Landis, one who realized that a lengthy public hearing over the *suggestion* of impropriety would hurt the NBA as much as Jordan. As a result, damage to both was minimal.

However, things could just as easily have gone the other way as they had with the Black Sox . . . and with one of the most famous nonissues in all of sports history.

Joe Namath:
"Guilt by Association"

In 1969, Joe Willie Namath stunned the sports world by making good his pregame boasts and leading the sub-underdog New York Jets to a 16-7 victory over the powerhouse Baltimore Colts in Super Bowl III. They weren't just supposed to lose, they were supposed to be demolished, and it was the greatest upset in the history of the game—perhaps in all of sports history.

Even more than before, in the wake of the victory, swinging "Broadway" Joe was a media darling, and it's likely that his well-chronicled womanizing rubbed conservative, smooth, perennially tanned Pete Rozelle the wrong way . . . almost as much as Joe's financial interest in Bachelors III.

Namath had been the co-owner of the East Side saloon for less than a year. He had bought and renamed the faltering Margin Call with friend Ray Abruzzese because, he says, "We wanted a club where we could go and where our friends could go and have a good time." The other one of the "III" was co-manager Bobby Van (no relation to the late entertainer); the other manager was Joe Dellapina, whom Joe describes as "Husband I."

Joe had fun there and says that, sure, the club attracted all types of people: "gamblers and judges, socialites and secretaries." The important thing, he says, is that he didn't fraternize with the riffraff. He went because "I could always find my friends there, and they could find me." Joe even played on the Bachelors III softball team, just so he could spend more time with people whose company he really enjoyed.

But Rozelle got his nose out of joint because he didn't like the "undesirable" patrons who sometimes came there and used the phones to make bets—as though Bachelors III had a corner on the market. Rozelle had gone relatively lightly on Detroit Lions star defensive lineman Alex Karras and superstar Green Bay Packers running back Paul Hornung back in 1963, when they admitted placing modest bets on NFL games and were suspended for a season. Both men were welcomed back into the fold the next year and were approved by the league to serve as color commentators on NFL broadcasts after they rehired; indeed, the indiscretion was completely forgiven when Hornung was elected to the Pro Football Hall of Fame.

Of course, there *was* a difference. Karras and Hornung had admitted wrongdoing, said he never bet on games in which he was involved, and gave a radio interview in which he couldn't have been more contrite. Not Namath, who not only didn't know the meaning of the word but maintained his innocence. As a result, Rozelle took a harder stand with the Jets' star. He said that players simply "must not associate with gamblers or other notorious characters," and in June told the quarterback to make a choice: football or the restaurant business. Rozelle gave him two days to sell his share of Bachelors III. Outraged, Joe told him to take football and shove it.

Ed Garvey, head of the NFL Players' Association, was angry, claiming that Rozelle was just a public relations man who had "no conscience, no point of view, no philosophy." Joe agreed. "If I sold, I'd be wrong. I'd be giving in to Rozelle's theory of guilt by association. I'd be surrendering some of my basic rights just so that I could play football."

Actually, Joe had more to lose than just his football salary and endorsements, which added up to millions of dollars: he had just gone public with his Broadway Joe's restaurant franchise, and that would certainly be hurt if he weren't on the field playing. (He says that a few days later, he gave a waitress a $20 tip on a drink and, though appreciative, she told him he shouldn't throw away his money like that. He just laughed and said, "You should have seen how much I threw away last week!")

Rumors started to float, however, that Namath had used the incident to exit football because of his wobbly (to put it mildly) knees. Or that it was a smokescreen to allow him to exit gracefully rather than be investigated for reportedly having thrown two games in 1968, when he threw five interceptions per. (He denies any kind of a fix: "Hell, you'd have to be an idiot to make it that obvious!" he says. The charges *are* ludicrous.)

Feeling some heat and not wanting to appear intransigent, Rozelle contacted Namath a few weeks later and asked to meet with him. When the quarterback walked into his apartment, the first thing the commissioner did was ask him to sign some photos for his daughter and a friend. The guy had nerve.

The men talked semantics. Namath claimed he'd done nothing wrong. Rozelle replied that Namath simply hadn't done anything illegal. Namath said he'd stay away from the gamblers and crooks, and had instituted security measures to keep the place as clean as possible. But that wasn't good enough, and nothing came of the meeting.

Namath thought of showing up at training camp on July 13, getting suspended, and suing. He thought of going to play in Canada. Ultimately, however, he felt he owed something to his teammates and the investors who had put up the money for the Broadway Joe's enterprise. He went back to see Rozelle with a compromise: he'd sell his interest in Bache-

Joe Namath just a year shy of fifty—still full of impish good humor. His only complaint? "The knees *really* creak." (*Author's collection.*)

lors III, but retain the right to open other Bachelors IIIs in other cities. "Nobody undesirable had gone into places that didn't even exist yet," Namath pointed out. Rozelle accepted the deal.

Namath and Rozelle held a press conference, the commissioner wearing an expensive "got to protect the image of authority" blue suit, the quarterback in jeans.

The commissioner began—and Howard Cosell snapped, "Hold it! My man's not ready."

"Fuck your man," Namath replied in jest.

When someone pointed out that a woman was present, the quarterback flushed and apologized—profusely and sincerely. It was a moment that seemed to define the meticulous correctness of the public relations king and the "aw shucks" athlete from Beaver Falls, Pa.

Namath's play in 1969–1970 was mediocre, and he missed a big chunk of the next season due to a broken bone in his wrist. However, when he returned after that—having seen for a second time, what life would be like without football—he put his heart back into the game. Though he never achieved the same heights of glory as in 1968, he ended up playing an impressive thirteen seasons, spending his last, in 1978, on the Los Angeles Rams so he could be in Hollywood, where he hoped to put some life into an acting career that turned out to be even weaker than his knees.

But Namath's personal fortune is safe, and he's presently married and involved in various business undertakings, as well as working as a football analyst for NBC. On April 29, 1992, he even got himself some new knees, undergoing bilateral replacement surgery in Manhattan. Today he describes himself as "very happy"—still recognized, still widely respected, and happy to be out from under the constant scrutiny of the press and watchdogs like Rozelle.

It's ironic that after all the publicity Namath and his tavern got, future superstars who grew up *watching* the gamblers-are-bad story unfold—from Pete Rose to, it appears, Michael Jordan—apparently learned nothing. As much as the absurd persecution of Joe Namath was a travesty, the failure of others to learn from it is an even bigger shame.

Mickey Mantle and Willie Mays: "The Banned Plays On"

As silly as the Namath affair was, this much can be said about Rozelle's decision: at least Namath was an active player. Whether or not Rozelle made the right decision, forcing Joe to sell, it was within his authority to do so.

The disputes between baseball commissioner Bowie Kuhn and Hall of Fame superstars Mickey Mantle and Willie Mays are a different matter.

During his playing career, which lasted from 1951–1968, Mantle was three times the MVP, regularly topped the league in home-run hitting, and in one season—1956—won the triple crown by leading the league in home runs (52), RBIs (130), and batting (.353). He was a switch-hitting slugger who remains one of the greatest fan favorites in the history of the game.

Willie Mays played from 1951 to 1973 (with two years off to serve in the military), and is arguably the greatest all-around athlete in the history of the game, spectacular at the plate or in centerfield. Mays doesn't think that his backwards, over-the-shoulder catch against the Cleveland Indians' Vic Wertz in the 1954 World Series was the greatest catch he ever made—but those who witnessed it disagree.

Along with Joe DiMaggio, these are the living players who personify baseball to fans and the general public alike. But Bowie Kuhn had a bone to pick with them, and he let it cloud his judgment.

While Mays was working as a coach for the New York Mets, earning $50,000 a year, he was approached to work at Bally's Park Place casino in Atlantic City as a "greeter," saying hey to the high rollers and signing autographs, playing a little golf. The pay would be $1 million spread over ten years for ten days work a month. Former fighter Joe Louis had made a comfortable living doing the same thing for Caesar's Palace in Las Vegas, and Mays didn't see anything wrong with it . . . especially since, as an employee of the casino, he would be forbidden by state law from gambling within 100 miles of the casino.

Mays recalls that when Kuhn found out about what he was offered, "He told me I couldn't take the job and stay in baseball." Mays felt that was ridiculous. Several team owners also owned race horses: wasn't that "worse"? Besides, Mays had been doing this sort of thing for years for The Dunes in Las Vegas, albeit only for room and board and not for pay.

Kuhn's rationale was that by working for the casino and for baseball, Mays might be a target for gamblers looking to "get to" players to throw games or help them make odds. Mays felt this was ridiculous. Would quitting baseball rob him of access to players if he wanted to get to them?

This wasn't the first time Kuhn had killed a Mays deal. Several years before, Willie had been offered the chance to play in Japan and Kuhn worked hard to deep-six the deal. He felt it would be catastrophic if American superstars were allowed to "defect" for the yen, would cause a wholesale desertion by major players.

Mays had been outmaneuvered in the Japanese deal; he wasn't about to be pushed around again. He took the job and was banned though, through legal channels, he twice tried (and failed) to be reinstated.

And then . . . déjà vu.

In 1983, Mickey Mantle signed a $100,000-a-year contract to do basically the same thing for the Claridge Hotel in Atlantic City. Upon learning of this, Kuhn once again swept down like the God of Virtue and told Mantle that if he took the job he'd be banned.

"What would I be banned from?" Mantle replied. He was working as a batting instructor for the Yankees during spring training, but says that what that "really amounted to was a two-week paid vacation." He admits he really didn't give much instruction, stating, "We just kidded around."

Mantle held a press conference to announce his deal to serve as "Director of Sports Programs" for the hotel. As he finished up, a messenger was waiting with a letter from Kuhn, banning him and self-righteously chiding him for not having taken a job with a company like Mister Coffee, the way Joe DiMaggio had done. (Mantle later shrugged, saying he'd have had no problem with that, but "nobody like Mister Coffee had offered to hire me.")

Of course, Kuhn had conveniently overlooked the fact that DiMaggio was co-chairman of the Hall of Fame Golf Tournament, which was sponsored by the Riviera Hotel in Las Vegas. But then, Kuhn was a selective kind of guy where baseball's heroes were concerned. In 1981, a check of old stats revealed the fact that in 1910 Napoleon Lajoie had hit .383—better than that year's title holder Ty Cobb. That meant Cobb didn't win nine straight batting titles, as recorded, but had three before Lajoie and five after. Kuhn refused to adjust the records accordingly. *That's* not dishonest? He's also the man who, in 1971, gave in to the TV networks by allowing World Series games to be played at night, despite players' concerns about the effect the cold weather would have on their effectiveness. Despite the fact that it happened to be damn chilly when the first night game was played, Kuhn stubbornly sat there without a hat or coat. There weren't a lot of tears on the field or off when Kuhn left the game in 1984 and was replaced by California travel agent Peter Ueberroth, who held the job until 1989 and (rightly) focused *his* wrath on players who used cocaine.

In March 1985, six months after becoming commissioner, Ueberroth called Mantle and Mays to join him at the Waldorf Astoria Hotel for an announcement: the players obliged and there, before a horde of pleased reporters and fans, the commissioner declared that "the world changes" and said he was lifting the ban against the players "who are more a part of baseball than perhaps anyone else."

The players were delighted, and Mays remarked how it was ironic that they'd broken into the sport together and were now returning together. When asked later, Kuhn said he disagreed with the decision—as if anyone much cared.

For once in the long, sad history of Sports Babylon, a story had a happy ending.

Charles Barkley:
"Great Expectoration"

Amid all the death and brutality, the self-abuse and pain athletes have caused others, one recent story stands out as a tribute to the best and worst of Sports Babylon: the best in the sense that it was, all things considered, a minor sin; the worst in that the "authorities" overreacted in a way that's almost comical, given all the corruption that goes on elsewhere.

In fact, in an era when teams tend to close ranks around drug users and accused rapists to protect them from the press, fans, and even legal retribution, Philadelphia 76ers forward and rebound *meister* Barkley has *got* to wonder if someone's got it in for him. Compared to what happened to him on March 21, 1991, some of the figures in this book have gotten off easy.

Coming into the fateful game, the six-foot four-inch forward hadn't exactly been a favorite of the press or NBA. For seven seasons, he'd been one of the most dependable but outspoken players in the NBA—outspoken about teammates, coaches, the league, opponents, you-name-it. Because his mouth and celebrity status made him such a target, he took to packing heat when he's in public ("I'll do anything—*anything*—to keep my family safe," he says), and that got him into some highly publicized trouble in August 1988.

After talking to some Atlantic City, New Jersey, kids about the dangers of drugs (he's also an outspoken critic of cocaine), Barkley was headed home and got himself pulled over for speeding. The trooper decided to check out the car for drugs (she must've thought, "How *else* could a black man afford a nice car and spiffy clothes?"), and found the gun. Though Barkley had a Pennsylvania license, this was New Jersey and he was arrested.

The charges were later dropped, and the trooper caught flak from the courts for having searched his car for no good reason. In the meantime, however, Barkley was scourged in the press.

In the spring of 1989, he was back in the headlines when his younger brother Darryl suffered a stroke brought on by drugs. Not only did Barkley hurt for his sibling, but as he puts it, because he's a celebrity, "If someone in my family gets in trouble, I'm in trouble."

Now it's March 21, 1991, and the dome-topped bad boy was winding up his seventh season in the NBA. The Sixers were playing the New Jersey Nets at the Meadowlands Arena, neither team doing spectacularly well that night, and a fan was shouting "nonstop vulgarity" near the baseline. Every taunt was heard loud and clear by the players, and Barkley was really getting riled.

Finally, the forward got so frustrated he did something he rarely did: he turned, shouted back at the slob, and then spit "in his general direction but mainly toward the floor." Or so he thought.

Unfortunately, the tired Barkley "had no control" over his expectoration. Instead of going nowhere in particular, the spit landed right on an eight-year-old New Jersey girl, Lauren Rose, who was sitting with her parents near the heckler.

Now, Barkley loves kids. He hasn't got much use for most adults, but children are another matter. He's got a young daughter of his own, who was just shy of two years old when the incident occurred, and said that having her made him love kids even more.

Barkley wasn't aware that he'd hit anyone until after the game, which the Sixers won 98-95. An usher had complained about his actions; when he heard exactly what had happened, Barkley was "sick."

He immediately did the right thing: he called and apologized to her and to her father. He bought them season tickets for the next year, and invited them to be his guests at an upcoming Easter Seals function. He says that they were nice and understanding about what had happened, "nothing like the asshole whose tirade had tripped my switch." He also apologized publicly, stating that he would never hurt a blameless soul like Lauren—though "assholes," he said, were another matter.

The Roses considered the case closed, and Barkley expected that he'd probably get a wrist-slapping from the NBA. He was partially right: Commissioner David Stern slapped him, all right, with a $10,000 fine and a one-game suspension that cost him another $39,000. He was excoriated in the press, on TV, on radio talk shows, made to feel "like shit," he says, "booed, cursed, and crucified almost everywhere I went."

Again.

The much-beleaguered Barkley took a this-too-will pass attitude, and learned at least one important lesson: henceforth, he would be very careful about the kind of dribbling he did on the court.

Roger Maris:
"Crown of Thorns"

For a kid growing up in New York in the late 1950s, early 1960s, there was nothing—nothing—more exciting than the race between New York Yankees teammates Mickey Mantle and Roger Maris to see who (if either) would be the one to win the Home Run Derby, break Babe Ruth's record for smacking the most homers in a single season.

Old-timers said it was nothing compared to the race Ruth and Lou Gehrig had had in 1927, the year the Bambino hit his record (though Gehrig had actually been ahead of Ruth by one home run as they entered the last month of the season). But this was a time of the young, of JFK, of Elvis Presley—of the old guard giving way to the new, and the race for Ruth's 60 home-run record monopolized the sports pages and the hearts of sports fans everywhere.

Maris was an amazing all-around athlete who had signed with the Cleveland Indians straight out of high school, taking their $5,000 bonus instead of accepting a scholarship offered by the University of Oklahoma. He smacked 14 home runs his rookie season, and 28 the next. Traded to the Kansas City Athletics, Maris went to the New York Yankees in 1960 in a trade that involved sending pitcher Don Larsen to the Athletics.

One of the greatest moments—and greatest photos—
in sports history: Maris finishes his swing as he wal-
lops his sixty-first home run to break Babe Ruth's record. The historic hit came in the fourth inning, with
Maris at bat for the second time. (*AP/Wide World.*)

In his first year with the Yankees, Maris hit 39 home runs (one less than Mantle), though he won MVP honors with a whopping .581 slugging percentage. When the Yankees lost the World Series, manager Casey Stengel was fired and Ralph Houk took over, solidifying the batting order that spread terror throughout the American League, with Maris batting third and Mantle fourth.

The pair's bats sizzled in 1961, and before long it became clear that both had a shot at Ruth's record. In the home stretch, with 53 home runs under his belt to Maris's 56, Mantle came down with an infection that left him weak, then bedridden; when he came back, he hit another home run and that was it. (As though 54 home runs is *bad*. Only that year, folks.)

Maris went all the way, hitting his sixty-first home run off Boston Red Sox pitcher Tracy Stallard in the last game of the season. What happened, then, was amazing: not only did the cheering stop, but the backlash against Maris was amazing. There was a sudden feeling among far, far too many "fans" that the Yankee newcomer had no right— no *right*—to go after the record of the greatest Yankee of them all. How *dare* he? Who did Maris think he was?

What he thought he was was a ballplayer who went out there and did the best job he could.

Maris had never been the most talkative guy in the world and he didn't curry relationships with reporters (This, in marked contrast to the Babe, who was a press favorite and used reporters like he used balls at batting practice, easily putting them wherever he wanted.)

"He hated public attention," Mantle recalls; even when he blasted his sixty-first home run, teammates literally had to push him back onto the field to wave his cap at the cheering crowd.

He was also a perfectionist, and never hid the

disgust he felt for himself—disgust that reporters misinterpreted as petulance or snit. "You can always do better than you're doing," he said at the time, and said that when he wasn't doing his best he became frustrated because "I want it to be made right then and there."

On top of his often punishing desire to do better, the attention of the home-run race got to him—the police escorts, crowds of fans, constant press of reporters. As a result of his misunderstood temperament, Maris didn't get the adulatory press the easygoing Mantle and many of his teammates got, which only made things worse—as when a reporter who obviously knew nothing about the mechanics of home-run hitting once asked how a guy who was hitting .269 that season could possibly be closing in on Ruth's record. The startled Maris just looked at him and replied, "What are you—a newspaperman or a goddamn idiot?"

Mantle says, "It really got crazy," and resents that the press went so far as to invent a rivalry with Mantle that couldn't have been more bogus. The men shared an apartment with outfielder Bob Cerv—himself a home-run ace—and Mantle says, "All my feuds should be as nice as the one I had with Roger." It was, he says, "Pure fiction."

The slugger began losing his hair because of all the tension, and found it difficult to concentrate on playing. He hit his fifty-ninth home run with eight games to go—but didn't tie Ruth's record until the 159th game. Nothing happened the next two games, and the pressure to do it during the final game was enormous. That he rallied and succeeded shows just what a champion the man was.

Yet, as nerveracking as the season itself was, the aftermath was even less pleasant. At a time when he should have been basking in the glory of his achievement, Maris had to contend with the nonsense heaped on him by fans and by Commissioner Ford Frick.

In 1960, Branch Rickey sought to establish a third league, the Continental League, feeling that there were many cities that would eagerly support a major league franchise—including New York, which was still fiercely bitter about having lost the Dodgers and Giants to California just three years before. In response to Rickey's efforts, Major League Baseball underwent a major expansion (giving the Mets to New York) and the schedule had to be increased so that each team would get an equal number of cracks at each other, at home and away.

In a remarkable display of narrow-mindedness, Frick ruled that since Maris had knocked out his runs playing in a 162-game season, and Ruth in a 154-game season, the record must be qualified with an asterisk, explaining that fact.

Maris was hurt, and Mantle was furious. "I thought it was a ridiculous ruling," he says, and points out that that same year, Sandy Koufax broke the National League strikeout record that Christy Mathewson had set in 1903 on a *140*-game schedule. Yet, there was no star adorning the beloved Koufax's record.

Fans who regarded Maris as a carpetbagger were also on his case for having had to face "easier" pitchers: the expansion had left the major leagues shy of top-drawer pitchers, and Maris often faced some less-than-magic performers.

They also pointed out, vis-à-vis Mantle, that Maris had a distinct advantage batting third. Pitchers were forced to throw relatively good balls to Maris in an effort to try and get him out: no opponent wanted to throw around Maris, walking him, then have Mantle step to the plate. The result was that Maris had his pick of much better pitches.

But what was irksome about the Frick ruling and

the rancor of the fickle fans was that they'd failed to take into account the factors working *against* Maris—for example, the fact that Ruth had played all of his games in daylight, which makes the ball easier to see than under night-lighting; the fact that players are *fresher* during afternoon play; and that in crisscrossing the country, players tend to get jet-lagged but still have to get out there and play (Mantle says, "One of the worst things about baseball is all the traveling.") And though Maris faced more mediocre pitchers than Ruth had, it's also true that he faced more *fresh* pitchers, because the use of relief pitchers (often more than one) was becoming more and more commonplace.

The following season, Maris caught a *load* of raspberries from fans for a film he made with Mantle, *Safe at Home!*, in which Mickey acted him off the screen (relatively speaking) and Maris came across as a big stiff. He still managed to hit more than 30 home runs, but hurt his hand the next season, an injury that subsequently benched him for over half of the 1965 season. He underwent surgery off-season, was traded to the St. Louis Cardinals in 1966 and, away from the scrutiny of the New York press and the outspoken fans, led the sixth-place Cardinals to National League championships in 1967 and 1968—after which he retired from the game.

Maris died of cancer in 1985; he was just fifty-one years old.

Because of all the bullshit—and there's no other word for it—Maris has never made it to the Hall of Fame. Former Yankees first baseman Moose Skowron says of the snub, "People . . . forget that Roger was an excellent base stealer and a superb right fielder. History never gave him his due." Pitcher Ralph Terry, who also played for the Yankees that historic year, says, "Roger was the American League MVP two years in a row. He was a genius at breaking up double plays with his slides into second. I can't remember a ball ever getting by Roger or Roger making a bad throw.

"It's a disgrace that Roger Maris isn't in the Hall of Fame."

Asked how he himself felt looking back on the events of 1961, Maris once said, "I'm not bitter. Maybe I wasn't the chosen one, but I was the one who got the record."

Mantle agrees. He says he was there for a lot of amazing records: Joe DiMaggio's 56-game hitting streak, Don Larsen's perfect World Series game, and many more. He says today, however, "The single greatest feat I ever saw was Roger Maris hitting his 61 home runs."

The absence of Maris (and Pete Rose, among many others) has made the Hall of Fame about as valid as a barometer of world-class play as the Oscars are of world-class filmmaking. In the hearts of those who were lucky enough to see him play, and who watched him triumph over the kind of scrutiny that would have sent even Bill Clinton packing, Maris will always be one of the giants.